# 100 MORE WEEKEND WALKS IN BRITAIN

Produced by AA Publishing

Designers: Design 23

Contributors: Charles Aithie, Steve Ashton, Chris Barber, Jackie Bates, John Baxter, Wilfrid Capper, Kate Chevallier, Paddy Dillon, Heather Freeman, Michael Gerrard, Susan Gordon, David Hancock, Derek and Eve Hancock, Des Hannigan, Leigh Hatts, David Herman, Tony Hopkins, Charlie Hurt, Christopher Knowles, Peter Lambley, Tessa Lecomber, Helen Livingston, Cameron McNeish, Andy Murray, Séan O Súilleabháin, Brian Pearce, Ben Perkins, Mark Richards, Erica Schwarz, Roger Smith, Roland Smith, Rebecca Snelling, Colin Speakman, Donald Stokoe, Paul Stonehouse, Clive Tully, David Winpenny



Reprinted in this edition September 1997

ISBN 0 7495 1305 5



Published by AA Publishing (a trading name of Automobile Association Developments Limited, whose registered office is Norfolk House, Priestley Road, Basingstoke, Hampshire RG24 9NY; registered number 1878835).



Colour separation by Daylight Colour Art Pte, Singapore
Bookblock printed by Graficromo, Cordoba, Spain
Ringbinder by MĊ Services, Kidderminster

# *Essential Information for Walkers*

All the routes have been carefully researched, but despite our best efforts to ensure accuracy, changes may occur at any stage during the lifetime of the book. Landscapes change: features mentioned as landmarks may alter or disappear completely, and paths may become muddy or overgrown.

It is important to note that some of the routes pass close to dangerous features in the landscape and need care, especially if children are with you. Our walks follow public rights of way and established paths, tracks and bridleways wherever possible, but the routes sometimes include stretches along a road. Some of the routes are around the coast. Please remember that, although exciting places to visit, cliffs are by their very nature dangerous, so stay away from the edge. Walking on the seashore, be aware of the tide: it can rise with surprising speed. When seas are rough, keep well away from the water.

The walks have all been carefully selected to take you through attractive and varied areas of the British and Irish countryside, and to be enjoyable both for experienced and occasional walkers. While the approximate distance is always stated, the time taken to do the walk will vary with the individual. Do wear sensible clothes for the conditions; and you will need comfortable footwear that will withstand wet and possibly muddy or slippery conditions.

With the information for each walk, we indicate the conditions you should expect – for example, whether it is a gentle stroll on reasonably level ground, or a more challenging walk on rougher terrain. If a walk includes any particularly steep hill stretches, or other hazards such as stiles, we have indicated this. Where possible we have also listed nearby facilities for refreshments, and the nearest public access toilets. Listing in this guide does not imply AA inspection or recognition, although establishments may have an AA classification.

The National Grid reference for the start of each walk is given below the walk number; this relates to the larger scale Ordnance Survey maps (1:50,000 and 1:25,000), which walkers may like to use in addition to this book.

Places are suggested where you may be able to park. These have all been checked by our researchers and were found to be practicable. However, these suggestions are not a guarantee of any right to leave a vehicle parked, and if no distinct car park exists, walkers should park carefully and considerately where they can. Remember that it is the responsibility of the individual to ensure that their vehicle is safely and not illegally parked, and that it does not obstruct other traffic or access.

Respect the country code and keep dogs strictly under control. Please keep to the designated paths, and if you open a gate, please close it after you. Be particularly careful not to discard cans, bottles or food because these are a hazard to wildlife as well as being an eyesore. Do not discard lighted cigarettes, matches or anything else that could cause a fire.

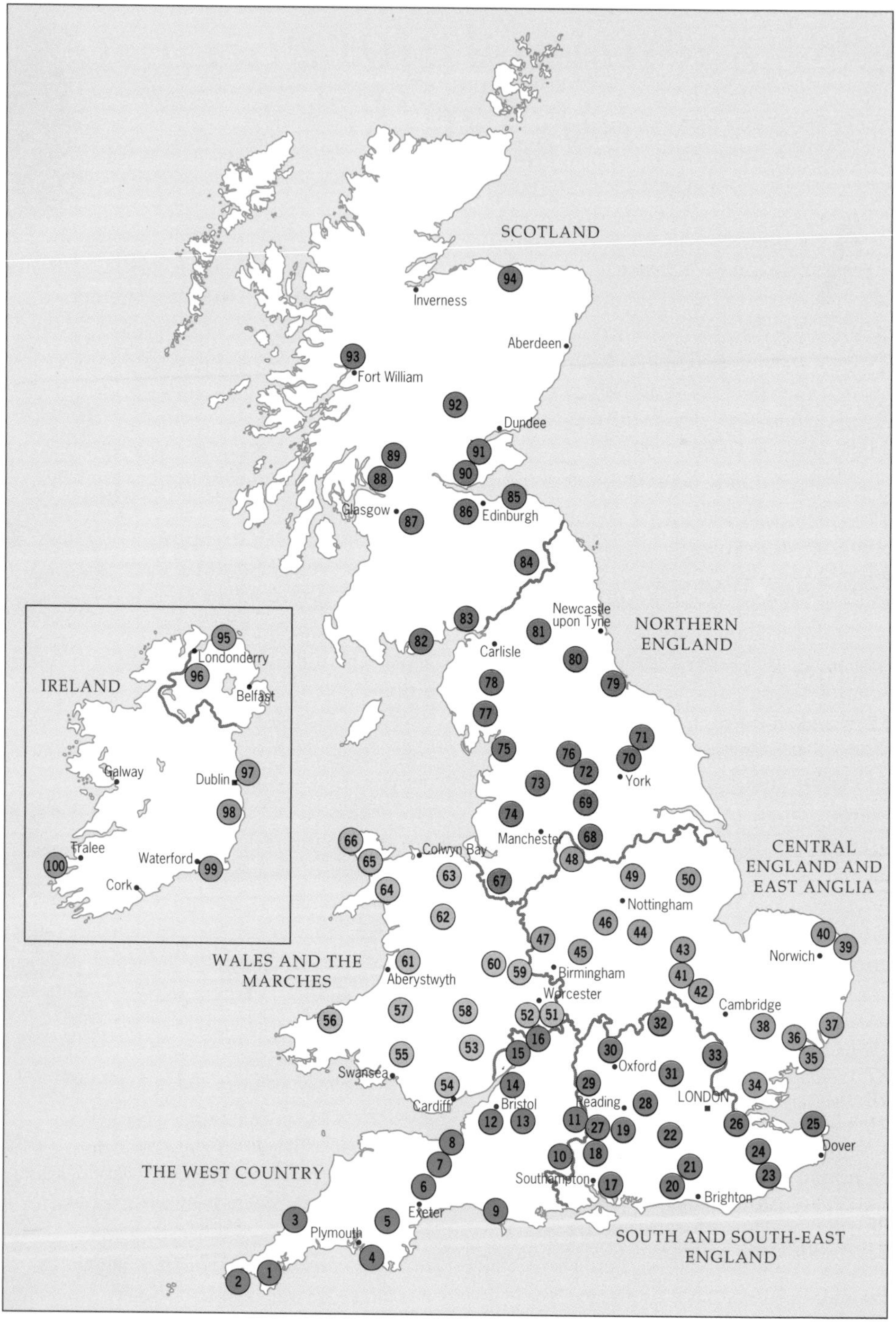
SCOTLAND
Inverness
Aberdeen
Fort William
Dundee
Glasgow
Edinburgh
NORTHERN ENGLAND
Newcastle upon Tyne
Carlisle
York
Manchester
CENTRAL ENGLAND AND EAST ANGLIA
Nottingham
Norwich
Birmingham
Worcester
Cambridge
Oxford
LONDON
Reading
WALES AND THE MARCHES
Colwyn Bay
Aberystwyth
Swansea
Cardiff
Bristol
THE WEST COUNTRY
Exeter
Plymouth
Southampton
Brighton
Dover
SOUTH AND SOUTH-EAST ENGLAND
IRELAND
Londonderry
Belfast
Galway
Dublin
Tralee
Waterford
Cork

# The Walks

# Reading the Landscape

## by Paul Sterry

Any walk in the countryside can be enhanced by some knowledge of the landscape through which you are travelling. Seasonal changes affect every aspect of the landscape, and the time of year can have a crucial influence on what will be seen on your walk. To observe the changes, try visiting a few of your favourite walks during each of the four seasons for comparison. Whatever the time of year, you can be sure that there will be something of interest to see.

Although some plants and animals are found in a wide range of habitats, others have more specialised needs and may only occur in one particular type of habitat. Some obvious examples are aquatic plants, which are only found in freshwater habitats, and birds such as nuthatches and tree-creepers, which are more or less restricted to woodland areas.

The walks in this book explore just about every sort of habitat found in Britain, and the notes below will help you know what to look out for in each type of landscape, at different times of the year.

### Freshwater

Spring is an excellent time of year to visit freshwater habitats. From as early as February, frogs and toads go to ponds, lakes and canals to spawn, invariably returning to the area in which they themselves were spawned. When spawning is in full swing, seething masses of frogs or toads and their spawn may be found. If you wait patiently in a suitable location, you should hear the males' quiet, croaking calls.

During April and May many of our water birds start to nest among the vegetation that is just beginning to emerge around the margins of the water. Slow-flowing rivers and streams sometimes harbour little grebes, rather secretive birds which build floating nests of vegetation attached to water plants. Their larger relative, the great crested grebe, prefers sizeable lakes and gravel pits but builds the same sort of floating nest. It can sometimes be found in the vicinity of nesting coots and moorhens.

Insects begin to make their annual appearance in the spring as well. Having spent the previous nine months or so as nymphal stages in the water, dragonflies and damselflies emerge as adults. There are different species associated with the variety of freshwater habitats but low-lying ponds and lakes are usually the most productive. A good way to see them is to visit the pond early one spring morning. Search carefully among the vegetation at the margin and you have a good chance of finding newly emerged dragonflies and damselflies. In this stage they are usually rather docile but remember they are also extremely delicate and should not be handled. Other springtime insects include mayflies. To see them, visit a low-lying river at dusk in May – you may be lucky enough to see a swarm of males dancing over the water.

By the summer, the dragonflies and damselflies can be seen mating and egg-laying over the water. If you sit and watch carefully, you may see pairs flying in tandem or females forcing their abdomens underwater to lay the eggs. Many of these insects fall victim to hungry broods of waterside birds. Reed warblers and reed buntings take their toll and even young moorhens are not averse to a tasty water insect.

It is at this time of year that waterside flowers are at their most colourful. Although species such as marsh marigold have already flowered and set seed by late spring, a much wider variety of flowering plants can be found from June to September. Yellow flag, great willowherb and purple loosestrife are among the more striking species to be encountered.

On balmy summer evenings, there are few things more pleasant than to take a stroll along a river bank or beside a lake. The air is refreshing, and as the dusk falls you may be lucky enough to see bats hunting for insects over the water – several species hunt in this manner in southern England. If you have mixed feelings about having close encounters with bats remember that every time they catch an insect there is one less mosquito or midge to bite you! One of the walks in the book takes you near the famous bat roost in the Greywell Tunnel on the Basingstoke Canal. Although this is most important as winter refuge to these flying mammals, bats can always be seen in the summer months too.

As autumn approaches, the insect-eating activities of the bats are adopted by swallows and martins which gather over water to feed, particularly at dusk. They congregate around freshwater habitats prior to migrating south to Africa in September. Autumn is a good season for admiring and photographing the reflection of trees in the water. Keep a look out for attractive patterns of floating seeds and leaves.

At first glance, freshwater habitats in winter might appear dead and lifeless. This is far from true, however, and birdwatchers in particular are often in their element. The numbers and variety of ducks build up on lakes and reservoirs, the birds having moved south from more northerly parts of Europe. Among the common species such as tufted duck, pochard and gadwall, look for unusual ones such as smew, goosander and scaup.

Because much of the emergent vegetation has died back, winter is often a surprisingly good time of year to take a net with you and go pond dipping. The larval and nymphal stages of freshwater insects will be numerous and you should also find water snails. Beside rivers and streams in upland areas, the lack of leaf cover on the trees can make the observation of resident grey wagtails and dippers easier than at other times of year.

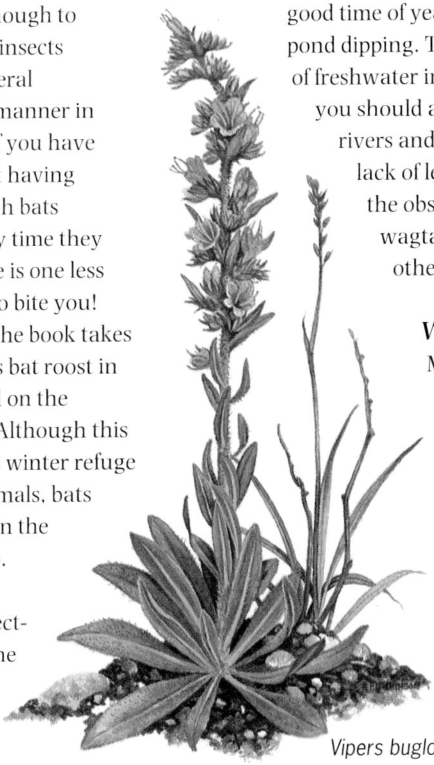

*Vipers bugloss*

### Woodland

Many of the walks in this book pass through areas of woodland. These vary in character from deciduous forests of native species such as beech and oak, to the rather monotonous ranks of conifer plantations, comprising introduced species of trees. Although conifers in plantations have a limited wildlife appeal, in a few areas of highland Scotland remnant pockets of native Caledonian pine forest can be found, harbouring a unique and varied combination of plants and animals.

Although woodlands are fascinating places at any time of year, many people find that spring is the most rewarding season. From late March until June, the ground layer of many deciduous woodlands hosts a colourful carpet of flowers. Bluebells, ramsons, wood anemones and wood sorrel often cover large areas, and keen-eyed observers may find early purple orchids in small clumps here and there.

An early morning walk in the woods can reward you with a rich dawn chorus of birdsong, and this is the time of year when fox cubs first emerge from their dens to play. Look up into the leaf canopy of the trees and shrubs you encounter and you may see the nibbled holes caused by the myriad caterpillars in the woods. If you want to investigate further, take an umbrella with you. If you hold the open but inverted umbrella under a spray of leaves and give the branch a sharp knock, a shower of insects will fall into the umbrella. These can then be easily observed, but remember to put them back on the leaves when you have finished.

*Primrose*

By the time summer has arrived in the woods, you will encounter family parties of birds such as blue tits, wrens and robins. The birds time their nesting so that the young birds fledge just as the woodland insects are at their most abundant. Most noticeable among these are the butterflies that fly along sunny glades and visit the flowers of brambles. Speckled woods and ringlets are widespread, and in a few places you might be lucky enough to see one of several species of fritillary. As you pass by the trunks of the trees, keep a lookout for camouflaged moths resting on the bark.

Autumn is the season for colour in our native deciduous woodlands. The leaves of maple and ash contrast with those of oak and beech, and change almost on a daily basis through September and early October. Nuts and berries are produced in abundance and woodland birds and mammals such as squirrels search the leaf litter for this fallen feast. Among the colourful leaves, there will be a wide range of fungi. If these are your particular interest, time your woodland walk so that it occurs a few days after heavy autumn rain; this will have encouraged a sudden flush of fungi. Conifer plantations are surprisingly rich in fungi as well although the species will, of course, be different from those in deciduous woods.

Winter brings both plusses and minuses for the woodland naturalist. Gone are the woodland flowers and summer migrant birds. The leaves have also long since fallen, but this can prove to be an advantage. Deer can be much easier to see at this time of year, as can the mixed flocks of resident birds such as tits and nuthatches which feed among the branches. Resident tawny owls are often very noisy at this time of year, mostly after dark. During the day, they roost among the branches and are often quite conspicuous. Small birds also spot them more easily, and the agitated alarm calls of blackbirds and tits may show you where an owl is roosting.

*Bullfinch*

### Heath and Moorland

People have exploited woodland resources for centuries, and in areas of southern Britain where woods were cleared on impoverished, acid soils, a new type of habitat – heathland – gradually developed. Characterised by ling, bell heather and gorse, this is a fragile and vulnerable habitat.

In spring, the flowers of common gorse burst into life and fill the air with a heady fragrance of coconuts. Heathland birds such as stonechats and yellowhammers perch on tall sprays and sing loudly to advertise their territories. It is at this time of year that the heathland reptiles are easiest to see. On sunny days in March and April, adders and common lizards, recently emerged from hibernation, bask in the warming rays.

*Great plantain*

By July and August, the flowers of ling and dwarf gorse predominate and sometimes turn whole slopes into a blaze of purple and yellow flowers. Butterflies such as graylings and silver-studded blues occur in these habitats and are easiest to see early in the morning when they are less active. As the season progresses, spiders' webs and their silken strands become more and more obvious. They are brought into stark relief when the first misty autumn mornings arrive, the webs becoming laden with water droplets. As autumn moves into winter, hoar frosts etch beautiful patterns on the heathland vegetation and webs.

Similar patterns of woodland clearance on acid soils in upland Britain have resulted in the creation of moorland habitats. Again, the characteristic species are members of the heather family but the birdlife is rather different. In areas from the Peak District northwards, red grouse are year-round residents. During the summer months, a variety of waders breed on the moors alongside meadow pipits and merlins.

## Grass and Meadowland

With grassland, the species of plants present depends on the underlying soil type: in this way, meadows on chalk-rich soils are generally much more colourful and herb-rich than those on acid soils.

Skylarks, an ever-present feature of grassland throughout Britain and Ireland, can be heard singing overhead at almost any time of day and almost all year round. For wildlife observers, meadows are at their best in the summer months. Butterflies such as meadow browns, small coppers and common blues, are often abundant and visit the flowers that bloom along the hedgerows and field boundaries and roadside verges. Grasses, which are flowering plants too, also flower in the summer months – as sufferers from hay fever know only too well.

For an interesting variation on grassland wildlife, take a walk on a summer's evening. Armed with a torch, explore the grass leaves for the caterpillars of marbled whites and skipper butterflies. You might even be lucky enough to see a glow-worm.

As the autumn approaches, grassy areas often produce a rich harvest of fungi unique to this habitat. Some are closely related to cultivated mushrooms and are delicious to eat; this is also true of ink-caps, parasol mushrooms and giant puffballs.

Others species may be poisonous, so make sure you are certain of your identification skills. Damp autumn mornings are also good for watching slugs and snails – because snails in particular need calcium for their shells, the species range is greatest on chalky soils.

## Coastline

The coast exercises a special lure for people who enjoy country walks. There is something bracing and inspiring about a cliff-top walk or indeed a walk along almost any part of the coast where the sea is visible.

Visit the coast in the spring and cliff-top flowers will be at their peak of flowering. In some places, thrift can turn whole slopes pink, while sea campion and scurvygrass flourish around rocky outcrops. This is the best time of year to tackle one of the walks that visits a seabird colony – the sight, sound and smell of thousands of birds such as guillemots, kittiwakes and razorbills nesting shoulder-to-shoulder will stay with you for a long time. If you are interested in the rich life along the seashore, then consult a tide timetable and visit a rocky shore around the spring equinox in March – together with the autumn equinox in September, the lowest low tides occur at this time of year, and the most interesting variety of animals and plants can be found.

Saltmarsh flowers are at their best in the summer months, with sea lavender and golden samphire putting on colourful displays alongside the more subdued greens of saltwort and sea purslane.

As autumn approaches, the saltmarshes and estuaries come alive with migrant waders and wildfowl returning from the nesting grounds in northern Europe. Some of these migrants pause for a few days before continuing their journey southwards while others remain on British estuaries throughout the winter. This time of year can be extremely productive for the beachcomber, especially on an exposed stretch of sand. Winter gales often dump huge amounts of flotsam on the high tide line, along with an array of strange and colourful shells.

*Badger*

## Wildlife in Man's World

For thousands of years, humankind has had a profound influence on the environment – so much so that there is almost no part of the British landscape that can be said to be entirely untouched, with the possible exception of some of our estuaries, coastal cliffs and highest mountain tops. Although to describe the landscape of Britain as man-made is perhaps overstating the case, almost all the habitats we find around us are at the very least man-influenced. For example, native deciduous woodlands have been felled or selectively managed for centuries, chalk downlands were created by woodland clearance and intensive grazing, and heathlands came about after woodland clearance on acid soils.

In recent decades, with the advancement of technology and consequently of our ability to alter or destroy landscapes, the pace of change has accelerated considerably. While many of these changes have had an adverse effect upon our wildlife, it has to be said that some of our native plants and animals are extremely adaptable and have coped admirably with the change.

One of the most significant human influences in modern Britain is that of farming. The varied practices employed around the land have helped shape the regional landscape in often distinctive ways as land is drained to take livestock, for example, or fields are enlarged to make the best of mechanised farming. Intensification of farming methods has, however, taken its toll on wildlife diversity. Hay meadows now often lack the herb-rich qualities of half a century ago thanks to seeding and herbicide application, and many former arable 'weeds' are now botanical rarities.

Despite these adverse changes, arable land and grazing pastures sometimes support flocks of birds in winter such as lapwings, golden plovers and rooks. Lapwings formerly bred in far greater numbers than today, the growth of winter wheat effectively excluding them because they like wide open vistas when breeding. New approaches such as set-aside schemes, where land is taken out of intensive production, and the provision of unsprayed headlands, while flawed in many people's view, may be the start of a trend to a more enlightened approach to integrating wildlife and farming.

There has also been a tendency over the last few decades to remove hedgerows, resulting in 'prairie' landscapes in many regions of intense arable farming. Where they do survive, hedgerows provide important sanctuaries for wildlife. Birds that would otherwise nest along woodland edges find them ideal habitats and berry- and nut-bearing plants grow in profusion. The informed wildlife detective can even tell the age of a hedge by its species composition. Walk along a 30 metre stretch and count the number of different woody species - each species corresponds roughly to a century of age.

From the naturalist's point of view pine plantations are relatively poor habitats, partly because the plantation species is often alien to Britain, and also because of the uniform age, single species and dense planting regime of the trees. However, recent interest in recreating woodlands of native species, some for recreational purposes and some a short-term coppice for fuel, may help redress the balance.

The road network in Britain has had a major impact on the landscape, not only in terms of the direct effects of road construction, but also in terms of the end result – far more people than ever before can visit the countryside. Partly because of their inaccessibility to humans, motorway and dual carriageway verges often serve as havens for wildlife – in a sense unofficial nature reserves. However, many of the walks in this book also encounter rural roadside verges. Here, a microcosm of the wildlife of the surrounding countryside may be found. In a way, it is fitting that roadside verges have a role to play in natural history terms since it is by road that most of us travel the countryside in the first place.

*Common toad*

# Frenchman's Creek at Helford

## WALK 1

CORNWALL
SW759261

*Moorings on the Helford Estuary*

A woodland walk to the quiet banks of the notorious Frenchman's Creek, immortalised by Daphne du Maurier in 1941, in her famous novel of that name.

**START**

Helford is about seven miles east of Helston, following signs for The Lizard and St Keverne, then Manaccan and Helford, along a narrow, winding single-track road (congested in the height of summer). There is a car park just outside Helford – only residents are allowed to drive into the village.

**DIRECTIONS**

Leave the car park and turn right down the lane to the ford and bridge. Do not cross the bridge, but continue up the lane in front of cottages and bear steeply left to follow a path behind a thatched cottage. Follow the path through the woods.

At a fork go right across a small stream and through an opening. Continue up a short incline and cross a stile into a field. Keep to the field edge and at Kestle go through the farmyard (can be very muddy), then through a gate between barns and Kestle Cottage. Cross road and continue down a broad track, signposted 'Frenchman's Pill'. At end of farmhouse wall, turn into field through gate and bear left, proceeding down a steep, woody incline. Turn right at the fork at bottom of hill to reach the head of Frenchman's Creek. Bear right and follow path along the creekside – beware of 10ft drop to the water! Turn right at a gnarled oak tree just beyond a plank bridge. Go up wooden steps, continue upwards and the path levels out to give magnificent views. Continue

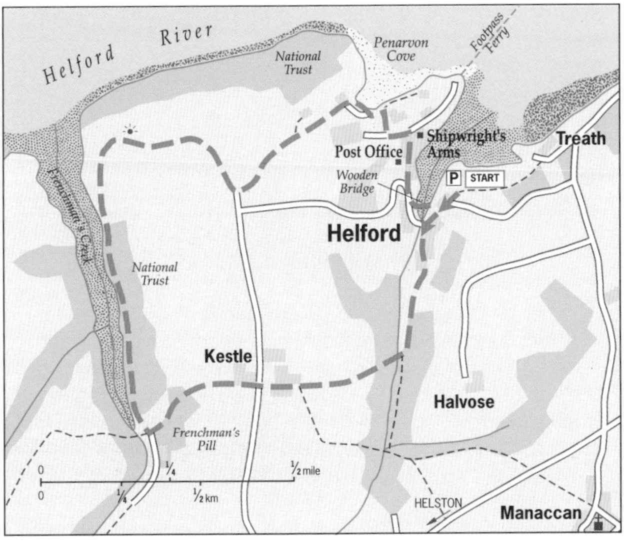

along and past field, cross a wooden stile amidst bamboo and turn sharp right up a track. Turn right at a T-junction.

Follow field edge and just beyond a cattle grid go immediately left down a lane, signposted Penarvon Cove. Keep straight on at the fork, passing through a gate to reach the cove. Cross top of beach, then follow a track leading up through trees. Cross a road-end on your left and proceed through a gate to follow a short path behind some houses. Turn left at end of cottages down a track. Bear right to pass Shipwright's Arms. Follow lane through village. Cross wooden footbridge and turn left to return to the car park.

*The path through Pengwedhen Woods*

**Frenchman's Creek**

Daphne du Maurier used the creek for a meeting between a local beauty and a French pirate, bestowing an air of romance on what is undoubtedly a perfect venue for such an assignation. The narrow inlet may be less endearing to romantics at low tide, but the wading birds which come to feed on the mud flats would not agree.

**Helford**

This lovely riverside village has retained its subtle beauty, and some of the best of its surrounding countryside is in the care of the National Trust. There has been a ferry to Helford Passage across the river since ancient times, and this makes a pleasant trip.

*Pintail*

**Information**

The walk is two and a half miles long
Level most of the way with some short, very steep sections which require care
A few stiles and cattle grids to cross
No road walking other than through Helford Village
Picnic places in woods and at Penarvon Cove
Toilets at car park
Pub at Helford

**What to look out for**

There are many water birds in the muddy creek bed at low water. These include redshank, grey heron, cormorant and several types of duck in winter months. The woods are full of smaller birds as well as the larger green and great spotted woodpeckers, while buzzards may be seen wheeling above the open fields. Springtime visitors can enjoy the colourful daffodil fields at the top of Penarvon Cove.

# *Readymoney Cove and Combe Haven*

**WALK 2**
CORNWALL
SX110512

A short walk, but one with some steep sections, unavoidable in this beautiful and complex area of coast.

### Information

The walk is one and a half miles long
Good paths but some steep sections
No road walking
A few stiles to cross
Seasonal dog ban at Readymoney Cove; must be on leads through Alldays Fields
Seasonal refreshments at Readymoney Cove
Seasonal toilets at Readymoney Cove
Picnic spots at Coombe Haven and Readymoney Cove
Swimming at Readymoney Cove

**START**
The National Trust car park at Coombe Farm is reached by turning down Lankelly Lane, signed Lankelly and Coombe, off the A3082 just outside Fowey.

**DIRECTIONS**
Leave the car park entrance and turn down the second track on the right, signed 'Coombe Haven ¼m'. Fifty yards before a metal gate, at signpost, go over a stone stile on the right, signed 'Coombe Haven', and follow the steep path down through the trees to reach the beach at Coombe Haven.
From the beach go left along the coast path up a short, very steep section at first, over a stile then out along the edge of Alldays Fields. Look behind for a view of the lighthouse. Where the fields end by a small memorial stone (dedicated to G James Allday, who gave fields to Fowey in 1951), go through a metal kissing-gate.
Follow the main path to a junction with several paths. Just short of the junction, to the right, a short steep path curves up to the Rashleigh Mausoleum. The next path on the right leads out to St Catherine's Point and Castle (open to visitors).
Follow the main path in Covington Woods where it curves down to the left (this can be muddy and slippery). Bear round to the right and go down to Readymoney Cove. Facing seaward, turn right and go to far end of the beach, where steep steps and a steep path lead back up to the junction by the mausoleum. Alternatively retrace your steps up the less steeply sloping track.
At the junction of paths below the mausoleum turn right up three steps and across the flat remains of a building. Follow the path through the trees of Covington Woods, ignoring

### What to look out for

Fowey is a busy yachting and boating centre and there are always vessels coming in and out of the estuary, including fishing boats. They make a fine sight through the woods at St Catherine's Point. The plant and bird life of the area is prolific. There are strong contrasts between the reedy foreshore at Coombe Haven and the salt-resistant plants like thrift, scurvygrass and sea campion of the open cliff, with woodland flowers and the ash, beech and sycamore of Covington Wood.

*The rocky foreshore at Combe Haven*

side paths, to reach a fork after 250yds. Bear left at another fork in another 250yds. At the edge of the woods, turn left, go through a kissing-gate, then follow a grassy track across cliff-top fields directly ahead. The track curves gently right to a stile and metal gate. Cross the stile and go down the lane to turn left into the car park.

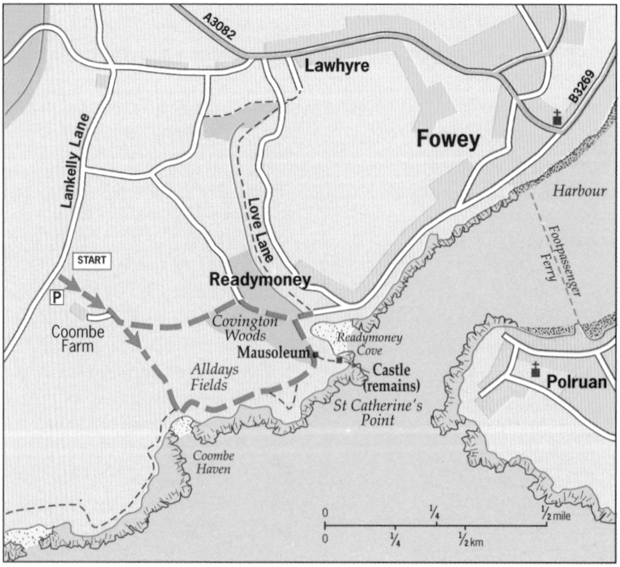


**Readymoney Cove**

This little beach was a busy harbour in the past. There is a stony lane (called Love Lane) leading down to it through Covington Woods, its surface worn into ruts from the days when carts plied to and from the cove collecting landed goods, sand and seaweed, and delivering lime from the old kiln, which is now a shelter.

**The Rashleigh Mausoleum**

The Rashleigh family have been closely associated with Fowey and its environs for hundreds of years. The mausoleum was erected in the 1870s and members of the Rashleigh family are buried beneath the flagstone memorials. Family pets are said to be buried near by.

WALK 3
CORNWALL
SW941799

# The Rumps and Pentire Point

An exhilarating coastal walk through National Trust property, with glorious views of the North Cornish coast and the Camel Estuary; the route includes a circuit of an Iron Age fortified headland.

**Information**

The walk is just over four miles long
Walking is generally easy, with some short, steep sections
No stiles, but several gates
Dogs must be under strict control where sheep are grazing; dogs banned on local beaches from Easter to September
Take care with children where the path skirts the cliff edge
Wooden seats along the way and grassy areas on The Rumps provide good picnic spots.
Toilets and refreshments at New Polzeath

*The Rumps seen from Cliff Castle*

START
From Wadebridge take the B3314 and follow signs for New Polzeath. At a cross-roads ½ mile before New Polzeath, turn right down a narrow lane to Pentireglaze. Follow the road where it bends left in front of cottages, go over a cattle grid and, 200yds ahead, turn right into a National Trust car park.

DIRECTIONS
Leave the car park by the back corner, where there is an information panel and National Trust collecting box (please contribute). Go up a stony path, then keep alongside a wall to reach a gate in the opposite field corner.

Beyond the gate, turn left along the coast path, taking particular care for the first 50yds where the path is close

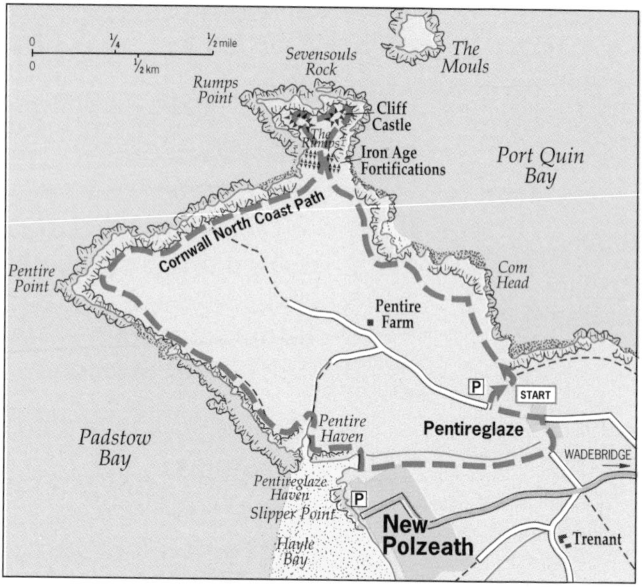


to the cliff edge. Keep to the main coast path for about ¼ mile to reach the double-headed promontory of The Rumps, where the defensive embankments of Iron Age fortifications still survive. A circuit of the promontory can be made by following the path alongside its eastern edge, from where there are splendid views of Mouls Island just offshore. Take care on steeper slopes.

Leave The Rumps by the entrance gap in the embankment, then follow the broad track that runs right and uphill to where it merges with an upper path. Continue to a gate, level with a trig point, and pass through. Where the path forks beyond the gate, take the right-hand branch to Pentire Point.

Just before the Point, turn left, following the low wall, and continue along the coast path for ¼ mile. Pass above the narrow inlet of Pentire Haven (short rocky descent) and continue along the coast path to Pentireglaze Haven.

At the far side of Pentireglaze Haven beach, turn left along a wide track, passing a house on your left. Where the track loops back to the right, keep straight ahead along a grassier track. Keep straight on through fields, passing through several gates, to reach a road. Turn left, walk through Pentireglaze, and follow the track left to return to the car park.

**Mining**
Lead was mined near Pentireglaze from the 16th to the 19th century. The National Trust car park actually lies within spoil heaps from an old lead mine.

**The Rumps**
The headland is a classic example of an Iron Age promontory site, fortified across its narrow neck by banks and ditches. Wooden huts would have been situated just inside the entranceway. The site was probably established some time after 500 BC and abandoned by the middle of the 1st century AD.

**Pentire Point**
In 1936, the glorious western slopes of Pentire Point above the Camel Estuary were divided into building plots and put up for sale. Conservationists, both locally and nationally, raised sufficient money to buy the headland and then presented it to the National Trust, to ensure preservation and public access.

## What to look out for

Goldfinches, stonechats and whitethroats are common here, and kestrels hang motionless in the updraught above the cliffs. On the western side of Pentire Point, oystercatchers throng the tidal rocks, and seals may be spotted in the restless waters near The Rumps. In spring and summer the cliff slopes are vivid with pink thrift, white bladder campion, and the lovely pale blue squill.

# Noss Mayo – Revelstoke Drive

**WALK 4**
DEVON
SX541466

A good, mostly level walk round the southern headland of the mouth of the River Yealm, passing through the charming creekside village of Noss Mayo. Most of the walk is along the broad and amenable Revelstoke Drive.

### Information

The walk is about four miles long
Level, easy walking with a long upward incline at the finish
Short section of quiet road walking
Several stiles
Pubs in Noss Mayo
Good picnic spots along the first part of Revelstoke Drive and at Cellar Beach

### START

The National Trust car park is reached from Noss Mayo via Netton Farm. The way is signposted from Noss Mayo but not generously – and Devon lanes can be confusing, particularly on the way back. Navigators should be on their toes!

### DIRECTIONS

Leave the car park through a gate in the far left-hand corner. Go down the lane and cross a stile to turn right onto the coast path (superb views). At the entrance to the prominent Warren Cottage, go left through a gate and along a short section of path, then through another gate to rejoin the broad drive.

Follow the coast path over a few stiles, continuing round Gara Point and enter Brakehill Plantation. Go through a gate by a National Trust sign indicating the end of The Warren property and continue past some old coastguard houses. Just past here a path leads down quite steeply to the left to Cellar Beach, which is worth visiting.

Continue on the main path

*Cellar Beach, just a short detour from the walk*

### What to look out for

Watch for boats and ships out to sea, and for yachts coming in and out of the River Yealm. Seabirds such as gulls, terns and gannets also pass along the coastal section. This area was a managed rabbit warren in the 19th century and rabbits can still sometimes be seen on the grassy open spaces. The woods on the second section of the walk are full of bird and plant life.

past the distinctive Battery Cottage. The way leads on, with lovely views of the river, through Passage Wood and Ferry Wood to reach the surfaced lane which is followed for about ½ mile into Noss Mayo.

Continue to the head of Noss Creek. Bear left up the road, then go right to reach a large car park with an adjoining children's play area. Beyond the car park entrance follow the rough track uphill, past hillside cottages on the right, and continue for about ½ mile, passing a farmhouse on the right. At a T-junction turn left to reach the car park almost immediately on your right.

### The Revelstoke Drive

Revelstoke Drive is a remarkable Victorian feature – the inspiration of Edward Charles Baring, Lord Revelstoke, who owned the surrounding Membland Estate. The Drive is part of a nine-mile circular carriageway round the estate, built near the end of the last century by local fishermen during slack winters. Lord Revelstoke would drive his house guests by carriage round the drive to view his domain.

### The Great Mew Stone

This rocky island lying to the east of Gara Point takes its name from the 'mewing' of the seabirds that have colonised it for centuries. The Mew Stone was occupied from 1774 when a convicted criminal was banished there with his family for a seven-year term. When the family eventually left one daughter remained, married and raised a family there. The last known inhabitant kept a rabbit warren on the island during the early 19th century. Not surprisingly, he was also a smuggler!

*The head of Noss Creek at Noss Mayo*

### Noss Mayo

This lovely riverside village dates from medieval times. Its sheltered position and good anchorage on the River Yealm probably guaranteed close connections with smuggling, which was rife along the South Devon coast during the 17th and 18th centuries.

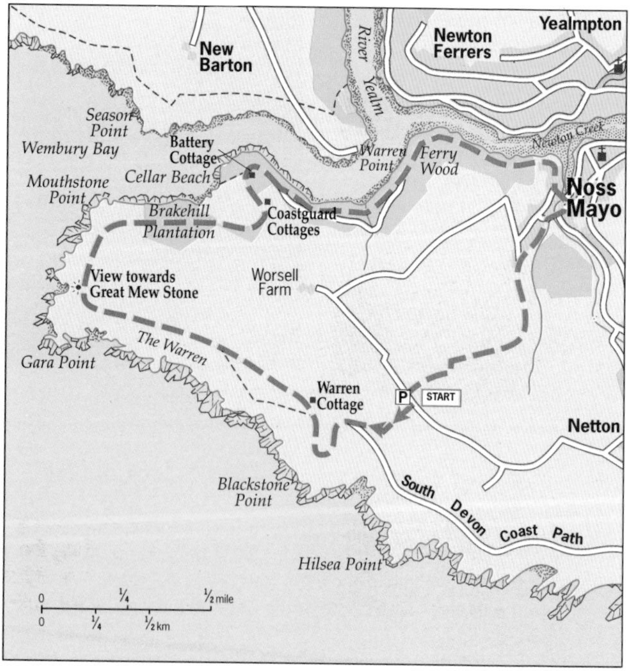

# Postbridge: Dartmoor's Ancient Stones

A walk at the heart of Dartmoor through woods and moorland, visiting prehistoric sites on the way.

**WALK 5**
DEVON
SX656772

**Information**

The walk is three miles long
There is a slope up into the woods and two short but very steep rocky sections.
The ground can be muddy
Short sections of linking road between paths
Take-away café and pub at Postbridge; cream teas at hotel
Picnic places in Bellever Forest and on banks of the East Dart River at Postbridge

START
The Forestry Commission car park at Bellever is reached from the B3212 (Two Bridges road) in Postbridge by turning south down a narrow lane by the main Postbridge car park.

DIRECTIONS
From the entrance to the car park turn left and walk up the road keeping straight ahead at the junction. Pass the Youth Hostel on the right and continue past some farm buildings to follow a short, but awkward rocky path up to a gate. Go through the gate and continue up the path. At the next gate, labelled 'Lichway', turn right, and follow the broad track, also signed 'Lichway', and after about 100yds, bear left to reach a crossing and follow a muddy track for about 100yds. Turn right along the forestry track. About 150yds up the track look out for the remains of a burial chamber just off to the right.
Continue for about 200yds (a track on the left leads into the trees to a well-preserved burial cist). The main track continues for 100yds, then follow a path leading left through the trees and into the open for 400yds to a stone circle.
Return to the main track. Continue until the mature trees end, and where the area has been recently cleared and replanted, divert to the left along an almost indistinguishable path which leads in about 500yds to the large open area of Kraps Ring settlement. Return to the main track and continue downhill to go through a

*The woods near Postbridge*

*Postbridge's famous clapper bridge*

wooden gate. Bear right to a minor road. Turn left and immediately right to reach the main road for Postbridge (toilets in car park opposite). Go into Postbridge to view the famous clapper bridge. Twenty yards back up the road from the clapper bridge, go left through a gate with stone stile. Follow the path signed 'Bellever' and after 50yds go through another gate and uphill to the right on a short, steep rocky section. Where the path reaches open ground at the top veer off towards the right along a faint but straight wide path. This runs alongside the approach road to Bellever. Continue on the path in company with the road to Bellever and in about 600yds cross a track and continue along the road back to the car park.

**In misty conditions avoid the path from the clapper bridge across the open moor; return instead along the verge of the minor Bellever road, reached on leaving the forest before Postbridge.**

### Ancient Sites

The many ancient sites on the first section of the walk date from the Neolithic and Bronze Ages. The stone cists contained burial remains and were once covered with earth and stone mounds known as 'barrows'. The substantial settlement at Kraps Ring would date from roughly the same period, though may also have been used in the Iron Age.

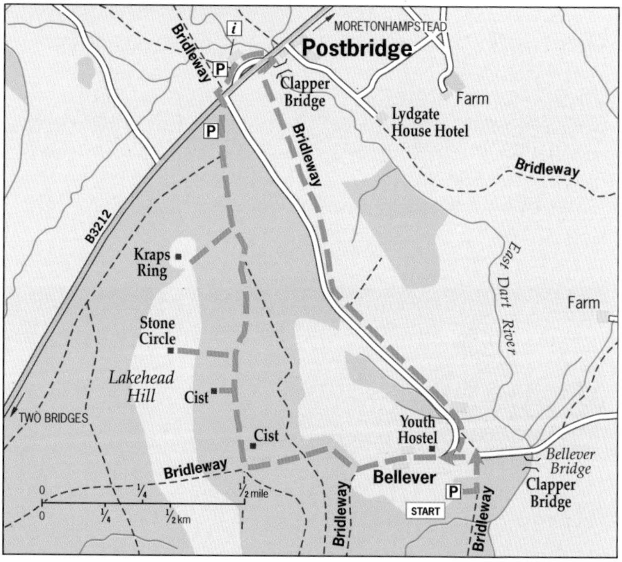


## What to look out for

Conifer woods encourage birds like crossbills, siskins and redpolls, while the open moors are home to meadow pipits,merlins and ring ouzels, best looked for in springtime. The sturdy little Dartmoor ponies can be seen on the open moorland.

# *Tiverton: the Canal and Railway*

**WALK 6**
DEVON
SS961126

The remnants of two great industrial transport systems – a canal and a railway – on the outskirts of Tiverton combine to create a delightful and interesting walk, enjoyable at any time of the year.

### Information

The walk is about two miles long
Level, easy footpaths along canal and old railway line
One short flight of steps and one longer flight
A short section of road
Convenient benches along the canalside for picnics
Cafés at Canal Basin

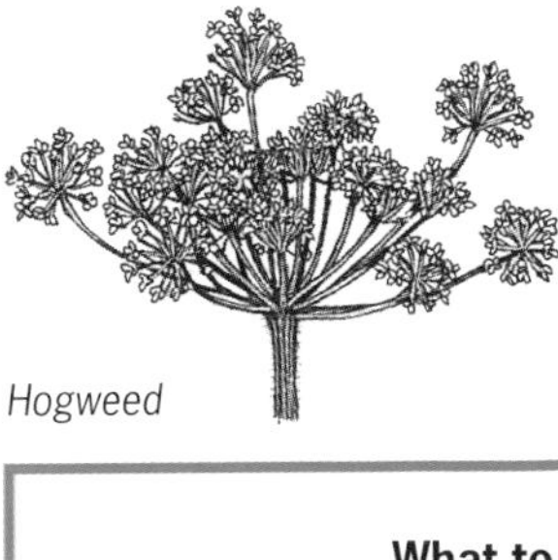

*Hogweed*

**START**
The walk begins from the Old Station car park on the eastern edge of Tiverton. From the A361, turn onto the B3391 and on reaching the large roundabout at the entrance to Tiverton follow 'Town Centre' signs down Blundells Road. At a smaller roundabout turn left, then immediately left again into the car park.

**DIRECTIONS**
Leave the car park through an exit in its far right-hand corner. Turn left and continue along the road for about 300yds, passing a small link road (Old Road) on the left. A few yards further on turn left down a tarmac path to reach a metal gate on the right. This gives access to the old railway line which is now a cycle track and walkway. Follow the tree-lined walk way for about ½ mile to where a road bridge spans the old line. Go up the steps on the right to a road. Turn right and walk a few yards up the road to where a signposted track goes off to the right. Go along the track to cross Ford Road onto a continuation track, which leads up to a children's play area and a grassy open space. Just

*By the Grand Western Canal*

### What to look out for

The woodland alongside the old railway line is alive with birds and rich with wildflowers. There are ducks and other water birds on the canal, while butterflies and dragonflies favour the moist verges of the canal bank. There is achance of seeing the horse-drawn barges of the Grand Western Horseboat Company which runs trips along the canal during the season.

*Narrowboat trips are a popular attraction on the canal at Tiverton*

abreast of the swings, go left down a passageway, then turn right into a cul-de-sac of houses.

From the right-hand corner of the cul-de-sac go up another passageway to a short flight of steps, which lead up and onto the canal path. Turn right and follow the canal to where it ends at The Grand Western Canal Basin, taking the steps down to the Grand Basin car park. To regain the Old Station car park from the Canal Basin car park it is necessary to cross the main road to the pavement opposite. Turn right and at the bottom of the hill recross the road to the Old Station car park.

**Old Railway Line**

The first section of the walk is along the route of a branch line railway built in 1848. This line took over much of the traffic of the Grand Western Canal which gradually declined. In turn the railway was closed as road transport increased – a pattern repeated throughout the industrial transport network of Britain.

**The Grand Western Canal**

The 11-mile Grand Western Canal that runs east from Tiverton is the remnant of an ambitious scheme to link the Bristol Channel and the English Channel by building a network of canals and rivers. The Tiverton branch was opened in 1814 at a cost of over £220,000. It was used mainly for transporting limestone and coal to feed the limekilns at Tiverton Basin.

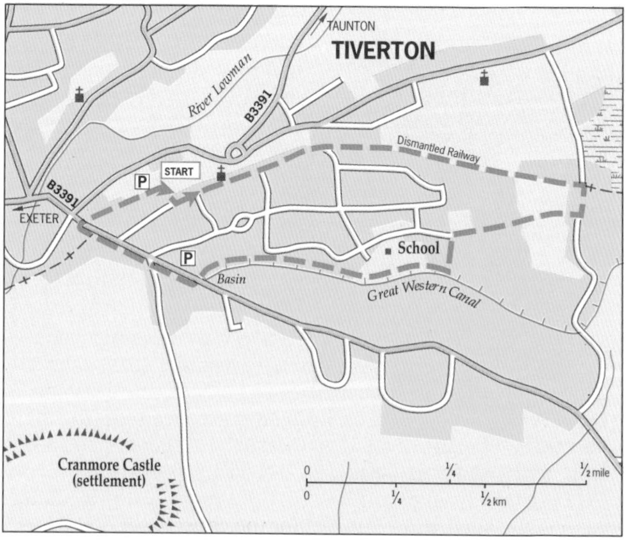

# The Somerset Moors: North Curry

This walk follows the banks of the River Tone through Somerset's willow-growing area. It includes the picturesque village of North Curry and part of the waymarked Curry Moor Trail.

**WALK 7**
SOMERSET
ST316268

### Information

The walk is about four miles long
A lot of stiles
Dogs must be on leads
The Bird in Hand pub has a covered patio and beer garden
Seats and picnic area in Queen Square

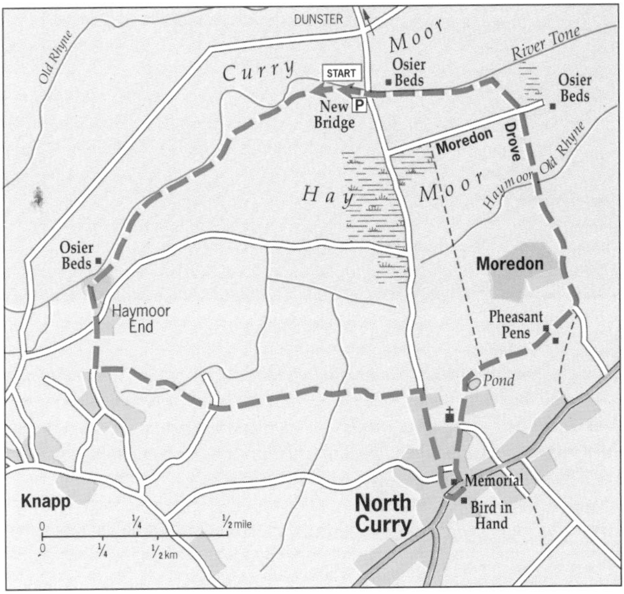


START
The walk starts at New Bridge car park, one mile north of North Curry and seven miles east of Taunton. From Taunton take the A361 towards Street and turn right one and a half miles beyond Durston. The car park is half a mile further, on the far side of the bridge.

DIRECTIONS
From the car park take the gateway marked 'TDBC Trail'. Walk across the field to the gate on the river bank and repeat with the next field. Keep to the bank through another five gates or stiles, passing an osier bed on the left. Beyond are some old orchards. At the end of the first orchard turn left through a gateway and into the field between the orchards. Turn right over the stile (waymarked) and keep to the left of the field beyond. Go through the gate and up the road past the cottages.
Before the next buildings turn left over the stile and follow the waymarks over the fields. After eight more stiles and a gate, cross a bridge with a stile, and walk straight ahead up the field to a stile in a corner of the hedge at the top. Heading for the church, there are two more stiles before the road. Turn right into the village as far as the Bird in Hand pub. Turn back past Queen Victoria's memorial to Queen Square. Keep right down Church Road then left through the lych-gate into the churchyard. Keep to the right of the church and through the kissing-gate beyond.
Walk round the pond, along the side of the field and up stone steps to the stile at the end. Keep straight ahead up

*A watery channel, part of the Somerset Levels*

the next field and between the pheasant pens. Cross a stile and turn left down the lane and right around the lodge at the end. Descend the grassy track and continue onto the moor until the track (Moredon Drove) comes to a junction. Take the gateway ahead and cross the field to the river bank. Turn left along the bank, through two gates and over two stiles back to New Bridge.

**What to look out for**

Unimproved meadows have up to 50 species of plants and flowers in the rhynes include flag irises, marsh marigolds, lady's smock, meadow rue, ragged robin and arrowhead. Breeding birds include lapwing, curlew, snipe and kingfisher and there are many wintering wildfowl and waders.

**Somerset Moors and Levels**

The Levels were built up on clay deposited by the sea, creating the marsh, fen and bog land which is known as the moors. Flooded in winter, they became summer pasture (the meaning of 'Somerset'). For centuries they have been improved for hay meadows by cutting ditches known as rhynes. Haymoor Old Rhyne was built by the monks of Athelney in 1316.

**Osier Beds**

Willows have been cultivated here for more than two centuries for basket and furniture making and artist's charcoal. The willows are cut three years after planting, boiled, stripped of bark and soaked prior to weaving. The Willows and Wetlands Visitor Centre, two miles east of North Curry, explains the process.

*Kingfisher*

# The Quantocks: Holford Combe

**WALK 8**
SOMERSET
ST155411

Holford Combe was described by Dorothy Wordsworth, who lived here in 1797: 'Wherever we turn we have woods, smooth downs and valleys with small brooks running down them... The hills that cradle these villages are either covered with fern or bilberries or oak woods – walks extend for miles over the hilltops, the great beauty of which is their wild simplicity.'

**START**
Holford is ten miles west of Bridgwater on the A39. Turn off between the filling station and pub, pass the church and take the second turn on the right for the village green and adjacent car park.

**DIRECTIONS**
From the car park, turn back towards the village, then cross the stream and bear right to follow the track around the thatched cottages. Turn right up the road, which becomes a track. Further on the track crosses and recrosses the stream in the combe, but it is possible to keep to the left-hand bank most of the way. After a mile the stream has to be crossed and there is a meeting of streams and paths. Follow the track rising up the valley to the left of the left-hand stream.
At the top turn left. Keep straight on up the hill, ignoring the two paths to the left (views to Bridgwater and the Somerset Levels). At the top of this rise, where four paths meet, take the left-hand path. The path passes through and alongside the rampart of Dowsborough hill fort, hidden under stunted oaks. (A break in the trees to the right reveals views down to Holford, left to Exmoor and right to Hinkley Point power station and Weston super Mare beyond. On a clear they extend to the islands of Steepholm and Flatholm and the Welsh coast beyond.)
Turn right through the break in the rampart and follow the track down the ridge towards Holford. Keep along the crest of the ridge, then straight down through trees to the minor road at the bottom. Turn left along the road, which leads back to Holford Combe. Retrace your steps to the car park or fork right to circuit the village, keeping right to the main road, then left round the pub and right again to return to the car park.

*The leafy path at Holford Combe*

**Information**

The walk is three and a half miles long, four miles including the village
Easy walking, except for the half-mile climb to Dowsborough
The only road walking is in the village
No gates or stiles
Dogs should be on leads in the village
The Plough pub in the village has tables outside and there is a tearoom at the shop
The village green and Holford Combe are good for picnicking

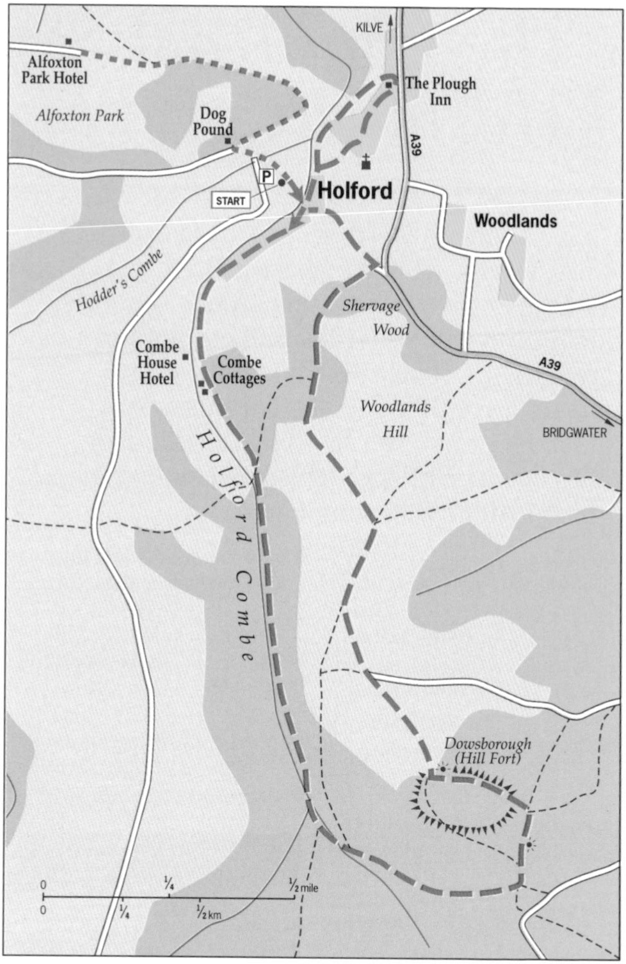


### Alfoxton

A mile along the road beyond the village green is the Alfoxton Park Hotel, once home of the Wordsworths. William rented the house to be near his friend Coleridge, who lived at Nether Stowey. Both wrote several poems here, although Wordsworth only stayed for a year, the owner of the house refusing to renew the tenancy because of Wordsworth's sympathy with the French Revolution.

Along the way is an old dog pound. A huntsman at the former kennels at Alfoxton was killed by his hounds whilst trying to silence them for barking at stray dogs. The Breretons, owners of Alfoxton, then erected the pound to keep stray dogs away from the kennels.

**What to look out for**

The area is renowned for its wild red deer, and you may see deer wallows in muddy patches near the stream. Bilberries, called whortleberries around here, grow amongst the heather and under the coppiced oaks and are ripe for picking in July and August.

### Dowsborough

This is a large prehistoric hill fort with an oval-shaped double rampart. It may be Iron Age, but there has been no excavation and it could have been occupied at any time from the Bronze Age to the Dark Ages. Roman coins have been found near by.

**WALK 9**
DORSET
SY560846

# Abbotsbury and Chesil Beach

From Chesil Beach, with its huge wall of shingle, the route skirts Chapel Hill, with an optional diversion to the Swannery, and climbs to St Catherine's Chapel before visiting the village or returning directly to the beach.

**Information**

The main walk is about two and a half miles long; three with a visit to the Swannery
Apart from a short, steep ascent of Chapel Hill, the going is fairly level
Road walking only if visiting the village
A few stiles
Picnicking on beach – please note: bathing is dangerous here
Refreshment and ice cream vans in car park (in summer season) and pubs, tea rooms and cafés in village
Toilets in car park

## START

Abbotsbury is on the B3157, eight miles north-west of Weymouth. Drive westwards through the village and follow signs to Subtropical Gardens and Chesil Beach. The car park is behind the beach.

## DIRECTIONS

From the car park, cross one of the wooden bridges towards the sea. Turn left and walk along the shingle for about 200yds. At a fork, follow sign 'Coastal Footpath and Swannery' through a gate, soon gaining a view of St Catherine's Chapel. After a while the path follows a stream.

After about 250yds look out for a stile on the right with a signpost to 'Swannery'. Cross the stile and start to skirt the hill, with a good view of The Fleet, a stretch of calm water enclosed by the bank. Pass a wartime pillbox and then go through a waymarked gate. Passing another pillbox on the right, follow the track across the field to a stone marker where a choice can be made.

(To visit the Swannery take the path downhill; either retrace your steps to this stone marker to rejoin main route, or take horse-drawn carriage to Swannery car park and walk on into village. To carry on round the hill to the village, continue straight on; to rejoin walk from the village, go west along main street, turning left to follow sign 'Chapel and Beach'.)

The main walk turns left and climbs very steeply up the hill.

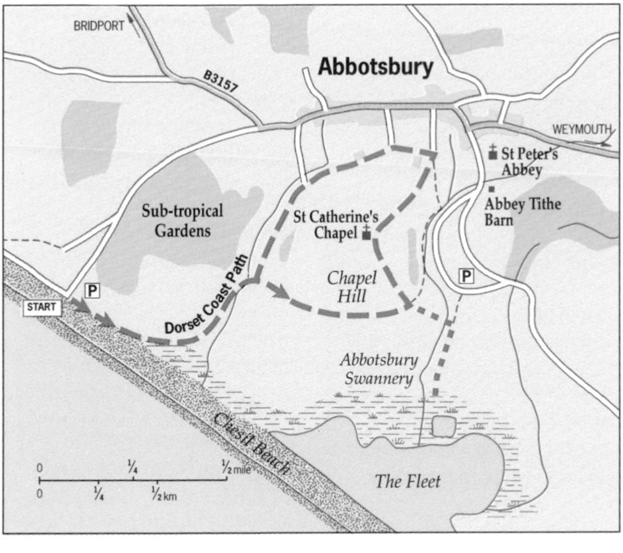

*The historic Tithe Barn at Abbotsbury*

crossing a stile, to the chapel (magnificent views). Enter the chapel from the far side. Follow the sandy track down towards the village past the farm and kissing-gate to join a lane. To visit the village, go straight on; retrace your steps to this point.

To return to the beach, turn left and left again. Pass some cottages on the right and after about 250yds go through a gate and turn left on to a track. Eventually meet the outward route by the stile and return to the car park.

**Chesil Bank**

This unique bank of shingle, up to 40ft high, extends for about 18 miles, from Bridport to Portland. The pebbles increase in size from west to east – so consistently that, tradition has it, a smuggler could tell exactly where he was in the dark. The bank is treacherous in stormy weather – during a particularly bad storm in 1824 one ship was carried right over the bank into the Fleet. Beachcombers have discovered parts of Spanish galleons and gold ingots.

**What to look out for**

From Chapel Hill look out for Abbotsbury Tithe Barn – about 600 years old and one of the longest in the country, it is now used for storing locally-grown water reed for thatching. In St Catherine's Chapel you will find the prayer used by women searching for a husband – St Catherine was the patron saint of spinsters. Terns and ringed plovers nest on the shingle, and the Fleet is home to brent geese, gulls and waders in winter.

**Abbotsbury Swannery**

Founded by monks in the 14th century, the swannery is a breeding ground for the only managed colony of mute swans. Several hundred can be seen at close quarters. There is a also 17th-century duck decoy. The swannery is open from April to October; for winter visiting telephone 01305 871125.

# *Old Sarum*

**WALK 10**
WILTSHIRE
SU139326

From the huge earthworks of Old Sarum, forerunner of the city of Salisbury two miles away, the walk crosses the watermeadows of the River Avon, skirts the village of Stratford sub Castle then makes its way back up to the ramparts.

**Information**

The walk is two and a half miles long
Steep climbs up and down the ramparts; otherwise level
Several stiles
Pub opposite entrance to Old Sarum; children's room and meals
Good picnic spots on Old Sarum
Toilets at Old Sarum

START
Old Sarum is two miles north of Salisbury on the A345. Either park in Old Sarum's car park (NB this closes at 4pm) or in the layby on the main road opposite the Old Castle pub and walk up to the car park.

DIRECTIONS
From Old Sarum car park cross stile and take the steps by the information board and toilets to reach the inner rampart. Turn left and follow the path, circling the rampart to reach the ruins of the old cathedral on the left. Just beyond the ruins, at the corner of the field, turn right into a gully and follow it down through a gap in the inner wall and across the embankment to the outer wall. Turn left and almost immediately take the path dropping steeply away to the right. Continue down the hill to a path and turn left. The path reaches a stile, but do not cross it – instead turn sharp right away from Sarum towards Stratford sub Castle. At the road, cross, and turn right. Take the first turning on the left, opposite a signpost to Devizes Road. The road continues over two small bridges and narrows to a tarmac path (views extend to Salisbury Cathedral). After crossing the River Avon turn right at the next path junction and continue with the river to the right (NB paths to the right are for fishermen only.)
The path eventually leads behind farm buildings to a road. Turn right and follow the road round to the right towards Salisbury. Shortly take the footpath to Portway by the sign for Stratford sub Castle. Follow the path diagonally across to the churchyard and on reaching the tarmac path turn left. Just before reaching the top of the path turn sharp right along the bottom of the embankment towards Old

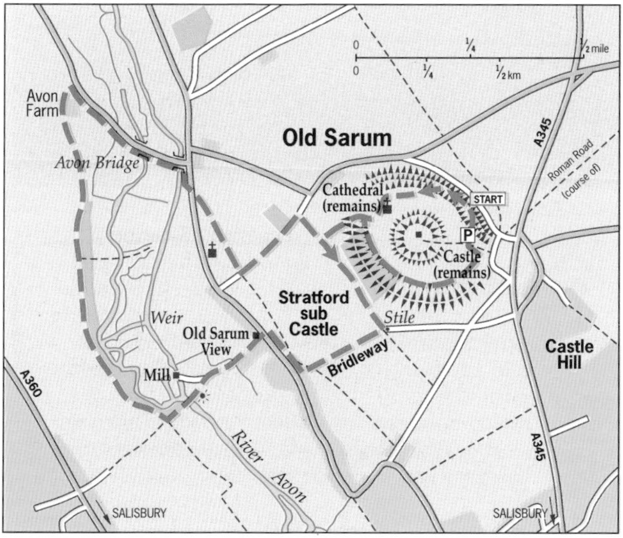

Watercress

Sarum. Turn up the hill to the left and retrace your steps to the outer embankment. Turn right and follow the outer wall back to the car park.

**Old Sarum**

Originally a prehistoric hill fort, Old Sarum grew through Roman, Saxon and Norman times, eventually becoming a major medieval settlement with a castle, a cathedral and a bishop's palace. Today there is little remaining, but the foundations of the cathedral can be clearly seen, and there are ruins of the bishop's palace in the inner bailey. Most of the excavated finds can be seen in Salisbury's museum.

**Stratford sub Castle**

This ancient village – its name recalls the days when there *was* a castle above it – had a fulling mill in the 13th century. Its church dates from the 13th and 15th centuries, although the tower was rebuilt in 1711.

*Old Sarum was once an important medieval city*

**What to look out for**

Gliders and light aircraft from the nearby airfield can often be seen circling ahead. The flat fields neatly divided by straight hedges to the right, after leaving Old Sarum, are the remains of a Roman settlement. Swans and geese inhabit the watermeadows of the Avon, particularly in winter, and there are pollarded willows and fine views across to the spire of Salisbury Cathedral. Watercress grows by some of the streams, and wetland flowers such as ragged robin and hemp agrimony flourish in the meadows.

# *Beside the Kennet and Avon Canal*

## WALK 11
WILTSHIRE
SU276618

A gentle walk from Wilton Windmill along the Kennet and Avon Canal to the picturesque villages of Great and Little Bedwyn, returning through rolling farmland and mixed woodland, and with an optional detour to see the beam engines at Crofton.

### Information

The walk is about seven miles long.
Gentle walking with no steep gradients.
Can be muddy in winter, so stout footwear is necessary.
There are pubs in Wilton and Great Bedwyn; the Harrow at Little Bedwyn is half way along the walk.

### START
The walk starts at Wilton Windmill, which is signposted from the A338 and Wilton. Park in the road-side car park serving the windmill.

### DIRECTIONS
From Wilton Windmill follow the road downhill towards Wilton village. At the T-junction turn left and, after about 100yds, take the bridleway on the right. (To see the beam engines, continue at * below.) Take the footpath which leads sharply right 50yds along the bridleway.
At the field, bear left along its edge and, just after passing beneath telegraph wires, bear right towards a water-trough and elder tree. Continue in this direction along a rather indistinct path; a wood soon appears on the horizon. Cross the stile into a small field and, before entering the wood, look left for a view of Tottenham House, former home of the Earl of Cardigan. Follow the meandering path through Wilton Brail: it becomes clearer. At the edge of the woods a broad grassy ride opens out to the right; cross this and look for an iron gate and squeeze-stile, ahead and to the left. Go through

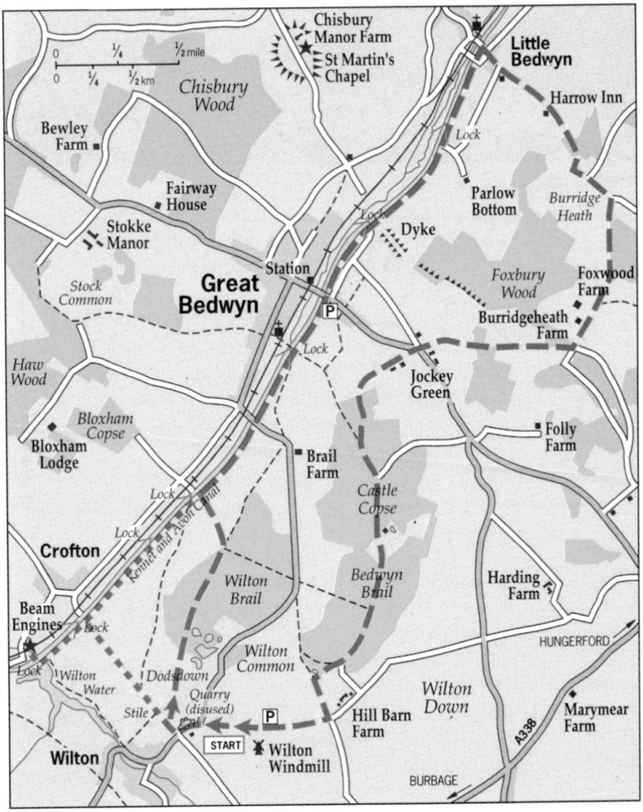

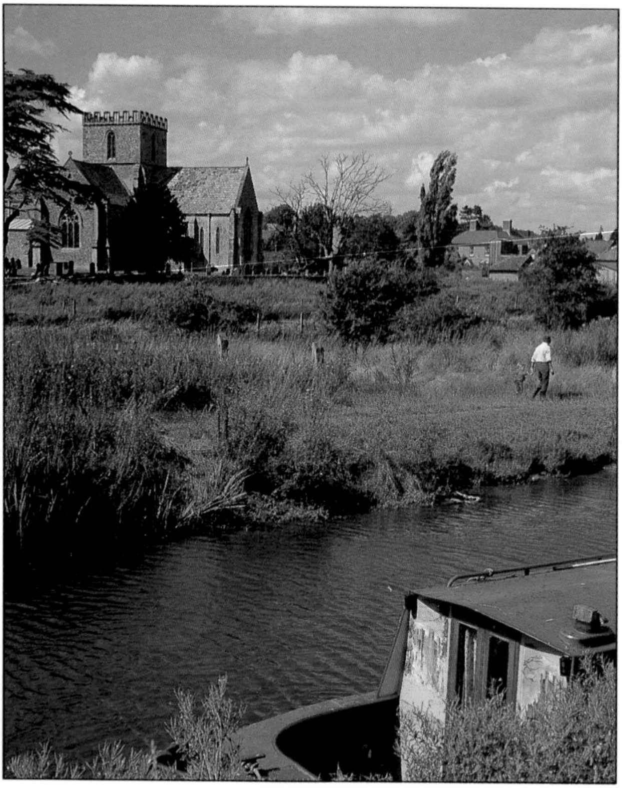

*Great Bedwyn church, from the canal*

### What to look out for

Crofton Pumping Station houses the two oldest working beam engines in the world still in their original building. Dating from 1812 and 1845, they were installed here to pump water to this, the highest point of the Kennet and Avon Canal, which links the Thames to the Severn. Open on summer weekends. Tel: 01672 851639.

the stile and proceed downhill with the fence on your left. At the bottom of the field pass through the gate and turn right along the towpath. Follow the canal for about 2½ miles to Little Bedwyn.
In Little Bedwyn, by the footbridges over the canal and railway, turn right and walk up to the road. Continue straight on, past the Harrow Inn. After ½ mile, at the brow of the hill, turn right along a track, signed Burridgeheath and Jockey Green. Some 100yds beyond Foxwood Farm where the road bends sharply left, turn immediately right on to a farm track. In ½ mile cross the road at Jockey Green and take the track to Bedwyn Brail. Keep right of the farm buildings on a narrow path, and continue on up the field ahead. At a point of scrubby woodland, bear right and immediately left over a stile. Follow the path uphill across the corner of a field and enter the woodland, left, by a prominent oak tree. Follow the broad track through Bedwyn Brail, keeping to higher ground. In ¾ mile a broad ride on right gives a magnificent vista to Savernake Forest.
At the edge of the woods, the main path leads to a gate then veers left. Turn right after the gate, then bear left, keeping just inside the wood. After 50yds turn left, then right at the road. This brings you back to your start point.
*For a detour, continue on up the hill, enjoying fine views left of Martinsell Hill. Descend to the bridge and take the towpath to your left. Carefully cross the canal at Crofton Lock to see the beam engines; to rejoin the main walk take the towpath towards Great Bedwyn.

**Wilton Windmill**
The windmill was constructed in 1821. The sails turned for a hundred years, until in 1921 the mill fell victim to the advent of steam-generated electricity. Open on summer Sunday and Bank Holiday afternoons.

# *Chew Valley Lake*

The lake forms a lovely focal point to this very attractive walk, with its information centre, nature trails and picnic area.

**WALK 12**
AVON
ST573614

**START**
Chew Valley Lake is bordered on the southern side by the A368 south of Bristol. Start from the car park nearest the dam at the northern end of the lake, signposted 'Picnic Area'.

**DIRECTIONS**
Turn left along the main road and take the first right along Denny Lane. Shortly turn left over a stile onto a signposted public footpath. Follow this tarmac lane down into the valley and, just before the bridge and a sign, 'Strictly Private Property', take the signposted footpath on the right into the woods. Continue in the same general direction for about ¼ mile, through fields and across several stiles, with the river meandering along in woodland to the left. Eventually the path reaches the edge of Chew Magna at a gate and stile in the hedge. Go through the gate and turn right to visit the village, but otherwise head back diagonally in a south-easterly direction across the brow of the field you have just walked across. Go through a gate and follow the field edge to a stile in the hedge. Cross this and the road below and take the footpath (Pitts Lane) signposted opposite. Continue past a farm, through a gate and past another farm to reach a stile. Cross this and follow the left-hand field edge to a gate, marked 'Public Footpath'. Continue along a narrow path, which can become overgrown, and go through another gate to reach an open area known as Knowle Hill. The walk continues in a southerly direction down the hill to reach a road. Turn right and immediately past

**Information**

The walk is three and a half miles long
Very few gradients, but some muddy sections
A lot of stiles
Pubs in Chew Magna
Café at car park
Picnic area beside the lake
Toilets at car park

*Coot*

**What to look out for**

The lake is an important inland site for wintering wildfowl, including a small but regular flock of Bewick Swans, and there are displays on wildlife at the car park.
Thousands of tufted ducks, pochards and gadwall can be seen from October to March. The members of the sailing club are often active on the lake, and anglers can be seen on the banks, fishing for brown and rainbow trout.
Pitts Lane is a fascinating example of an ancient hollow lane, with properly layered hedges containing a variety of species – the more species there are, the older the hedgerow.

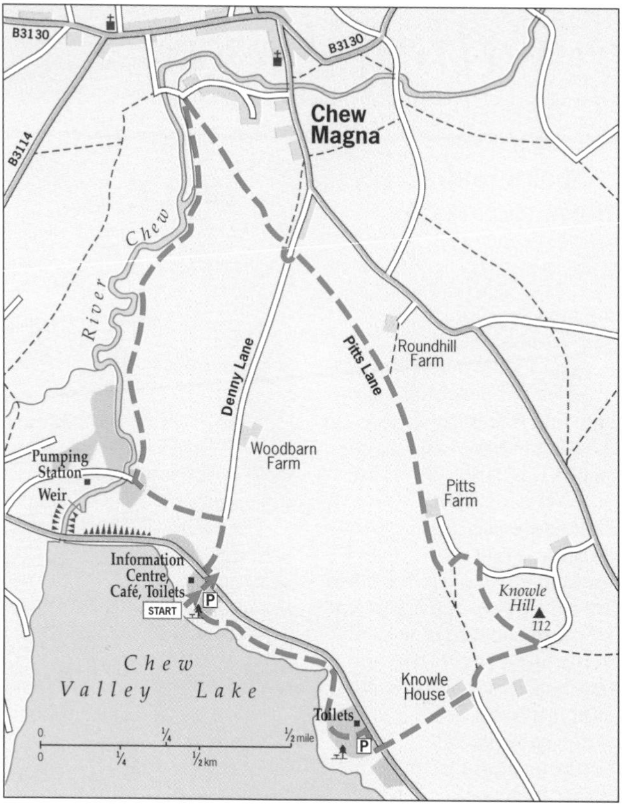


Knowle House turn right, as signposted, into the courtyard and between the two buildings and go through a gate on the left into a field. Carry on towards the lake, now in view, and follow the path to reach the main road. On the opposite side, to the right, is the entrance to the lake's lower car park. Follow the lakeside path to return to the upper car park.

**Chew Valley Lake**
The Bristol Water Company began construction of the lake in 1950 and six years later it was opened by HM The Queen. One of the largest artificial lakes in the south-west of England, it has a perimeter of ten miles and yields about ten million gallons of water every day. Now a Site of Special Scientific Interest, the lake is very popular with birdwatchers.

*The view from Knowle Hill*

# The Canal and River at Bradford-on-Avon

## WALK 13
WILTSHIRE
ST825607

A pleasant and undemanding stroll along the well-maintained towpaths of Bradford Canal and the river, with plenty of opportunities for refreshment breaks.

### Information

The walk is three miles long
Level, easy walking on good paths
One stile, if extension to walk is taken
Dogs should be kept on leads
Pub and seasonal teashop at Avoncliff; also teashop at Barton Farm; pubs, restaurants and teashops at Bradford-on-Avon
Picnic tables by the river at Barton Farm

*Cuckoo*

### What to look out for

There is always something to see on the canal and river – narrowboats, dinghies, birdlife and anglers. At a right angle to the large Tithe Barn is its much smaller predecessor.

**START**
The walk starts from the railway station car park in Bradford-on-Avon.

**DIRECTIONS**
Go through the gap at the far end of the car park, turn left along the river bank across the open area to a broad tarmac path which runs parallel with the river. Follow this path until it joins the canal opposite a swing bridge. Turn right along the canal bank, and continue to a clearly marked right turn leading down to the river. (To reach the aqueduct at Avoncliff continue along the path.) Turn right and follow the river bank back towards Bradford. After climbing the stile, keep to the right around the pumping station and up to the canal bank. Turn left at the swing bridge and follow this path until it leaves the canal bank and joins the road. (At this point you may take a detour to Bradford Lock by crossing the road, turning right, and then going through a gate on the left. Retrace your steps and re-cross the road.)
Turn left along the road for a short distance, then turn left through a small gate and head towards the tithe barn within Barton Farm Country Park, entering through the gate to the right of the beech tree. After visiting the barn, rejoin the river path, turn right and go under the railway bridge. Continue along the bank, and turn right beside the swimming pool to return to the car park.

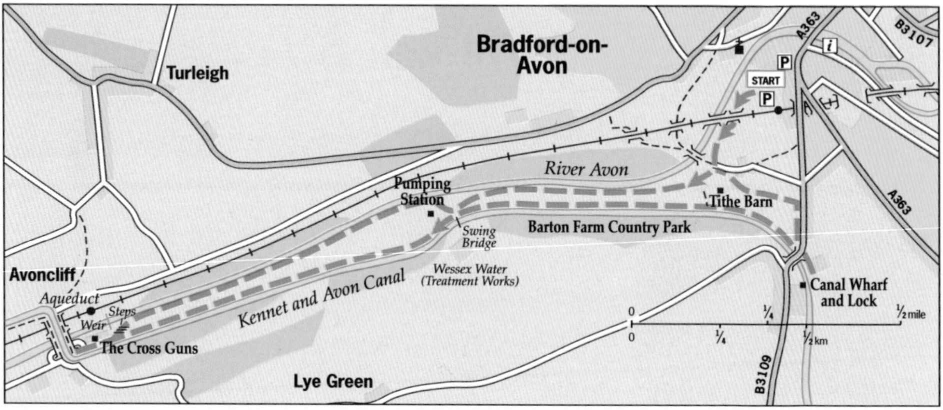


**Barton Farm Country Park**
Now in the care of English Heritage, the huge Tithe Barn forms the focal point of the complex here. Built in the 14th century, the barn originally belonged to Shaftesbury Abbey and was used to store the tithes of grain elicited from the estate's tenants. Thousands of stone tiles cover the roof and immense, but exquisitely graceful, timbers support the weight. The complex now houses craft shops and refreshments.

**Bradford's Blind House**
Originally used as a chapel, this tiny stone building on the ancient town bridge is thought to have become a prison at some time in the early 18th century. Such places were sometimes referred to as 'blind houses' because there were no windows, and conditions inside were abominable. It is possible to obtain the key from a nearby shop and go inside.

*The old stone bridge in the centre of Bradford-on-Avon*

# *Oldbury-on-Severn*

**WALK 14**
AVON
ST609925

An undemanding walk on absolutely level ground, with the Severn estuary providing interest for the first part – it is well worth taking binoculars.

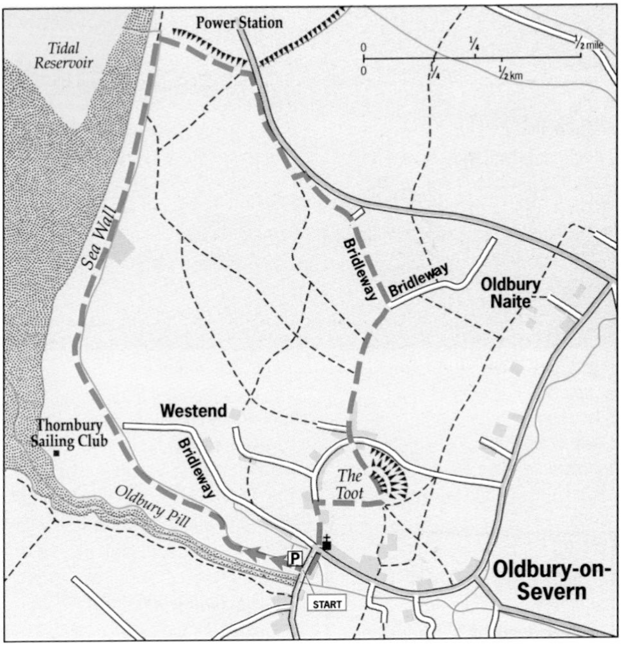


### Information

The walk is three miles long
No road walking and no gradients, but very muddy in places
Several stiles and one gate to climb
Pubs in Oldbury

**START**

Oldbury lies on the south bank of the River Severn, about three miles north of the Severn Bridge. Park in the car park in Church Road, by the bridge, opposite the Anchor Inn.

**DIRECTIONS**

On leaving the car park, go through the pedestrian gate to the right, signed 'Thornbury Sailing Club'. Follow the road to the clubhouse, passing the sluice gates to the left, and turn right along the sea wall. Continue for about ¾ mile, with the nuclear power station looming ahead. On reaching the power station, turn right along the signposted path, and continue until reaching a road.

Turn right here then shortly right again, where signposted, and climb the gate into a field (there are usually cattle here). Follow a field edge on the left side, to a stile by a ruined building and continue on to two gates. Go through the left-hand gate, then turn right along the track just before reaching the road. This bridleway can be very muddy indeed.

Where the track divides, turn right. The lane turns into a metalled road. Continue to the fork and take the public footpath signposted almost ahead, between houses. Cross two stiles before reaching The Toot. Cross the double stile in the right-hand corner and continue straight ahead to reach a stile hidden in the hedge. Cross this and head for the stone stile between stone walls.

Continue to steps, and reach the road. Turn left past the Ship, then cross into Church Road to return to the car park and start point.

*A safe mooring near the bridge*

**The Toot**
Oldbury Camp, otherwise known as The Toot, is an Iron Age hill fort. Covering about ten acres in all, it has a double bank and ditch on the north and east sides, and a single bank on the west. The discovery of coins here indicates that it was in use in Roman times, too. Now it is an integral part of the village; footpaths cross it and it is partially encircled by streets and housing.

**What to look out for**

There is always something to watch on the river estuary, with all manner of craft including tugboats, dredgers and sailing dinghies from the Thornbury Sailing Club. Birdwatchers will find plenty to interest them, and with luck will see cormorants at any time of the year. The Severn is an important refuge for winter visitors which may include dunlin, curlew and ringed plover.

**Oldbury Church**
Perched on a hill in the flat plain alongside the Severn, Oldbury's church can be seen for miles around and is a useful landmark throughout the walk. It is dedicated to Arilda, a local saint in Saxon times. The only other church in the country bearing her name is at Oldbury-on-the-Hill, about 15 miles away. Views from the churchyard are superb, and it is possibly to make out the route of the walk from here.

*Grey plover*

# May Hill and Clifford's Mesne

## WALK 15
GLOUCESTERSHIRE
SO699227

A simple climb to a viewpoint commanding panoramic views – west to the Black Mountains and east to the Cotswolds – this is a walk of constant change; a bumper package of exercise and wildlife interest.

### Information

The walk is three miles long
About 200 yards of ascent
Minimal minor road walking at beginning and end
Dogs should be on leads
Pub at start of the walk
Picnic on May Hill summit

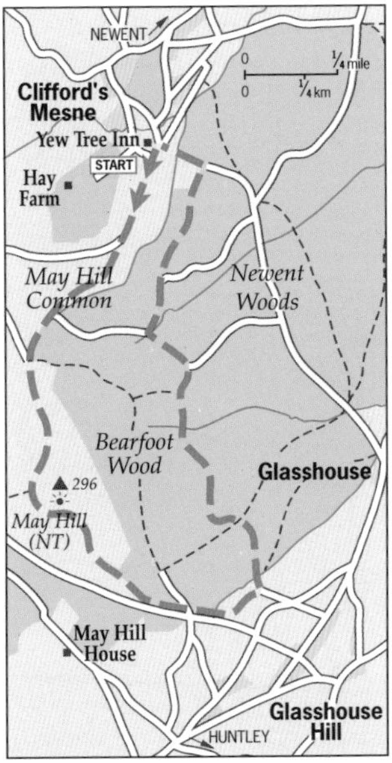


START
Park directly above The Yew Tree Inn in Clifford's Mesne.

DIRECTIONS
Follow the tarmac lane steeply uphill to a cattle grid to enter May Hill Common. Twenty yards further on, a sign ('May Hill') directs left. Ascend to a bridle-gate and on to May Hill. Follow the broad path slightly left through the wooden posts leading up the gentle ridge to the 971ft summit. Pass round the western perimeter to the right of the pine plantation (far-ranging views). Continue to the Silver Jubilee plaque, about 30yds into the trees. Leave the hill in a southerly direction by walking from the plaque, passing to the right of the stone triangulation point and heading towards the right-hand edge of the pine wood ahead, keeping to the meandering beaten track towards the River Severn. The path descends to a bridle-gate. Entering the lane, descend beyond a cottage and then pass to the left of a water tank, continuing to a fork. Take the left lane (a bridleway which can be muddy) leading down beside a solitary cottage with a large conservatory. Meeting a road at the bottom, go left (waymarked) to pass a gate and, ignoring paths to left and right, keep ahead on path marked '193', which winds through the predominately coniferous Newent Wood. In about 150yds, just before the track ahead rises to the left, go right, then in 20yds turn left. At the next track junction keep left uphill. At the second track junction, in 650yds, turn left uphill, then in just over 300yds turn right downhill. In another 200yds or so branch left and at the end of the track cross a stile and turn left onto the lane to return to the start point.

### What to look out for

The area is renowned for the wild daffodils that carpet fields and line hedgerows giving such joy to spring rambles. Check for signs of badgers and foxes in Newent Wood – they sometimes leave footprints on muddy tracks.

**May Hill**

The name May Hill is said to derive from the custom of neighbouring parishes contesting ownership of the hill on May Day. May Hill Common, but not the summit ring, belongs to the National Trust. The conifer plantation on the summit, which gives distinction to the pudding-shaped hill, was supplemented with new stock to celebrate Queen Elizabeth II's Silver Jubilee in 1977. The panorama ranges over the Forest of Dean, the Black Mountains in Wales (Waun Fach at 2661ft is the highest hill in view), the Malvern Range, the broad spreading Severn vale and the Cotswold escarpment.

**National Birds of Prey Centre, Newent**

Just over a mile north of Clifford's Mesne on the minor road to Newent, is this fascinating centre, open from February to November, which is home to eagles, hawks, vultures, falcons and owls. Weather permitting, there are flying displays every day, demonstrating the ancient skill of falconry. The centre has breeding aviaries, a falconry museum, gift and coffee shops.

*A peregrine-crossed lanner at the Birds of Prey Centre*

*A stand of trees at the summit of May Hill*

# The Severn Way

**WALK 16**
GLOUCESTERSHIRE
SO846278

A splendid riverside ramble which loops back via an old canal and the hilltop village of Apperley. A natural extension north along the Severn Way embraces Deerhurst, with its remarkably intact Saxon church and nearby chapel.

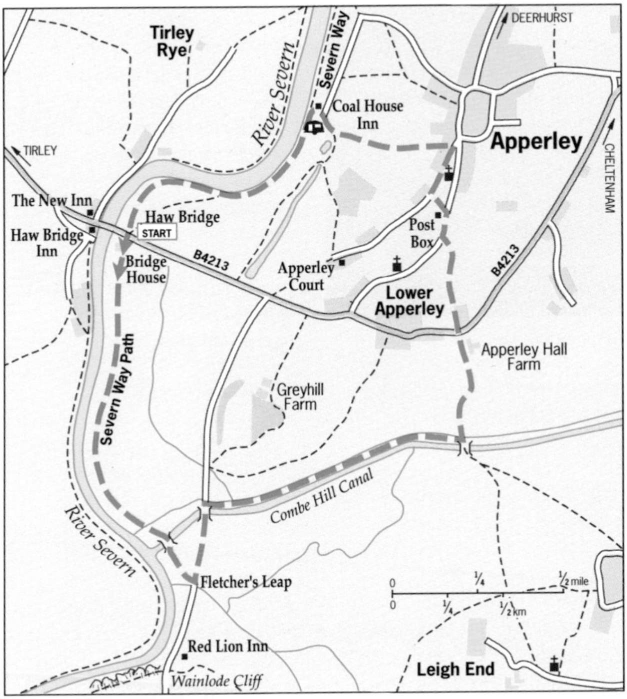


**Information**

The walk is about four and a quarter miles long, with an optional two-mile extension
Mainly level, with one slight ascent
A few hundred yards of very minor road
A lot of stiles, some rather wobbly
Dogs must be on leads
Riverside pub en route at Apperley for bar snacks and morning coffee; no children's room, but tables outdoors; also the New Inn and Haw Bridge Inn at walk's end
Picnic places along the riverbank

**START**

The walk begins five miles south of Tewkesbury, via the A38 and B4213, signposted 'Apperley' and 'Tirley'. Park carefully near the gate on the east side of Haw Bridge on the B4213.

**DIRECTIONS**

Cross to the wicket gate (waymarked) on the south side of the B4213, passing through the yard of Bridge House. Crossing the stile, signposted 'Severn Way Path', enter the long riverside meadow. After 500yds cross stile in left-hand hedge, then keep right and proceed along the riverside flood bank via stiles and gates. After the new floodgate the path sweeps round a pylon to a stile/gate and bridge over the old Coombe Hill Canal. Passing the old lock, keep right along the river and continue to the stile leading onto the road at Fletcher's Leap (to the right are Wainlode Cliff and the Red Lion Inn).

Turn left, following the road north to the bridge over the old canal. Beyond this turn right through the bridlegate on Warren Way path (Coombe Hill Canal Nature Reserve). Proceed along the inter-stream causeway (rough in places), through Cobney Meadows for ¼ mile then turn left over a stone and brick footbridge and along a winding lane leading up to the road by Apperley Hall

*The river from Haw Bridge*

Farm. Cross directly to the facing bridleway, rising steadily uphill, and on joining the minor road turn right. At the post box cross the stile left, traversing the pasture towards the white-painted house. A stile gives access into a metalled lane. Turn right, passing the church, duck pond and green and seeking the footpath immediately after the two new houses, via a gate to the left.(To visit Deerhurst, a mile distant, continue north along the village street then take footpaths down the hill; return along the riverbank on the Severn Way.)

The main walk continues due west beside the fence to a waymarked stile, descending into a valley, crossing two further stiles en route, to the open road at The Coal House Inn. Follow the road, left to the river to join the Severn Way. Turn left (right if you are returning from Deerhurst), through the waymarked Severnside Caravan Park via a stile, with two further stiles to negotiate to complete the walk.

**What to look out for**

Both the Severn-side section and old Coombe Hill Canal are exceptionally interesting locations to study wildlife, a fascinating blend of marine and moorland birds, from gulls through to curlews, swans, geese, ducks, herons and kingfishers.

**Odda's Chapel**

This rare survival from the Saxon period was dedicated on 12 April 1056 and was built by Earl Odda in honour of his brother Aelfric. It is now in the care of English Heritage. The priory church of St Mary is considered one of the most important monuments of Anglo-Saxon England, founded in the 7th century and becoming established over the next three centuries. Originally a Benedictine monastery with a 30,000 acre estate, it was here, in 1016, that King Canute made a treaty with Edmund Ironside. The chapel is open at any reasonable time.

**The Severn Way**

The Severn Way was created by Gloucestershire County Council in 1989 and the east bank path is currently waymarked for 50 miles south of Tewkesbury with the distinctive 'Severn Trow' symbol. Eventually there will be a walkers' route along most of its 200-mile course from Plynlymon Fawr to Bristol. In this county there will be paths on both banks.

In 1430 an Act of Parliament named the river the 'King's Highway of the Severn' because three-quarters of its length was navigable. It is famous for its elver (baby eel) fishing (see elver deterrent notice at the end of the Coombe Hill Canal) and its tidal 'bore', beloved of surfers and canoeists.

# A Longer Ramble at Hamble

**WALK 17**
HAMPSHIRE
SU483068

The walk starts in the famous yachting centre of Hamble and incorporates a short ferry crossing, some of the finest river and woodland scenery in Hampshire, and takes in the picturesque village of Bursledon.

**START**

The walk starts from the village of Hamble, 7 miles from Southampton. Park in the main square of the village, or at the pay and display car park on the harbour.

**DIRECTIONS**

Walk down the main street of Hamble to the water's edge, and wait on the pontoon, opposite the Bugle pub, to cross over on the Warsash ferry.

On the opposite bank turn left along the footpath beside the river. This path continues without interruption for 2½ miles to Crableck Marina. Continue past a car park and follow the path through trees and via a squeeze-gate. Cross

*The marina at Hamble*

### Information

The walk is about six and a half miles long.
Walking is mostly on level and easy ground, but some short, steep hills.
Many squeeze gates.
Some walking along busy road – dogs must be on a lead here.
Ferry times to be checked.
Many good picnic spots along the river bank.
Refreshments available in Hamble and Bursledon.

### What to look out for

The salt marshes are rich in wildlife, with brent geese, gulls, oystercatchers and redshank in the winter. Purslane and sea lavender can be seen here in the summer.

the marina hard-standing, leaving the wooden office of the marina on your right. Shortly, pass through two squeeze gates. After a mile, the path widens out to emerge at houses and the car park of Lower Swanwick marina. Follow the lane for 300yds up to the main road. Turn left here, keeping Moody's Boatyard on your left. Turn left into Church Lane, and then bear left, following signs for Bursledon Station.
By the station go a steep, narrow lane with bollards across, which leads up to a

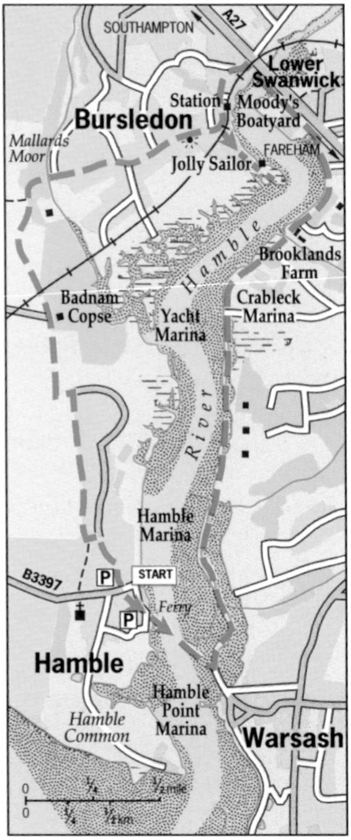


green. A short detour left here will take you to the Jolly Sailor Pub. Otherwise, bear right and continue along the High Street through Bursledon. At a narrow gateway half way up the street there is an excellent viewpoint.
Continue, and bear left at the small green (marked by a phone box). Cotinue past the Vine Inn and a junction, and where the road bends away right, follow the footpath between houses, through a squeeze gate, down hill.The path emerges at a narrow, surfaced lane, and after 50yds drops down a steep path (signposted) on a track. Turn left to cross to a footbridge and Mallards Moor wood. Continue climbing through here, to emerge at a concrete road. Cross over this and, bearing right, follow the high chain-link fence (crossing a railway bridge) until the path emerges at a road. Continue left here and pick up the signed path on the right, about 100yds beyond the sharp left-hand bend sign. The footpath continues for another mile between two fences across the disused airfield and along the backs of houses. Bear left at the large hangar by a grassy triangle, following the path down to the road. Turn right and follow the road back to Hambledon village centre and the car park.

**Bursledon**
With poor roads and no bridge until 1880, but sheltered waters and deep anchorages near The Jolly Sailor, Bursledon's growth depended on the river. Shipbuilding has taken place here since medieval times. The Elephant Boatyard was named after a ship built here for Lord Nelson.

*In-shore rescue boat*

# Chilbolton

**WALK 18**
HAMPSHIRE
SU383389

A lovely walk of a good length that takes in the watermeadows of the Rivers Test and Anton.

**Information**

The walk is four miles long, with a shorter alternative
Easy, mainly level walking
No stiles
Dogs must be kept under control, particularly on Chilbolton Common
The Mayfly pub, near the car park, offers food and a pleasant riverside garden

START
Chilbolton is east of the A3057, five miles south of Andover. Start from West Down car park at the southern end of the village, just off the A3057.

DIRECTIONS
Cross the road and follow the Test Way ('TW') sign to Totton, along the trackbed of former railway. On reaching the road turn left – take care as this road can be very busy. (For a shorter walk turn right and almost immediately right again. Follow the road to the bridleway signposted right and continue with the route

*Crossing the second bridge*

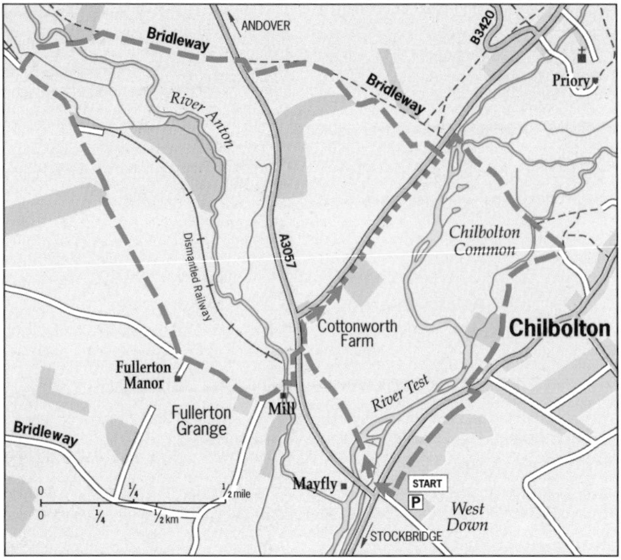

Hemlock

directions at * below.) Having crossed the bridge, turn right along the road to Longstock. Keep on this road (not turning off to Longstock) and continue up the hill. Opposite the drive to Fullerton Manor, turn right and follow the field edge. Continue in a straight line across the field as signposted. On reaching the old railway line trackbed, turn left to a cross-track.
Here turn right through a gate. Cross the river and at the end of the path through woodland turn right through a gate. Cross the main road and turn right into the corner of the field. Follow the fence uphill and continue on the bridleway to emerge on to a road. Turn left and after a few yards turn right along the signposted bridleway.
*Continue across two bridges to Chilbolton Common. At the far side of the common turn right, pass the white thatched cottage, go across the playing fields and follow the path to meet the road. Turn left, cross the road and take the path leading across West Down to return to the car park.

### Chilbolton Common

This lovely open area, between the villages of Wherwell and Chilbolton, is typical of the watermeadows that used to be a feature of all Hampshire's chalk rivers, and the common is designated a Site of Special Scientific Interest. For centuries the common has been grazed by cattle, and it still is.

### Wherwell

A number of legends are attached to the nearby village of Wherwell, but the most famous is that of the cockatrice. The story tells of a duck's egg which hatched into a cockatrice – a sort of cockerel with a serpent's tail. The creature grew to be enormous and devoured villagers, until a reward was offered to anyone who could kill it. A man named Green lowered a shining piece of metal into the monster's den and, thinking its reflection to be an enemy, the creature fought until exhausted. Green was then able to stab the beast to death.

### What to look out for

You can see swans and herons – and snipe in winter – on Chilbolton Common, where there is a rich variety of wild flowers. Watercress grows at the water's edge. There is evidence of the old railway line on the first part of the walk, which follows the trackbed of the former Andover-Romsey line, known as the 'Sprat and Winkle'.

# Greywell

**WALK 19**
HAMPSHIRE
SU722512

This is a very appealing walk with the attractions of water and bridges, castle ruins and a spooky sealed off tunnel which is home to hundreds of bats.

**Information**

The walk is just under two miles long
Level, easy ground
Virtually no road walking
Several stiles to cross
Pub in Greywell village for bar meals and morning coffee
Grassy area around castle suitable for picnics

## START

Greywell is five miles east of Basingstoke, just south of the A30. Start the walk from Greywell Pumping Station which lies to the east of the village along a minor road leading to North Warnborough and Odiham. There is parking for several cars on the approach road to the Pumping Station, but take care not to obstruct the gates.

## DIRECTIONS

Turn left on to the road and take the first track, signed 'Footpath' on the left. Cross the rickety stile by a gate at the end of the path, turn righ and keep close to the hedge. The ruins of King John's Castle can be seen over to the left. Cross the stile on to the canal towpath and continue right, to the swing-bridge. Turn left over the canal and continue towards the ford. Immediately before the ford take the footpath to the left, over a stile.

*The swing bridge on the River Whitewater at Odiham*

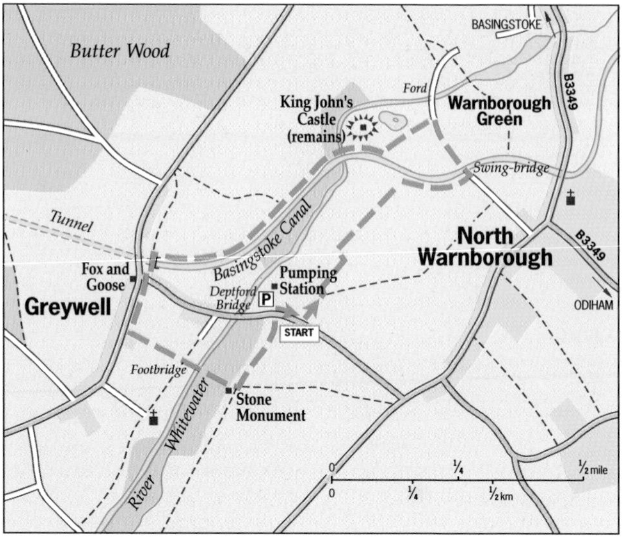


Cross the field and turn right on to the canal path over another stile, passing the ruins of King John's Castle and the remains of a lock before reaching the tunnel. Steps on the right lead down to the tunnel entrance, but take care as they can be slippery and end abruptly at the water. Turn left over the tunnel and follow the path to the road. Cross the stile and turn right on to the road, then turn left, opposite the Fox and Goose public house.

Continue through the village and, immediately before the first house on the left, take the footpath (not signposted) across the field. Go over the footbridge, signposted 'Wallace Memorial Reserve, Greywell Moors' then cross another stile. Turn left out of the woodland and continue through the field to the gate opposite the Pumping Station. Be sure to fasten this gate securely.

**King John's Castle**

A brief history of the castle is displayed on a board by the ruins – all that is left of the triple-storey keep forming part of a small fortress built in about 1207 by King John as a stopping place between Windsor and Winchester.

**A Tunnel Full of Bats**

Bats are always sure to capture the imagination, and although there is no access to the tunnel and its inhabitants cannot be seen, the very presence of these creatures provides an excellent source of interest on this walk. Just under ½ mile long, the tunnel is the biggest, and one of the most important of the known bat hibernation sites in Britain, thought to contain up to 2,000 bats of five species during the winter. Due to a spring here which keeps the temperature constant, and the collapse of the tunnel ensuring the colony is undisturbed, the bats are able to enjoy a unique micro climate. Plans to reopen the tunnel to canal traffic are causing much concern to conservationists.

*Leislers bat*

**What to look out for**

For over a century the Basingstoke Canal has been famed for its rich plant and animal life and whatever the time of year the most casual observer is sure to spot something of interest here. Among the most easily recognisable creatures are dragonflies: more than a dozen species are found on the canal. Kingfishers, moorhens, dabchicks, coots, swans, water voles, sticklebacks and perch can also be seen.

The profusion and variety of water plants is exceptional. Along the hedgerows blackberries, sloes and hazelnuts can be found in autumn.

# *Arundel Park and the River Arun*

**WALK 20**
SUSSEX
TQ018073

This easy walk links several of Arundel's main attractions. Without deviating far from the route you can feed the fish in a trout feeding pond, hire a rowing boat on Swanbourne lake, wander round the wildfowl reserve and round off the day with a visit to the famous castle.

**Information**

The walk is about three miles long
Level, easy walking
Half a mile of road walking, mostly on good verge
One stile
Dogs are not allowed around lake
Cafés along route; also Black Rabbit pub with garden
Picnic areas in Arundel Park

START
Arundel is on the A27 between Worthing and Chichester. Park at the Mill Road car park (charge) if you can't find free parking along the east side of Mill Road between the town and Swanbourne Lake.

DIRECTIONS
From the right side of Mill Road, where there is a wide path beneath an avenue of lime trees, go over a footbridge to the right of the stone road bridge. Stay in Mill Road for just a few yards before forking left onto a signposted path, passing to the right of the castle trout feeding pond. The path continues along the left-hand edge of Swanbourne Lake (from the far end it is possible to extend the walk up into Arundel Park, returning the same way) before doubling back to the right along the other side of the lake.
Rejoin Mill Road and turn left, passing the entrance to the Wildfowl and Wetlands Trust reserve on the right. In just under ½ mile, about 60yds before the Black Rabbit pub, turn right over a stile and double back along the river bank, with the perimeter fence of the wildfowl reserve on your right.
Where the river bends away to the left, turn right on a narrower path which brings you back to Mill Road. Turn left over the footbridge crossed at the beginning of the walk and retrace your steps to the start point.

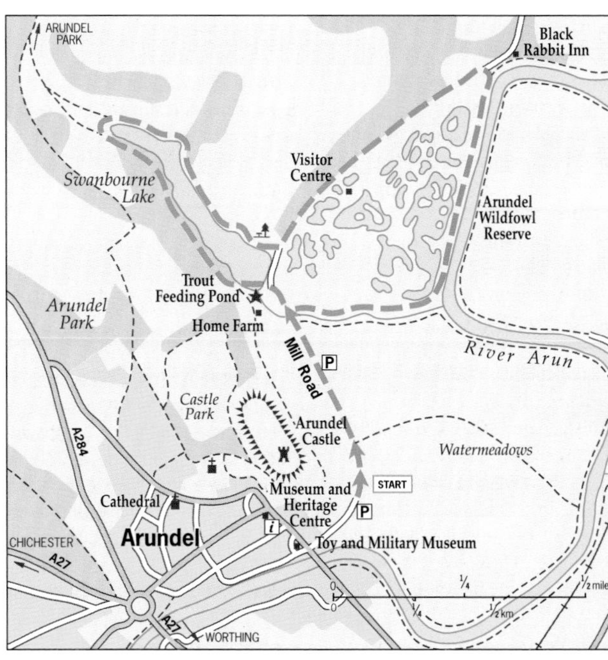

*Arundel Castle stands high above the River Arun*

**Arundel Castle**

The castle, seat of the Duke of Norfolk, Earl Marshal of England, occupies a superb situation, set high up amidst spacious parkland overlooking the River Arun. The first castle on the site was built in 1086, probably incorporating an even earlier Saxon fortress. It was dismantled by Parliamentarian troops in 1651 and what exists today is the result of a series of major restorations carried out over the following 200 years. The final work on the building was completed in 1903, using a style in keeping with the 13th-century original.

**Arundel Town**

The market town of Arundel occupies a steep slope overlooking the River Arun. It was once a busy port with a large trade in timber, but the river is now only navigable for small boats. Although the history of the town is closely linked with that of the castle, it has enjoyed an independent existence, being created a borough before the Norman Conquest. As well as its castle and wildfowl reserve, Arundel has an interesting Toy and Military Museum.

**What to look out for**

More than a thousand ducks, geese and swans from all over the world live in the 55 acres of pens, lakes and paddocks of the Wildfowl and Wetlands Trust, which is also a sanctuary for many wild birds. Wild diving duck are attracted by the clear pools, while waders come to feed in the watermeadows and man-made 'wader scrape'. Rarities include the shy water rail, which nests among the reed beds – listen for its grunting, squealing call. There are hides overlooking the different habitats as well as a large viewing gallery.

# Billingshurst

## WALK 21
SUSSEX
TQ086260

This walk follows field paths to visit a restored lock on the Wey and Arun Canal. It is a generally easy walk on level ground, but the paths can become overgrown, and route finding requires some concentration.

**Information**

The walk is three miles long
Almost all on level ground, though there is some rough ground; also one awkward plank bridge
Lots of stiles
Pubs and cafés at Billingshurst

**START**
Billingshurst is on the A29, London–Bognor Regis road. A free library car park opposite the National Westminster Bank is signposted to the west of the A29 in the centre of the village.

**DIRECTIONS**
From the library car park, go along the road to the left of the library. At crossroads go forward into Mill Way, later Arun Road. Between house numbers 46 and 48 turn right, up driveway, bearing left in front of a row of garages. Beyond the last garage, turn left (before stile) and follow path into copse. After about 100yds, where main path continues right into copse, bear left into the field by the signpost. Follow the right-hand field edge, turning left at a four-arm signpost; keep the hedge on your right. After 200yds follow signposts right, and after another 50yds follow sign left along an enclosed field for ½ mile. Turn right beside an overgrown pond and follow the path up between fenced fields. Cross over metalled track and continue forward, then after about 100yds go through a broken gate, bear left and down across rough pasture.

*Rowner Lock*

After 100yds, cross over a small stream (between two stiles). Turn left over a stile and climb across a meadow heading towards right-hand cottage, go through gate and cross over road. Cross stile ahead and proceed forward along fenced field edge. After about 250yds cross the stile by a shed and continue right, downhill along a bridleway to cross the river Arun over a sluice. Bear left and cross the water meadow to reach the Wey and Arun Canal at Rowner Lock. Retrace your steps from Rowner Lock, over the Arun, back up the bridleway to the shed. Return along

**What to look out for**

The walk passes former paddocks where grass and wild flowers have, at the time of writing, been allowed to grow unchecked, attracting lots of butterflies in summer, including meadow browns, gatekeepers and large skippers. The canal provides a haven for many water plants and insects, with a variety of dragonflies. You should see fish in the shallow water of Rowner Lock.

field edge to the road. Turn left and, after 100yds, go right along a track through farm buildings. Continue along the track for about ½ mile, ignore gate into field, continue left around field edge with copse on your left. Turn right on to a signposted footpath with a hedge on your right, and walk up through the buildings at Tedfold, turning left where signposted. Continue forward along public footpath through fields for about ¼ mile towards Billingshurst. At the houses, bear right along a paved alleyway and continue forward crossing over two cul-de-sacs. On reaching a small children's playground bear

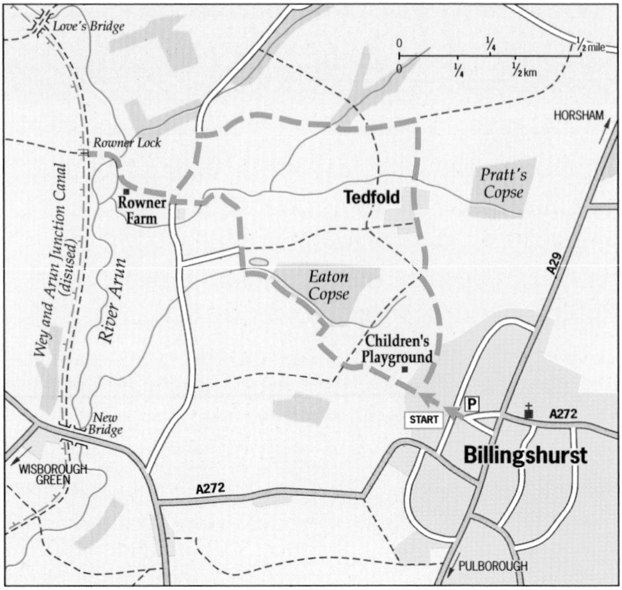

left to rejoin the outward route beside the garages. Retrace your steps to the library car park.

**The Wey and Arun Canal**
The canal was opened in 1816, but was never a commercial success, struggling on against growing competition from the railways until 1871. A hundred years later, the restoration of Rowner Lock was one of the first major projects undertaken by the Wey and Arun Canal Society, formed with the ultimate aim of re-opening 'London's lost route to the sea' over its entire 23-mile length. This goal is still a long way off, but much work has been completed – within walking distance of Rowner Lock are the reconstructed Northland lift bridge to the south and Love's Bridge to the north.

*The pretty village of Billingshurst*

# Shere

**WALK 22**
SURREY
TQ074478

This walk starts from the pleasant village of Shere and, combined with a visit to The Old Farm, makes a lovely day out.

**Information**

The walk is two and a half miles long
No road walking, but woods are popular with mountain bikers
No stiles
Seating by the church
Pubs and teashops in Shere
No dogs allowed at The Old Farm

START
Shere is just off the A25 east of Guildford. Start the walk from the village church. There is parking along the lane leading to the church.

DIRECTIONS
Walk to the end of the lane and take the footpath signposted to the right of the church. After 300yds at the gate continue straight ahead across the field to a small gate at the top. Continue along path beside trees, then cross the railway line and keep forward along path, through zig-zag gateway and across the next field. At the waymark post turn right along a narrow path by a high brick wall. Continue to the road and turn right opposite Burrows Lea Farm. After a few yards, by a house called 'High Fields', turn left along the signposted footpath. Keep on this path, taking the right fork where the path divides at the end of the houses. Continue to a road and carefully cross over onto a narrow path leading into the woods. Keep on this path through bracken and, on emerging by a track by a Thames Water borehole notice, bear round to the left to a lane, by a row of cottages. Turn right and carefully cross the unfenced railway line. Once over the tracks, take the path ahead. Keep straight on until reaching a triangle of roads, cross the road ahead and turn right onto the signposted bridleway, keeping on the main path through the woods (ignore paths to right). On reaching a fork, bear left down the path running through a hollow, down to the ford and passing under a fallen tree. Just before the ford and footbridge turn right through a gate, alongside the stream – the Tilling Bourne. Turn left out of the gate at the end of the field and keep straight ahead to the lane a few yards ahead. Turn right and continue right, past another ford, back into the village.

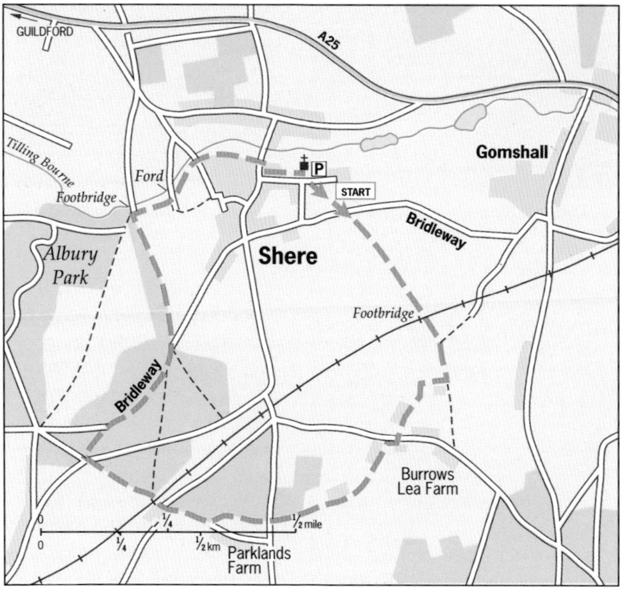

*Ford and bridge at Shere*

### What to look out for

Wildlife on the heathland includes stonechats, yellowhammers and common lizards; lucky visitors may see one of the adders who also make their home here. Listen for green woodpeckers in the woods. In late summer blackberries are abundant here.

**The Old Farm**
This working farm behind the church offers demonstrations every weekend in April, May and August. Sheep shearing, spinning, weaving, rope-making, threshing and corn grinding are some of the country crafts on display.

**Shere**
This is a delightful village well worth exploring. In the Malt House in Shere Lane there is a museum of local bygones dating mainly from Victorian times. The museum is open on five afternoons a week from Easter to September, other times by appointment.

**WALK 23**
KENT
TQ316843

# Rolvenden's Secret Garden

**Information**

The walk is just under two miles long
Several high stiles, and the path may be muddy in places
Dogs will need to be kept on lead in the fields
Pub (The Bull Inn) in Rolvenden for bar meals has a small garden; children welcome
Layne's Green suitable for picnics

From one of The Weald's prettiest villages, this walk goes through the churchyard to a wood where there is a glimpse of the original walled garden which featured in Frances Hodgson Burnett's *The Secret Garden*.

## START

Rolvenden is two miles south-west of Tenterden on the A28. Start the walk from Rolvenden church at the south end of the main street. There is some parking by the lych gate. Avoid the narrow lane by the war memorial.

## DIRECTIONS

At the main church door go right along the grass path at the side of the tower and, keeping to the right-hand side of the churchyard, follow a track to a kissing-gate (leave

*The church at Rolvenden*

on the latch or sheep may get through). Bear half-left down the line of oaks and climb up to a redundant stile. Keep ahead past three sycamore trees and head towards the stile on the edge of the wood – known as The Wilderness – following a path through the trees. On crossing the old Great Maytham driveway (gate on the left) there is the first glimpse of the walled 'secret garden' on the left. After another view the path runs gently downhill to a stile.

Turn sharp left to cross another stile and proceed along the side of a field. At the far end go over a stile (which has a dog gate) and follow an enclosed path. Beyond another stile, by a pond, continue in the same direction and go through two farm gates to the road at Rolvenden Layne.

Turn left, taking the pavement on the far side, to reach Great Maytham's main entrance. Continue on the road for a few yards to find a stile (with a dog flap) set back in the trees on the left.

Once in the field, pass two holly bushes and touch the field corner on the left. Keep ahead to pass between two tree clumps and join the outward path back to Rolvenden church.

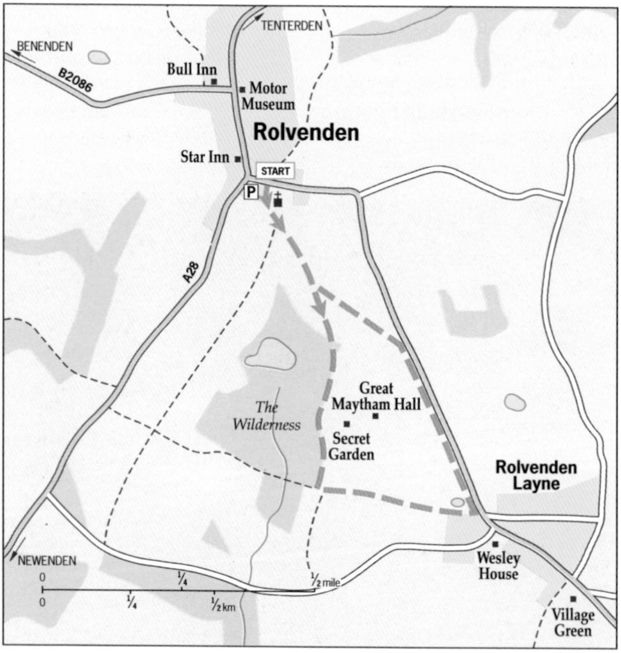


**What to look out for**

Rabbits abound in the field by the wood. In the churchyard, which is left partly wild, and on the woodland path there are summer wayside plants including common knapweed, spear thistle, creeping thistle, oxeye daisy and yarrow.

**Rolvenden**

Rolvenden has a wide main street lined with weather-boarded cottages. Its church was built by monks from Canterbury in around 1220 and has remained largely unchanged since 1480. The village, which has more than once been declared 'the best kept' in Kent, is known for its locally produced Korker sausages, invented in the butcher's shop opposite The Bull. Rolvenden has a small motor museum housing cars which take part in the annual London-to-Brighton Run.

**Rolvenden Layne**

When fire swept through Rolvenden in 1665 the population moved here to start a second village. Already here was the Tudor house where John Wesley preached in the late 18th century.

**Great Maytham**

Frances Hodgson Burnett rented this house in 1898 and it was a blocked-up door in the old walled garden that inspired her to write *The Secret Garden*. After her departure in 1907 the mansion was virtually rebuilt to a design by Edwin Lutyens. The garden and its door may be viewed on summer Wednesday and Thursday afternoons.

# From Cranbrook to Sissinghurst

**WALK 24**
KENT
TQ776362

A pleasant, easy walk in the Weald of Kent providing good views over the surrounding countryside, and starting from the attractive old town of Cranbrook.

**What to look out for**

The Union windmill shares your view over the green pastureland of the Weald of Kent on this walk. Look out, too, for the conical roofs of the Kentish oasthouses, familiar landmarks in this area.

**START**
Cranbrook lies 17 miles south of Maidstone on the A229. Free car parking in the Jockey Lane car park, off Carriers Road (off High Street by the White Horse pub).

**DIRECTIONS**
From the top right hand corner of the car park, follow the path left along the churchyard wall. Keep to hedge at the lower end of a playing field, and go down some steps to a road. Cross over, climb the steps opposite, cross a stile and follow the footpath to meet a concrete track. Continue straight

*The sturdy old windmill at Cranbrook*

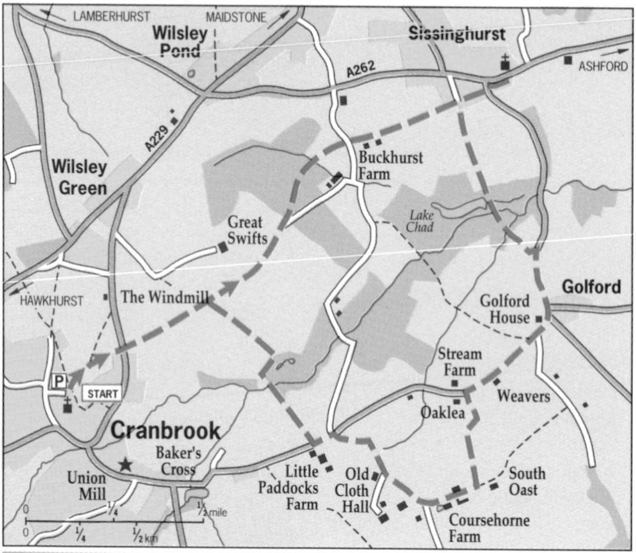


## Information

The walk is four and a half miles long
Fairly level walking, with several stiles and a few steep steps
Can be muddy
One short stretch of road walking
Pubs, cafés in both villages; pub in Sissinghurst welcomes children
Toilets in Cranbrook.

ahead, to cross a stile on the left. Follow the footpath down through woodland, to climb another stile. Cross the field to the stile ahead, and go down the steep steps to cross over a road.
Steps opposite lead to a track. Follow the track until the tracks cross near some houses: keep straight on via Playstole for the village of Sissinghurst.
Return to the crossing of tracks and turn left, to go down by a fence across the fields and into some woods (yellow bands on trees).
Pass Lake Chad on your right, following the worn path on the left, and cross over three footbridges by some fallen trees to a stile. Climb this and follow the direction of the yellow marker over a field, to pass through an iron gate to the road. Turn right and walk along the road to Golford crossroads, with Tollgate Cottage on the left. Turn right here and continue on this narrow road for 800yds. Pass by the first footpath sign on the left by 'Weavers' and continue to the footpath sign on the left at 'Oaklea', and follow this through the entrance. Continue ahead to pass through a small gate. Follow the left-hand edge of a playing field, go through a gap in the low railings onto a path, and through another low fence. Turn left and keep to the left of the school playing field to a marked stile with Coursehorne Barn on your right.
Turn right along a wide farm track with duck ponds on your left, and continue on to a tarmac access road by the entrance to Dulwich College Preparatory School to join a road. Continue past cemetery on right. Turn left at the T-junction and in a few yards, turn right over a stile. Walk down through a copse to bear right and cross a railed footbridge over a stream. Go straight uphill and follow around the copse to the right to find a worn path left uphill by a line of hawthorn bushes towards the line of conifer trees.
Turn left by gate to return to Cranbrook and the starting point.

**Cranbrook**
This small Wealden town was once an important centre of the woollen industry. It derived its name from the crane birds which frequented the local stream. There are a several fine buildings in the town, but the main attraction is the restored 1814 seven-storey Union Mill, which can be seen working on open days throughout the year.

**Sissinghurst**
This pretty Wealden village is often overlooked, but well worth exploring. The famous garden and Tudor mansion associated with this name are actually about 1½ miles further north-east (open from April to October, but not on Mondays).

# Reculver's Sea Bed Paths

**WALK 25**
KENT
TQ697224

This is an unusual walk around part of the old sea bed which separated Kent from the Isle of Thanet. The paths, built high above the silted channel, offer very easy walking and afford fine views in all directions – perfect for birdwatching.

**Information**

The walk is three and a half miles long
Level, easy ground
No road walking
No stiles
Pub at Reculver serves bar meals; children are welcome
Grassy area within ruins and by paths suitable for picnics
One café
Interpretation Centre for information

**START**

Reculver is a mile east of Herne Bay, just off the A299 Thanet Way. Start the walk from the King Ethelbert pub. There is parking near the end of the road, opposite the pub.

**DIRECTIONS**

Turn towards the sea and walk up the path leading to the ruins of Reculver's church. The path runs between the south side of the church and the grassed site of a Roman fort. Where the path runs down into the old shoreline go left towards the present sea-shore. Follow the sea wall and between crossing a stream and reaching a gate turn right to walk on to a high bank. The bank, known as the Rushborne Sea Wall, turns left round the back of Lobster Farm and runs in a south-easterly direction deep into the old channel. Continue, ignoring any turnings back to the sea. Look out for occasional waymark posts, and later follow the bank as it turns sharply south to reach the railway. Do not cross the tracks, but turn left along the high path running parallel to the line. Stay by the railway until crossing the River Wantsum then immediately turn left down the slope to follow a sea-level track alongside the water flowing towards the sea.
The path rises to meet the sea wall at Coldharbour Salt Lagoon. Turn left and follow the wide path back to the ruins of St Mary's Church which can be seen 1½ miles away.

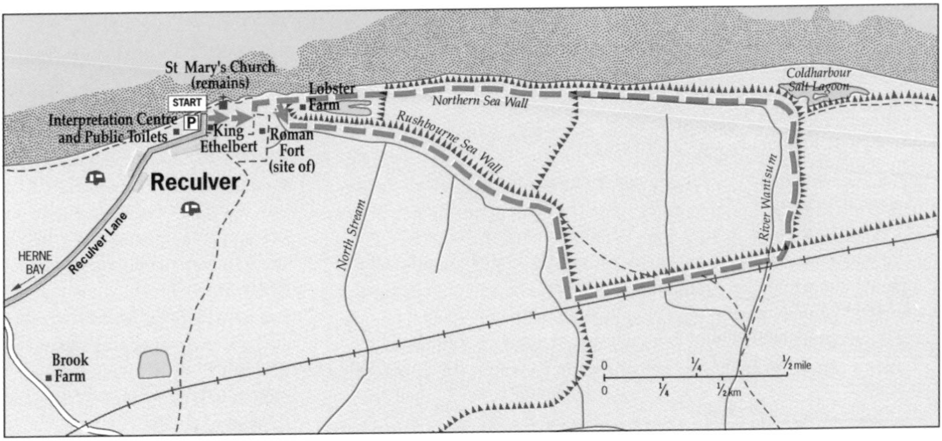

*The twin towers of Reculver's ruined church*

**Reculver**

Once this was Kent's most north-easterly point – when the Romans built a fort here in AD43 the sea was nearly a mile away, but by the Elizabethan era the headland had been so badly eroded that the sea was only a quarter of a mile from the buildings. By 1809 the cliff was so close that the villagers panicked and moved over a mile inland, building a new church there. The two 12th-century towers at Reculver are the remains of the original church, built as part of a monastery during the 7th century. Constant raids by the Danes eventually forced the monks to flee to Canterbury, but they gave their church to the community. When the villagers too were forced to leave by the encroaching sea, they left the two towers as landmarks for shipping. An annual service is held in the ruins in July.

*Goat's-beard*

**What to look out for**

The marsh is a resting place for hundreds of migratory birds. Kestrels may be seen, and there are reed and sedge warblers in the reedbeds in summer. Along the shore, terns fish in summer and brent geese arrive from Siberia in autumn. The grazing marshes and fields inland are renowned for sightings of birds of prey in winter, including hen harrier, merlin and rough-legged buzzard. Along the sea wall clovers and other wild flowers attract butterflies, and common lizards bask in the sun.

**Wantsum Channel**

The Isle of Thanet was once separated from Reculver on the mainland by a tidal channel a third of a mile wide. For centuries most crossings were made to the south where the Roman road ran to the sea opposite Sarre. By 1500 a programme of deliberate drainage, together with natural silting, had prevented shipping from using the channel, which has now shrunk to the River Wantsum drainage dyke.

**WALK 26**
KENT
TQ650546

# *Lullingstone Castle*

Artist Samuel Palmer called this area 'the veil of heaven', and historian Arthur Mee described the view down the Darent Valley as 'unique on the map of rural England'.

### START

Eynsford is five miles south of Dartford on the A225. Start the walk from the ford, just off the main road, opposite the church. There is a car park at the side of The Plough public house.

### DIRECTIONS

From the ford walk past The Plough and Sparepenny Lane, with Home Farm on the left. After the road bends, bear half-right up a slope and go through a gap by a gate.
Follow the footpath which rises half-right up the sloping field to cross the railway line. The path continues in the same direction to a stile near the end of a row of trees marking the line of a metalled farm drive.
Cross over to a second stile and continue half-right to a stile by a grass farm track.
Cross the stile opposite, which is slightly higher up, and keep by the fence on the left.
At the far end of the field cross another stile and turn left on to a narrow path which runs down the hill. In the wood there is a stile, then some steps before meeting a metalled lane. Turn right to visit Lullingstone Castle.
Beyond the castle gateway a 700yd riverside footpath leads to a visitor centre.
Retrace your steps back to Lullingstone Roman Villa and follow the lane, waymarked

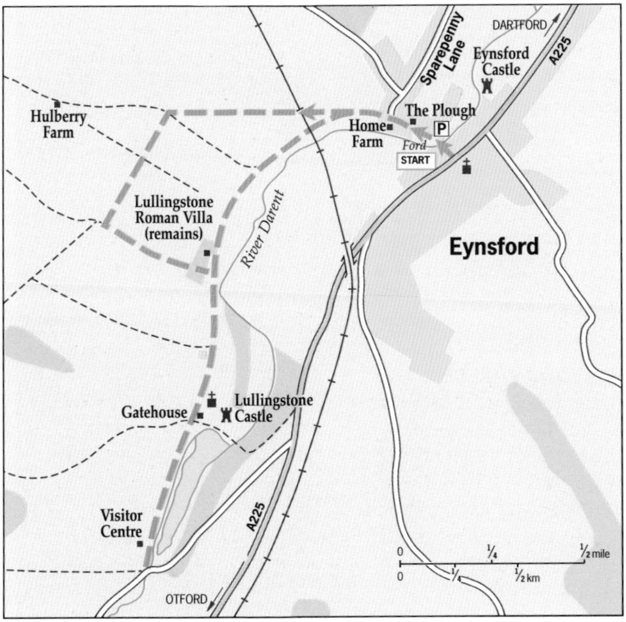


**What to look out for**

Home Farm breeds Highland cattle, which until recently were rarely seen outside Scotland, and from the top of the hill there may be the odd sighting of deer. Among the creatures along the river are water voles and damselflies. Birds include swans, kingfishers and herons.

*Short-tailed field vole*

## Information

The walk is just over two miles long
Several stiles
One unmanned level-crossing
The Plough at Eynsford serves special children's meals in the restaurant; children are also welcome in the bar, and there is a patio
Tea shop in post office
Café and picnic tables at the visitor centre

with a 'D' for the Darent Valley Path, passing under the railway viaduct to return to Eynsford.

**Eynsford**
The partly Norman church figured in the dispute between Henry II and Thomas à Becket when the archbishop appointed a new priest against the wishes of Sir William de Eynsford. His ruined castle (English Heritage), which incorporates Roman materials, can be visited. John Wesley used the narrow 16th-century bridge by the ford as an open-air pulpit.

**Lullingstone**
Altered extensively in Queen Anne's time, Lullingstone Castle has fine state rooms and beautiful grounds. The 15th-century gate tower was one of the first gatehouses in England to be made entirely of brick. Catherine of Aragon's pomegranate symbol can be found carved on the rood screen inside the little St Botolph's Church, known as 'the church on the lawn'. Visitors may go through the arch and over the lawn to visit the church even when the castle is closed. It was on this grass that the rules of lawn tennis were devised in 1873.
The Roman villa dates from the first and second centuries and includes an extensive bath complex. The mosaic floors are exceptionally well preserved. The site is roofed for protection, with additional exhibits in a lighted gallery.

*Eynsford from Hulberry Farm*

# *Walbury Hill*

**WALK 27**
BERKSHIRE
SU369621

### Information

The walk is three and a half miles long
Generally level ground but with one steep hill to go down and another very steep hill to climb
Very little road walking
No stiles
Plenty of grassy places for picnics
Dogs will need to be on leads

*Red-legged partridge*

This is an exciting, fairly strenuous walk with plenty of interest – and the views are magnificent! The gibbet on Gallows Hill holds a macabre fascination, while at 974ft Walbury Hill, crowned by its huge hillfort, is the highest chalk hill in Britain.

**START**
Walbury Hill is about five miles south-east of Hungerford, south of the A4 and east of the A338. Start at the car parking area between Walbury Hill and Gallows Down.

**DIRECTIONS**
Go along the wide flinty track across the top of Walbury Hill, crowned by its large hillfort. Continue along the track until you reach the road then turn right through the gate and go downhill along the bridleway to the left of the field with woodland down on your right. Go through the gate at the bottom of the bridleway and turn right onto the byway between tall bushes. Continue along this track past Lower Farm and the Keeper's Bungalow and onto the metalled road at Combe.
At the T-junction turn right and continue along the road for 500yds before turning left along the track to Wright's Farm. Carry on past the farm buildings, through the gates. Keep to the right-hand edge of the field going up the steep hill, ignoring the stile on the right by the tree.
At the top of the hill stop to admire the view and recover from the climb! Go through the gate and turn right along the edge of the woodland, ignoring the track immediately on your right. Turn right again when you reach the track on the top of Gallows Down. Continue along the track past the gibbet to the starting point.

### What to look out for

The downs are rich with wildlife, including foxes and deer, partridges and pheasants, and there are usually skylarks winging overhead in great bursts of song. This is chalk downland, and plenty of lime-loving plants grow amongst the short grasses, including wild thyme, marjoram, mignonette, small scabious and harebell. Birds of prey often ride the updraughts on Inkpen Beacon, but the only hanging you will see on Gallows Hill these days is from hang gliders; model aircraft enthusiasts congregate here too. From the top of the ridge (on a clear day) you can look into five counties: Berkshire, Hampshire, Wiltshire, Oxfordshire and Buckinghamshire.

**Combe Gibbet**
The siting of the gibbet on the top of Inkpen Beacon – known also as Gallows Down – was to expose those executed there to the gaze of

*Catching the thermals from Gallows Hill*

as many as possible, to let them be a mute and awful reminder of justice. It is a grim structure, a very high frame with a crossbar from which two felons could be hung side by side, as in 1678, when a man and woman were hung for a notorious murder. The present frame is not the original, but the latest in a number of replacements over the years, a grim landmark.

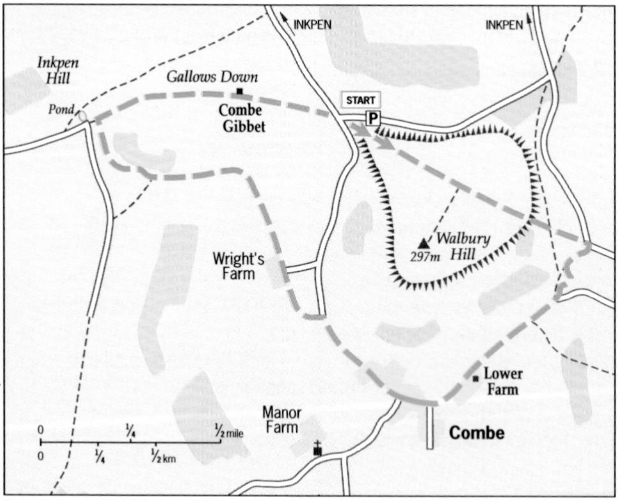


**Walbury Hillfort**

This is the largest Iron Age hillfort in Berkshire, the single bank and ditch which surround it enclosing an area of 82 acres. The main entrance was in the north-west corner, but there was another small one on the south-east side. The fort has not been excavated, but it is thought that the circular depressions inside it may be the relics of hut circles. An obvious choice for defensive purposes, the hill now offers magnificent views.

**WALK 28**
BERKSHIRE
SU825840

# *The River Thames and Hurley*

**Information**

The walk is just under two and a half miles long
Level, easy ground
A few stiles
Pub and hotel offering bar food in Hurley
Grassy areas to picnic beside the river

This leisurely riverside walk along the Thames, here replete with a number of islands, is particularly attractive and interesting throughout the year. The great river is alive with river craft and ducks.

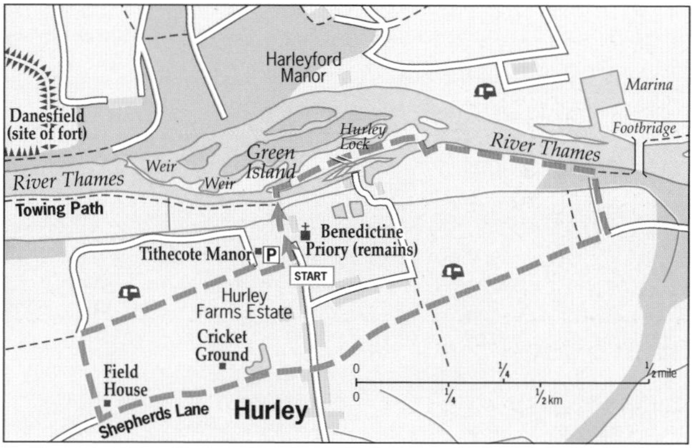


**START**
Hurley is on the southern bank of the River Thames just west of Cookham, off the A4130. Start from the village car park next to Tithecote Manor, opposite the church.

**DIRECTIONS**
Turn left out of the car park along footpath past Tithecote Manor heading towards the River Thames, with a red brick wall on your right.
After about 150yds go up and over the bridge over a branch of the River Thames to one of the many islands in this reach, and then turn right to follow the footpath to Hurley Lock.
Pass through both sets of lock gates and forward to bridge. Go over the bridge across the river and left to follow the riverside path beneath the horse chestnut trees along the edge of the meadows for about ¼ mile.
Go through the gate so that the private woodland is on your right and the river on your left. After 50yds, just before bridge, turn right down the path into the wood by the sign 'Private fishing only'. Cross the stile (or squeeze through the gap) and turn right along the track.

**What to look out for**

You'll find yourself watching the river traffic at Hurley Lock because of the sheer number and variety of pleasure cruisers on this reach.
There are large horse chestnut trees along the riverside meadows and in the private woodland.
There's plenty of wildlife, including jays in the woodland, and along the river there are Canada geese, mallards, coots and moorhens.
The medieval dovecot in the grounds of Tithecote Manor can be seen from the car park.

After about ¼ mile, pass a caravan site on your right, crossing cattle-grids at each end of the site.
At the far end of the caravan site, the track turns sharply to the right. At this point take the footpath on the left, overlooking the backs of houses, to the road into Hurley. Cross the road and go along Shepherds Lane past the cricket ground on the right.
After about ½ mile, at Field House, turn right down the right of way and cross the stile.
Go along the edge of the field to the track. Turn right over the stile along the track, with another caravan park to the left, and continue to road. Cross road and take the footpath opposite, by the old flint and brick wall of Tithecote Manor. Go over a stile and proceed to the car park.

**Hurley Lock**
The locks and weirs of the River Thames work together to make the river safe for navigation, and at the same time help to conserve water by regulating the flow. Hurley Lock is one of the 48 or so to be found on the Thames between Lechlade and Teddington.

**Hurley Priory**
Edward the Confessor's sister, Editha, is said to have been buried here in a Saxon church. This was rebuilt by the Normans before 1087 when a Benedictine Monastery was founded here. The monastery was suppressed by Henry VIII, the buildings passing to the Lovelace family, and all that remains is part of the cloisters, a fillet of the refectory, two barns and the dovecot.

*A quiet stretch of the River Thames at Hurley*

# WALK 29

OXFORDSHIRE
SP293866

# *The White Horse at Uffington*

### Information

The walk is about one and three quarter miles long
Easy ground with very gentle hills
One stile to cross
Grassy areas for picnics

This walk has something to interest everyone – the chalk-cut figure of the White Horse, the ramparts of Uffington Castle and the ancient Ridgeway footpath along the hills.

**START**

The White Horse is just off the B4507, six miles west of Wantage. Start from the large car park on Woolstone Hill.

**DIRECTIONS**

Go through the gate in the corner of the car park and take the path which bears right and uphill across the field.
Cross over Dragonhill Road to the chalky path opposite, bear left to see the White Horse and look down into the dry valley (the 'Manger') below.
Continue for a few yards before bearing right to the white trig point and Uffington Castle hillfort.
Turn left past the trig point and cross the stile onto the Ridgeway, a long distance footpath. Turn right along the Ridgeway to the point where another track crosses it. Turn right here for the return to the starting point (or continue ahead for about ¼ mile to visit Wayland's Smithy, a Neolithic long barrow; retrace your steps to this point and turn left for the car park).

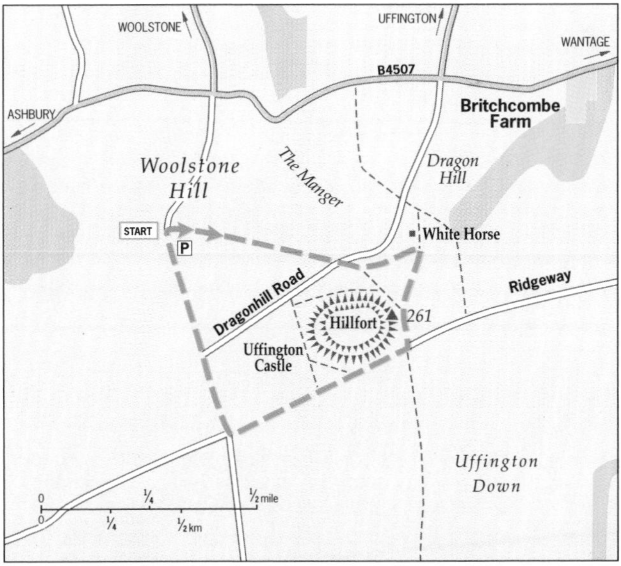


**The White Horse**

Some say that the White Horse was set up by King Alfred in AD871 to commemorate his victory over the Danes at the Battle of Ashdown, but most scholars believe it to be an emblem of the Iron Age tribe who occupied Uffington Castle.
There are many legends connected with the horse. In particular, it was thought lucky to make a wish while standing on its eye, though to protect the figure this practice is no longer allowed.
The horse measures 355ft from nose to tail and 120ft from ear to hoof, and its outline is cut two or three feet into the chalk, the trenches being some 10ft across. In the past the villagers of Uffington came up here every seven

*The chalky White Horse is seen most clearly from above*

years to 'scour' the horse, ie to weed the trenches. This was done with great festivities, with games and dancing, and the villagers would sing:

*'The owld White Horse*
*wants zettin to rights*
*And the squire hev promised*
*good cheer*
*Zo we'll gee un a scrape to kip*
*un in zhape*
*And a'll last for many a*
*year ...'*

**The 'Manger' of the White Horse**
This is a classic chalkland 'dry' valley (with no river), created during the Ice Age when the subsoil was frozen and the summer melt flowed down the valley as a stream. The grooves on the left are probably avalanche tracks.

**Uffington Castle**
Uffington Castle, an Iron Age hillfort crowning Uffington Hill, consists of two banks and an intervening ditch encircling a level grassy expanse of about 8 acres. From the ramparts there is an enchanting view over the Vale of the White Horse, with its scattered villages and patchwork of fields.

**The Ridgeway**
The Ridgeway was a trunk route in Prehistoric Britain, running along the dry top of the Downs rather than the marshy and forested vale. It is now a long-distance footpath which stretches from Avebury in Wiltshire to Ivinghoe Beacon in Buckinghamshire.

**What to look out for**

Chalk-loving downland plants such as wild thyme, marjoram and kidney vetch occur in profusion, and the site is good for butterflies from May onwards. The downland once swarmed with sheep, but their presence is less today.

**WALK 30**
OXFORDSHIRE
SP484206

# The Railway at Tackley

This is an easy walk with the attraction of three forms of transport – the railway, the canal and the route of a Roman road.

**Information**

The walk is two and a quarter miles long
Level, easy walking
One stile to cross
Very little road walking
Pub in Tackley
Grassy areas for picnics

**START**

Tackley is east of the A4260 to the north of Kidlington. Start from the station – there is room to park along the road here.

**DIRECTIONS**

Carefully go over the level crossing, then follow the bridleway signed 'Kirtlington' which bears right as it runs parallel to the railway, close by on your right, for about ½ mile to a junction.

(You can make a worthwhile detour to view the River Cherwell and the Oxford Canal. To do this, turn left and then right and follow the path over the river and the weir to Pigeon's Lock. Retrace your steps to rejoin the main walk).

The main route turns right, with a glimpse of the River Cherwell through the trees on your left. Continue under the railway bridge and then turn right over the stile signed 'Oxfordshire Way Footpath'. Cross the field with the railway now on your right, then bear left and cross the stile by the little footbridge under the willows. This is on the line of Roman Akeman Street.

Turn left over the footbridge and then right through the meadow, following the path to the left round the edge of the field.

Turn right through the gap and follow the path along the field edge. At the boundary go through the gates and across the track into a meadow with the mellow stone buildings of Court Farm on your left. Go through the gate onto the road and turn right into Tackley. Bear right at the green and continue

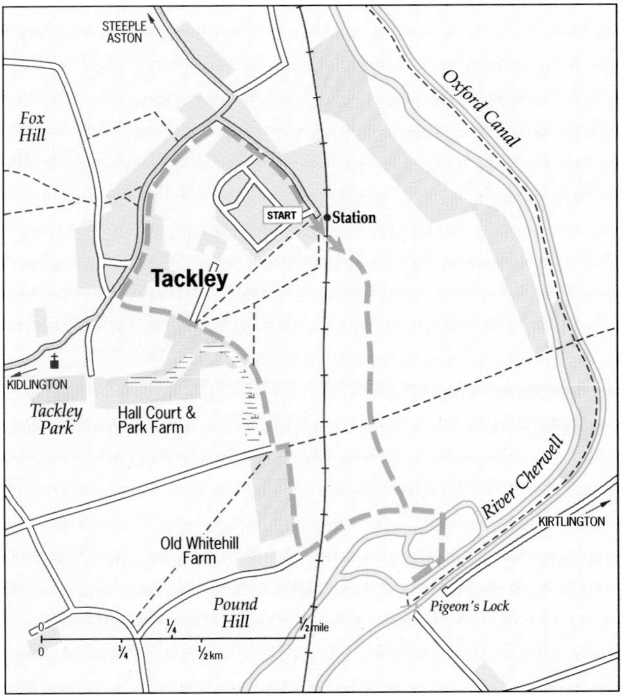

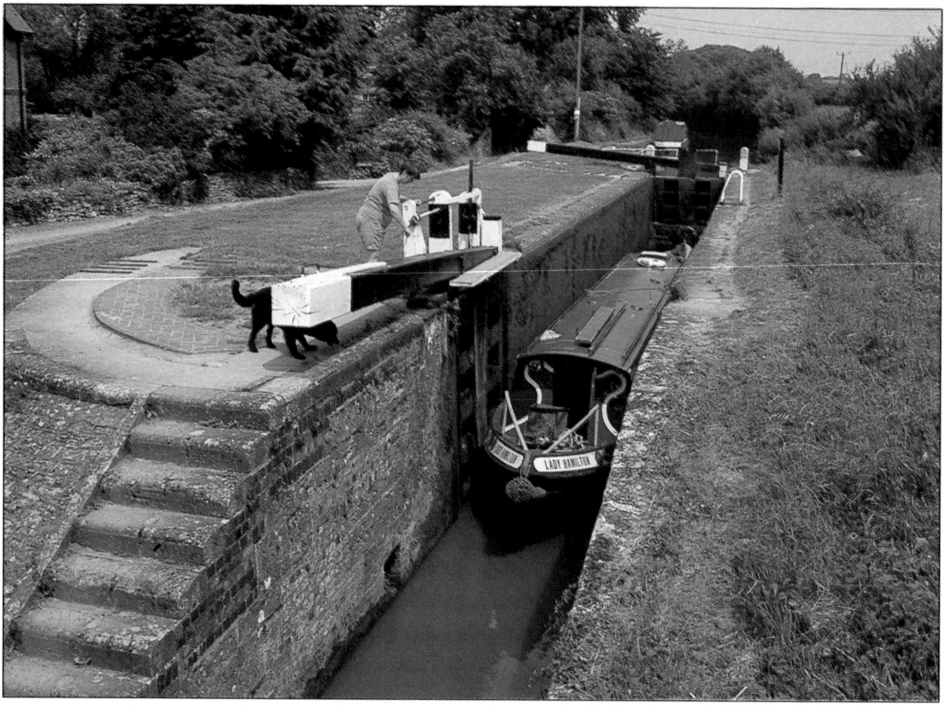


*Passing through Pigeon's Lock, on the Oxford Canal*

through the village to Nethercote Road (signed 'Station'). Turn right here to return to the starting point.

**The Railway**
The Oxford to Birmingham line was built by the Great Western Railway Company in 1850 to the 7ft broad gauge, later converted to the standard 4ft 8½ins. You can still see how far apart the two lines are, and how, over 140 years later, the line is still very busy.

**Roman Akeman Street**
Akeman Street is the name given to the Roman road which runs from east to west through the south Midlands to Cirencester and Bath. This road crossed the River Cherwell from Kidlington, and the walk directions locate the line of it. When you reach this point, look west and you will clearly see the raised bank on which the road ran.

**The Oxford Canal**
Opened on New Year's Day 1790, the Oxford Canal was built on a parallel line with the River Cherwell and the two waterways still share this pleasant valley.

**What to look out for**

The old gateway near Court Farm is dated 1620 and is ornamented with shields. A similar gateway, dated 1615, faces the road. This used to stand at the entrance to the demolished manor house. There is also a large 17th-century dovecot.
The River Cherwell and the Oxford Canal, with their rich vegetation of reeds and rushes, are a haven for wildlife, including ducks, herons and other waterbirds.

# Berkhamsted Common

**WALK 31**
HERTFORDSHIRE
SP994082

A varied and interesting walk, with the attractions of thickly wooded Berkhamsted Common, and the grassy earthworks of an ancient castle to explore.

**START**
Berkhamsted is on the A41, four miles north-west of Hemel Hempstead. Start from Berkhamsted Castle. There is room to park beside the railway or in the station car park.

**Information**

The walk is three and a quarter miles long
There are a couple of gentle hills
Some road walking on pavements
Several stiles to cross
Grassy places for picnics
Dogs should be kept on leads

**DIRECTIONS**
Walk up Brownlow Road with the castle on your right. Cross the road where it curves to the right and go up Castle Hill. Follow the public footpath by Berkhamsted Cricket Club. Continue along the grassy path between the fields in the bottom of the valley, crossing over four stiles. At the fifth stile cross a muddy track with Well Farm on your right, and continue up the valley towards the woods of Berkhamsted Common.
Cross the stile by the gate and go straight up the path to the woods.
Go into the woods over the stile, following the path uphill between the trees and the belt of bracken and silver birch, to the top of the slope. Turn left onto the wide path

*The verdant countryside of Berkhamsted Common*

*The ruined foundation walls of Berkhamsted Castle*

which crosses the path you are on, and immediately turn left again where the main path veers round to the right.

After about 50yds take the left-hand fork in the path and continue for about ¼ mile to a large oak tree. Brickkiln Cottage will be visible on your right. At the oak turn left to the stile at the wood's edge. Cross this stile and go down the edge of the field, over the next stile and up the side of the next field.

At the boundary cross another stile and continue along the field's edge past a small pond guarded by a stag-headed oak. Go through the gap and along the edge of the field, cross the stile by the gate and turn left into the hummocky meadow.

Go round the edge of the meadow, following footpath signs, to Castle Hill Farm and turn left down the track through the gate. Cross the road and bear left along the grassy footpath downhill. Continue along the pavement to the road junction. Turn left here and then right, back to the starting point.

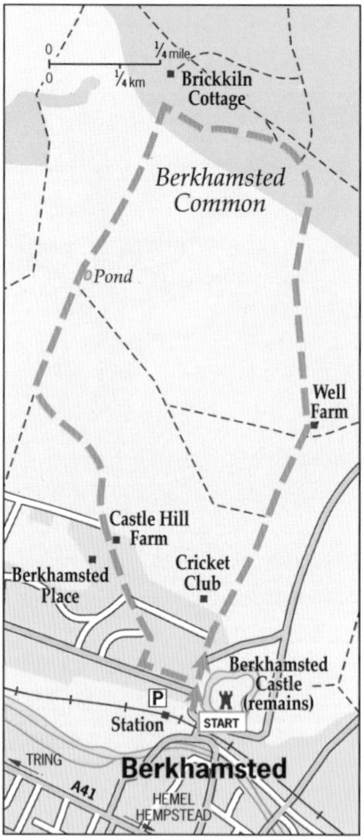


**Berkhamsted Castle**

Not much remains to be seen of this Norman fortress which William the Conqueror gave to his half-brother. It has been a ruin since Elizabethan times, when its stones were taken away up the hill to build Berkhamsted Place – now, too, demolished. Yet it was here that William received the submission of the Saxon nobles, following his famous victory at Hastings. The castle's most illustrious owner was undoubtedly the Black Prince, eldest son of Edward III.

In 1838 a large section of the outer defences had to be demolished to make way for the railway.

**Berkhamsted Common**

During the Middle Ages this was a common wood used for grazing, and most of it was included in the great park of Berkhamsted Castle. Today much of the area is National Trust property.

## What to look out for

Berkhamsted Common is a refuge for wildlife. Look out, in particular, for grey squirrels, and fallow and muntjac deer. The edible dormouse is found here, one of only a very few sites in Britain. In autumn you can find a lot of interesting fungi, both the bracket types such as oyster mushrooms growing on the trees, and species which grow on the woodland floor.

# The Ouse Meadows at Olney

**WALK 32**
BUCKINGHAMSHIRE
SP886504

**Information**

The walk is three and a half miles long
Level ground with one small slope
Several stiles to cross
Very little roadwalking
Pubs in Clifton Reynes and Olney
Grassy areas for picnics beside the River Great Ouse

A combination of riverside stroll and pastoral ramble, this lovely walk has lots of interesting features along the way.

**START**
Olney is on the A509 eleven miles north of Milton Keynes. Start from the layby on the A509 south of Olney, with Emberton Country Park on your left.

**DIRECTIONS**
Cross the A509 and go over a stile to the footpath. Turn right over a white stile and plank bridge and turn left along the edge of the field. Cross stile and follow the path straight across the next field, aiming to the right of the large willow. Go through the gap in the hedge and cross this field, which has a plank bridge in the middle. At the waymarked stile/bridge, cross into the meadow beside the River Great Ouse.
Bear slightly to your left aiming for the clump of trees on the river bend. Leave the trees on your left and go up

*The lofty spire of Olney church is a landmark for miles around*

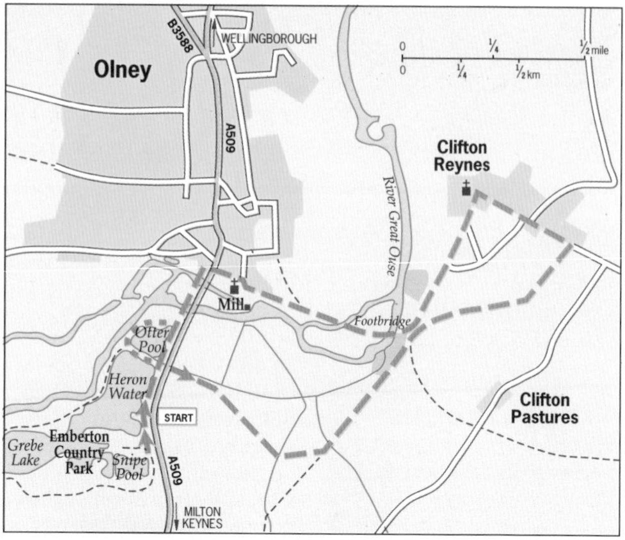


the slope to the track. Turn left and continue, going through a gate and past a line of bushes. Bear right beneath the horse chestnut trees and cross the stile. Go straight over the field and cross the next stile, then cross two more fields to reach the road. Turn left into Clifton Reynes.

Turn left through the village and bear left at the church, where the road becomes a track. Turn right through the gate and go diagonally across the field. Cross the stile and bear right down the grassy slope to the river, crossing by the footbridge.

Cross the meadow and another footbridge, heading straight for Olney church, with the river on the left. Go through the gate past the former mill house and bear round to the right, then through the gate to the church. Turn left through the churchyard to the main street in Olney.

*Water Rail*

Cross the road and turn left. Either return directly to your car or turn right for a detour through Emberton Country Park.

**William Cowper**

The town of Olney is inextricably linked with the 18th-century poet, William Cowper, who lived here for 19 years – the happiest in his sadly troubled life. His home is now a museum (open from Tuesday to Saturday and Bank Holiday Mondays). Cowper knew and loved this Buckinghamshire landscape well, and it featurs often in his writing.

Cowper frequently walked from Olney to Clifton Reynes to visit Lady Austen – who inspired him to write much of his best poetry – and stayed in Clifton Reynes with the rector and his wife.

### What to look out for

There is a rich wildlife in the watermeadows beside the Great Ouse and within the Emberton Country Park. Attractively landscaped from old gravel workings, the park consists of a series of lakes, frequented by migratory waders and wildfowl.

Olney Church has a large and impressive medieval tower with a 180ft spire, unusually lofty for Buckinghamshire.

On Shrove Tuesday the famous Olney Pancake Race is run, and has been every year since 1445 (except for a break during World War II), when a local woman apparently hurried to church still clutching her frying pan. The race starts at The Bull on the Market Square, pancakes being cooked at 11.30am with the tossing starting at 11.45am.

Participation in the race is limited to Olney residents, but of course anyone can go and watch.

**WALK 33**
HERTFORDSHIRE
TL396223

# The River Rib at Standon

This is a gentle, enjoyable walk, with plenty to see and do.

**START**
Standon is on the A120 about a mile to the east of the A10, six miles north of Ware and six miles west of Bishop's Stortford. Park in, and start from the High Street, which is south of the A120.

**DIRECTIONS**
Walk south down the High Street passing the church on your left, then bear left with the 'Standon Puddingstone' on your right. Keep forward and shortly turn right along the concrete road. When this turns to the left, go straight on along the grass track over the stream and through the belt of oak and ash trees. On reaching the field turn left and continue around it,

*The former paper mill at Standon*

### Information

The walk is two and a quarter miles long
The ground is mostly level and even
Virtually no roadwalking
One stile to cross
Pubs in Standon
Grassy areas for picnics by the river and on the village green

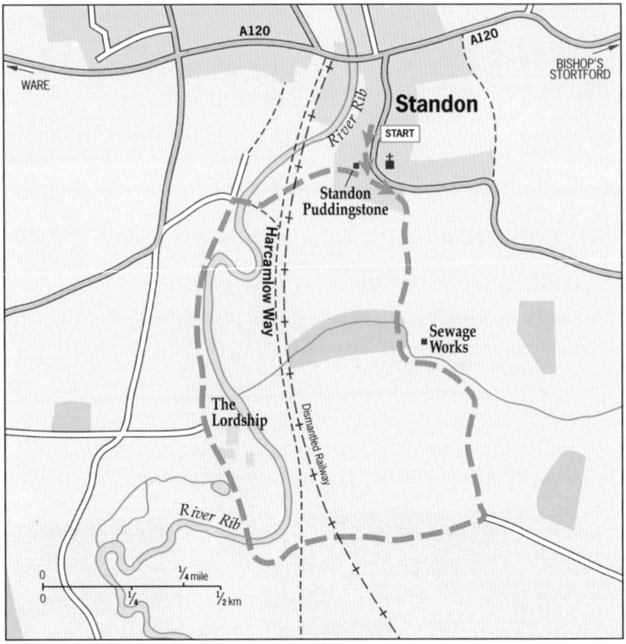


turning right at the corner, with the hedge always on your left. At the end of the field go through the gap onto the grassy track and turn right along it. At the next field boundary cross the old railway line. Continue, crossing the Harcamlow Way (not signed), to bear right and reach a stone bridge over the River Rib. Cross the river and go through the gate. Carry straight on along the little causeway over the meadow to join the track. Go through the gate, passing a large house, 'The Lordship', on your right and cross the track to a stile. Go over the stile and keep straight on through the meadows, with the river on your right. Go through the gate to the road and turn right to cross the river by the footbridge beside the ford. Continue past the old paper mill and straight on back to Standon.

### What to look out for

The old railway line, now almost unrecognisable, used to run north to Buntingford. The line opened in 1863 and closed in 1965.
The former paper mill, by the ford, was steam powered and worked turning rags into paper between 1713 and 1855.
The Standon Puddingstone, formerly in the church wall, is a lump of natural stone formed of many tiny flint pebbles from a river of long ago, cemented together with a natural cement.
Wildlife is abundant. Look out for grey herons by the river, as well as goldfinches, rabbits, water voles and kestrels.

**'The Lordship'**
This house in the peaceful river valley was the home of Sir Ralph Sadleir, gaoler of Mary, Queen of Scots, at Wingfield and Tutbury.
The present house is but a fillet of the splendid mansion of Sir Ralph's day, which was said to rival Hatfield House itself, both in splendour and in hospitality. Queen Elizabeth I stayed here on two of her famous 'Progresses' and James I, on his way to London and his new throne, stayed here with Sir Thomas, Sir Ralph's son, in 1603.

**The First 'Flying Man'**
In 1784 an Italian, Vincenze Lunardi, arrived in Standon by balloon, completing the first successful balloon flight in England. Setting out from Moorlands, some 30 miles away, Lunardi had completed this remarkable journey in just two hours.

# Hanningfield Reservoir

The central theme of this pleasant walk is water. It passes a large modern reservoir, now a haven for wildlife, and a small holy well, frequented by the devout in ancient times.

**WALK 34**
ESSEX
TQ737976

*Hanningfield Reservoir*

**START**
South Hanningfield is just west of the A130, three miles north of Runwell. Start from the grassy pay-and-display car park (closed November to March) near the landing stage overlooking the Hanningfield reservoir.

**DIRECTIONS**
Turn left out of the car park up the road to South Hanningfield. At the junction bear left into the village. Turn right to the footpath at the Old Windmill pub. Go over the stile behind the pub and turn left. Bear right across the field following the 'public footpath' sign.
Turn right and then left on the far side of the field, following the waymarks. Go over the stile onto the road. Turn right and then left over the stile beside the covered reservoir. Cross the field to the ash tree.
Go through the gap to the right of the ash tree and straight downhill past Fleming's Farm, seen to your right. Turn right over the stile and bridge and then left across the field, keeping the hedge on your left. At the field corner turn left and cross the stile. Go straight

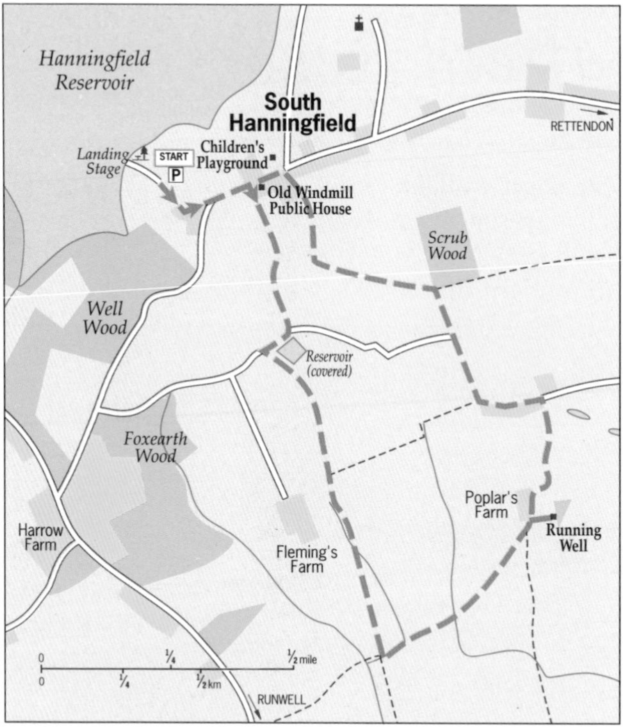


## Information

The walk is three miles long
The land is generally flat
Little road walking
Several stiles to cross
Dogs are not allowed at the reservoir
Pub in South Hanningfield with garden
Grassy area beside reservoir with picnic tables

ahead across the field and through the gap into the large field.
Go straight across this field to the stile. Cross the stile and turn left up the lane to Poplar's Farm.
At the concrete area, a detour over the gate on your right and across the field to the triangle of woodland takes you to the Running Well.
The walk continues past Poplar's Farm. At the road turn left past some houses. Where the road bears left take the stile straight ahead and go along the edge of the field towards the woodland. Turn left over the stile and head straight across the field, bearing to the right of the trig point.
At the corner of the field turn right along the boundary, keeping the hedge on your right. Go through the gap into the next field and head diagonally across to the stile, which brings you out opposite the playground.
Turn left onto the road back to the reservoir.

**Hanningfield Reservoir**
This important reservoir was created by the flooding of thousands of acres of farmland. The man-made lake, which cannot be seen easily from the road, has become an important nature reserve and over-winter site for waders and wildfowl.

**The Running Well**
This holy well has recently been cleaned and restored, and the annual Boxing Day walk along footpaths to the well has been revived. A book about the history of the well, *The Running Well Mystery*, was published in 1983 by The Supernaturalist of Wickford.

## What to look out for

There are spectacular views south to the Thames estuary during the central part of this walk.
The hedges and woodland harbour an extensive wildlife: look out for colourful pheasants, common partridges, rabbits and foxes. The reservoir site is well known to ornithologists; thousands of migrant wetland birds pass through in spring and autumn and ducks, in particular, are seen in winter in large numbers.

# *The Coast at Walton on the Naze*

This highly enjoyable walk around the Naze peninsula is of interest to all ages, with wildlife, lots of shipping and an excellent beach.

**WALK 35**
ESSEX
TM265235

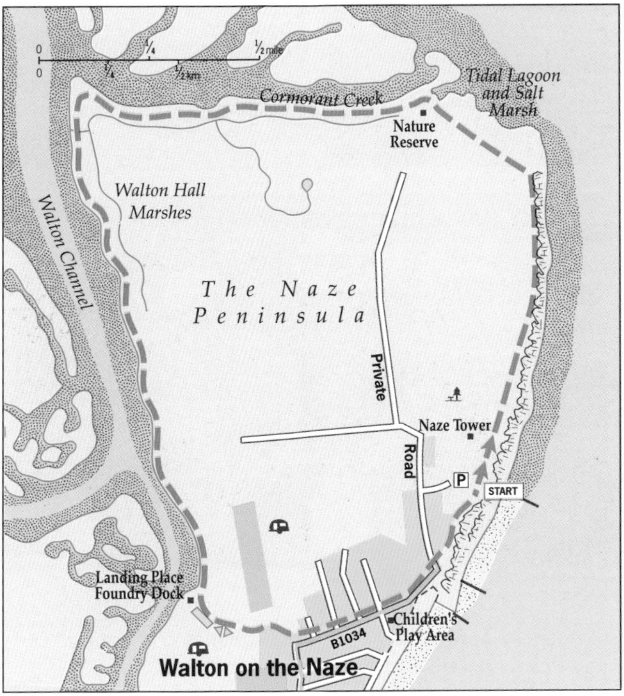


START
Walton on the Naze is north-east of Clacton on the B1034. Go through Walton and start from the large grassy car park (charge) at the Naze Tower.

DIRECTIONS
Turn left out of the car park past the café and follow the cliff-top footpath, with the sea on your right and Harwich and Felixstowe ahead across broad Hamford Water (the cliff down to the beach is crumbling into the sea so keep clear of the edge!)
Keep straight on to where the cliff merges with the beach and then turn left along the top of the dyke. A tidal lagoon and salt marsh stretch away on the right and the John Weston Reserve, run by the Essex Naturalist Trust, is on the left. Follow the dyke round

**What to look out for**

The Naze is renowned for the waders which visit its extensive mudflats. Among the easiest to recognise are curlews, bar-tailed godwits, oystercatchers and redshanks. Other wildlife includes the Essex skipper butterfly, found on grassy banks. The dyke is spot for watching the shipping – ferries, commercial vessels, pleasure craft, and the occasional Thames sailing barge. Fossils just fall out of the cliffs as they crumble into the sea, and while most are shells, shark's teeth are also being washed out of the clay.

*The Naze — a crumbling coastline*

*Colourful beach huts at Walton on the Naze*

**Information**

The walk is three and three quarter miles long
Level, easy ground; rather exposed to winter winds
No stiles
Road walking on pavement only
Grassy areas for picnics on the cliff-top

*Black-tailed godwit*

to the left, following the ever-widening creek, and left again at the next corner.

Continue along the dyke, with the open water of Walton Channel to the right and the expanse of Walton Hall Marshes to the left, to reach the landing place at Foundry Dock. Turn left along the footpath.

Proceed along the edge of the field, with the hedge on your right, as far as Naze Park Road. Turn left past the shops and telephone box to the children's play area. Just beyond the play area turn right towards the beach and then left to follow the cliff walk above the tearoom and beach huts back to the car park.

**Walton – Threat from the Sea**

Walton used to be 'Walton-le-Soken', but for many years now it has been Walton on the Naze. 'Naze', or 'nose', refers to the shape of the headland – and certainly old maps suggest that 300 years ago it was shaped like a snub nose. But this coast is falling into the sea; a print of Walton in 1787 shows the now vanished All Saints parish church towerless and about to succumb to the waves. The last great flood here was during the notorious storm surge of 1953, following which a new sea wall had to be built across the top of the 'nose', some way inland from the original. Land reclaimed by the sea is not a new problem here, indeed the whole of the little archipelago around Hamford Water (the 'Secret Water' of Arthur Ransome's tale) was formed in the past by the drowning of a low-lying stretch of coast.

# *The Stour at Flatford*

**WALK 36**
SUFFOLK
TM075335

This walk gives a taste of the countryside which so inspired the artist John Constable. Anyone familiar with his paintings will experience a feeling almost of *déja vu* when they see Flatford Mill, Willy Lott's House, the River Stour, and the view of Dedham Vale from Fen Lane.

**Information**

The walk is just under two miles long
A few stiles
National Trust tea room at Bridge Cottage

Gorse

START
Flatford is just off the A12 between Ipswich and Colchester. Take the B1070, avoiding the centre of East Bergholt, and follow the signs for Flatford. Start the walk from Flatford Mill car park (charge).

DIRECTIONS
Turn left from the car park onto the road (one way – traffic coming from behind). Towards the bottom of the hill, take the footpath behind the hedge, marked with a yellow arrow, which follows the right-hand side of the road (if it is very wet and muddy, you may prefer to stay on the road). The path, well worn and with overhanging branches from the trees to the left, goes uphill, emerging briefly onto the road from time to time. Continue straight on beside the field to reach a seat beside the road and a view of the Old Hall to the right.
Take the wide gravel track (Fen Lane) going left from the road, signed 'Private Road, Public Footpath to Dedham and Stratford' (somewhere along here Constable found the view for *The Cornfield*). Continue downhill, keeping to the main track, ignoring the footpath and stile off to

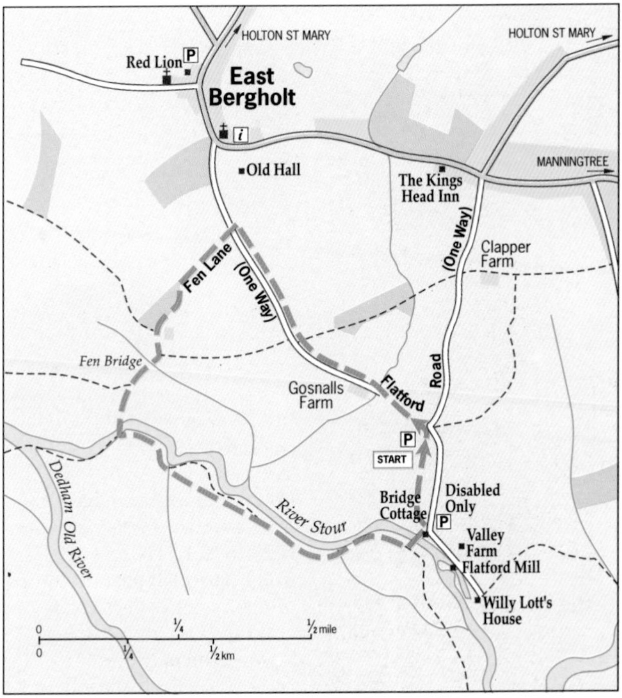

**What to look out for**

The hedge on the first section of walk dates back to medieval times. You can easily check its age by multiplying the number of woody species you can find in a 30yd section of hedge by one hundred years. This hedge contains field maple, elm, oak, hawthorn, holly and blackthorn.

the right at the bottom of the hill. The track bends left, and just beyond a junction with another footpath to the left, bear right and go over a bridge. Keep on the main track, which comes to a dead end with metal gates, then take footpath leading to the footbridge over the River Stour.

After crossing the bridge via two stiles, go left on to the path following the river bank. This is a well defined path across open fields with occasional lines of trees (where the path splits there is an option of following the river bank). Cross the stile. (The track off to the right leads to a river lock and a pretty view of Flatford Mill with the Stour in front; over the bridge, the lane to the right takes you to the other side of Flatford Mill, with the famous mill-pond and Willy Lott's House.)

From the bridge, take the road to the left, and then go left up some steps, following the path back into the car park.

**Flatford Mill**

Flatford Mill, built in 1733 and now a field study centre owned by the National Trust, provided John Constable with the inspiration for many of his fine paintings. Along the southern bank of the Stour is a view of the side of the mill, with its sluice gate and trees overhanging the river bank. On the other side of the mill is the quiet millpond, and Willy Lott's House beyond – a scene instantly recognisable from *The Hay Wain*.

**The Granary Collection**

This is a fascinating museum, displaying tools used by thatchers, blacksmiths, boat builders and wheelwrights, and a collection of cycles dating from the 1830s.

*The River Stour at Flatford*

# Marsh and Forest at Orford

**WALK 37**
SUFFOLK
TM424496

This is a delightful walk, taking in a stretch of the River Ore, a section of woodland and the charming village of Orford, with its imposing castle close to the start and finish. The birdlife on this part of the Suffolk coast is outstanding.

**Information**

The walk is just under four miles long
Mainly level
Little road walking
A few stiles and a gate to cross
Pub opposite car park, and pub and hotel in main village
Grassy area around castle suitable for picnics

**START**
Orford lies at the end of the B1084, ten miles east of Woodbridge. Start from the pay-and-display public car park at Orford Quay, opposite the Jolly Sailor public house.

**DIRECTIONS**
Follow the road down to the quay, and turn right signed 'Public Footpath'. Follow the path round to a gate, go through, and climb the steps, turning left onto the path along the riverside embankment. In the distance, to the left, are the multiple radio masts on Orford Ness, and further south, a hangar and structures that resemble pagodas – part of a World War I airfield.

After ½ mile, go over two stiles (about 80ft apart), and continue along the river bank around Chantry Point. Where the river turns to follow the west side of Havergate Island, turn right (public footpath sign 'Richmond and Orford'), and cross the stile.

Follow a wide track with fields on either side, and turn right where the track emerges on to a road. Just before the farm on the right ahead, take a sandy track to the left, signed 'Public Footpath'. Continue past a barn and a footpath sign to the right, keeping to the track which bends round to the

*A pretty corner of Orford*

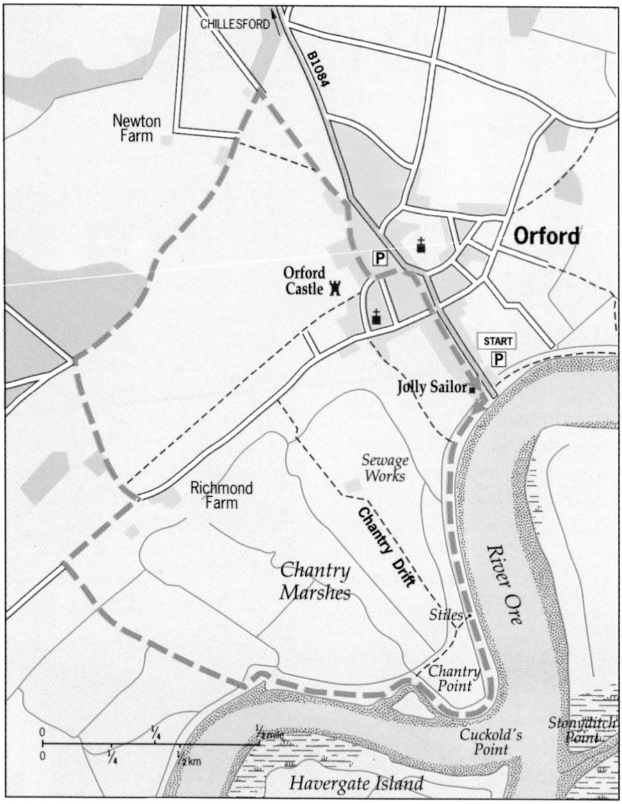


right at the trees. Follow the edge of the plantation, past the trees, and on past a small group of cottages on the left and a track leading to a farm on the left. Keep to the main track for the time being, ignoring the public footpath off to the right, which leads back to Orford.

The track is now gravel rather than sand. At the four-way 'Public Footpath' sign at the lodge turn right, with a forward view of the church tower and the yellow balconies of the fire tower in the distance. The track joins the road coming into Orford just past the tower, opposite the village sign.

Take the right fork down Mundays Lane to Market Hill. The castle is off to the right. Go left towards the church, and turn right down Church Street. This carries on into Quay Street, and back to the car park.

### Orford Castle

Built by Henry II in the late 1160s, Orford Castle has two major claims to fame. It is the oldest castle for which there exists any documentary evidence – in this case the Pipe Rolls, which are the financial records of the King's Exchequer. Secondly, it has the first castle keep to be cylindrical inside, and polygonal outside. This 'inside out' structure, reinforced by three projecting rectangular turrets, was designed both for all-round defence and to make it less likely to collapse should its foundations be undermined during a siege. The castle (English Heritage) is open daily except Mondays.

### What to look out for

Havergate Island, just across the river, is an important RSPB reserve and is one of the few places in Britain where pied avocets not only breed, but spend the winter. Thousands of other coastal birds can also be seen here year-round.

# Cavendish and Clare

An enjoyable rural ramble through the picturesque Stour Valley links these two charming villages, with a ruined castle, a vineyard and marvellous rolling countryside.

**WALK 38**
SUFFOLK
TL770451

**Information**

The walk is seven and a half miles long
Generally easy walking
Some stiles and steep gradients
Pubs and cafés in Clare and Cavendish
Good picnic spots along the river, and in Clare Country Park

START
Clare is on the A1092 between Haverhill and Long Melford, about 7 miles north-west of Sudbury. Park at Clare Country Park, signed along Malting Lane.

DIRECTIONS
Turn left out of the car park and follow the old railway path across a bridge over the River Stour, to turn immediately left through a waymarked gate (the Priory is signed left off the railway path, straight on). Continue alongside the river, cross a sluice gate (stiles) and proceed towards a brick building. Shortly, bear right across the meadow, to cross the river on a footbridge. Continue ahead to a lane. Turn left, then in 100yds bear left onto a waymarked bridleway. At a blue-arrowed board, turn right uphill.

*Pink-washed cottages at Cavendish*

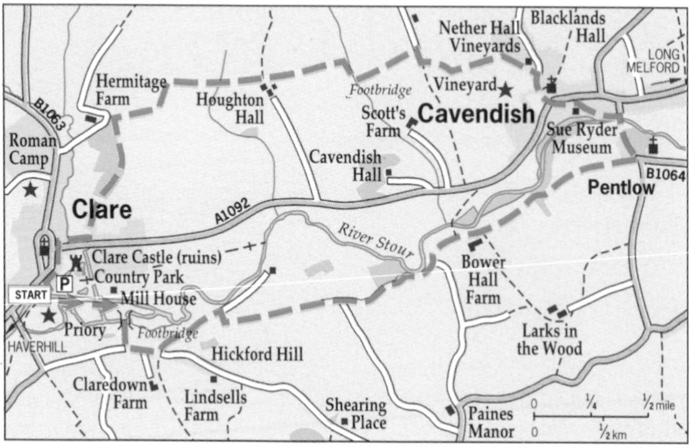


**What to look out for**

Many houses in Clare display the old craft of pargetting – the application of moulded plaster to timber frames. Look out for 'The Ancient House' by the church, with its intricate floral designs.

signed 'Pentlow', then follow the arrow left along the edge of open fields.

Continue on this path for over a mile, then bear left onto a farm road and pass in front of Bower Hall Farm. Remain on the defined track through fields and a copse, with views across to Cavendish, to reach a road (B1064) in Pentlow. Turn left along the footway towards Cavendish.

Cross the river and climb the first stile on the left, to follow a permissive path which runs parallel to the river. Cross a fence stile and footbridge, walk along a fence, then bear right by a further bridge, across lawns to a gravel drive. Turn left here to reach the A1092 in Cavendish.

Keep left, and soon cross the road to follow the lane beside the green, signed 'Vineyard'. Turn left towards Colts Hall, in front of Nether Hall Vineyards, and gently ascend out of the valley. Take the third arrowed footpath on the left, just beyond a cottage – the Stour Valley Path. Descend along the field edge to a footbridge and turn right, then left around a further field and climb towards Houghton Hall, hidden in trees. Keep right into the adjacent field, continue along the edge and pass a tank to join a good track with open views. Continue for ¼ mile with waymarkers, and soon descend towards Clare. At a junction of paths, keep to the field edge, soon to follow the path along the edge of scrub to join a track leading to the A1092. Turn right at the road, then left through the village, back to the start.

*Pargetting in Clare*

**Clare**

The history of this little market town centres on its Norman castle, of which only the motte and some masonry remains. The Country Park surrounds the site, and the old railway station is an information centre. The Augustinians founded their first priory here in 1248 and two buildings survive: the old infirmary and the church, both set in fine gardens near the river.

**Cavendish**

The expansive slope of the green is set off by the pastel washes of the thatched cottages which surround it in this picture-postcard village, once the ancestral home of the Dukes of Devonshire. The magnificent Old Rectory is now the headquarters of the Sue Ryder Foundation, and houses a museum illustrating its work. Open all year, daily.

# *The Dunes at Winterton*

**WALK 39**
NORFOLK
TG498197

**Information**

The walk is five and a half miles long
Mostly level ground, though dune walking can be harder, and groynes to negotiate on shoreline
Some road walking on quiet lane
Café at car park in summer, pub in Winterton
Toilets in village
Beach ideal for picnics

A pleasant walk through dunes and farmland that shows a flat landscape is not necessarily a dull one.

**START**
Winterton lies about 8 miles north of Great Yarmouth, on the B1159. Start the walk from the beach car park at the eastern end of the village – a charge is made in summer.

**DIRECTIONS**
Walk back towards the village and turn right before the first bungalow. Continue across the sand hills and tun left on to a track between two houses. Go striaght ahead at the crossroads and continue on this track towards East Somerton for about ¼ mile, passing Winterton church and farm buildings on the left. The track bends right past Manor Farm and a ruined church, and bear right on the concrete track beyond Burnley Hall. At the next junction bear left, and turn right just before the trees. Continue on this roadway for about ½ mile, and turn right on to a rough track.

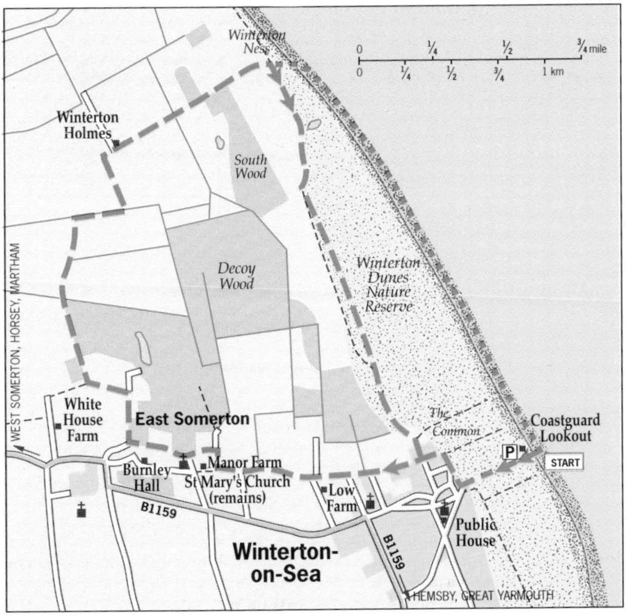


After a short distance, turn left, keeping the hedge on your left, towards some farm buildings. Turn right here, keeping the buildings to your left, and follow the track towards the sea, reaching a gate on your right beyond some trees. (For a slightly longer walk, go straight ahead here to cross the dunes, walking back to the car park along the shoreline.) Pass through the gate, and follow the track along the back of the sandhills for just over a mile, back to Winterton. Follow the track between two houses, and at the crossroads turn left to retrace your route to the car park.

**A Storm-wracked Coastline**
Often appearing deceptively peaceful, this stretch of coast was notorious for its

*The tall tower of Winterton Church serves as a good landmark*

shipwrecks in stormy weather. The 18th-century writer Daniel Defoe reported that half the village of Winterton was built of timbers from wrecked vessels, and in one winter's night 200 coal ships were lost offshore. Tombstones in the church bear witness to the many lives lost at sea.

The sea has also invaded this coastline, breaking through the dunes and flooding the land. Since the most recent flooding, in 1938, the dunes have been reinforced with concrete in some places.

**What to look out for**

The dune system is a National Nature Reserve, and rich in a variety of wildlife. The drier areas of the dunes support heather, and ferns and other wetland plants grow on damper patches. Watch out for adders. Little terns nest on the beach, so keep to the main track and observe all warning signs to avoid disturbing them.

**WALK 40**
NORFOLK
TG392180

# *Ludham Marshes*

### Information

The walk is about three miles long
Level, easy ground, but can be very muddy and slippery by marshes; care needed beside dykes and reed beds
A little road walking on a no through road
No stiles
Dogs should be kept on leads
Pub offering bar snacks in Ludham, with garden; also a small café in the village
Grassy area by staithe suitable for picnics, also one or two places along route
Toilets by staithe

An interesting and easy walk, close to one of the Broadland waterways and providing fine views across traditional grazing marshes.

**START**
Ludham is about 14 miles north-east of Norwich. From Wroxham, take the A1062 to Ludham, continue through the village centre, then shortly afterwards take the turning on the right, signposted 'Womack Staithe'. There is parking on the staithe near the shop and toilets.

**DIRECTIONS**
From the staithe, walk on down the lane beside the moorings, past some attractive houses on the right, until you come to the 'County Sailing Base'. Immediately on the left-hand side of the Base is a footpath (do not take the track marked 'bridleway' which is to the left of the footpath). The footpath runs along a low bank, with Womack Water on the right; to the left are extensive grazing marshes. After about ½ mile, at a cottage, the path turns left and then runs alongside the River Thurne, though separated from it by a bank of reeds. After about ¼ mile chalets can be seen on the far bank, and the path soon leaves the river by a pumphouse. Cross a dyke on a plank bridge, taking care at either end where it is a little rough, then turn left along a grassy track which is bordered on either side by dykes. After about ¼ mile, go

*Marsh thistle*

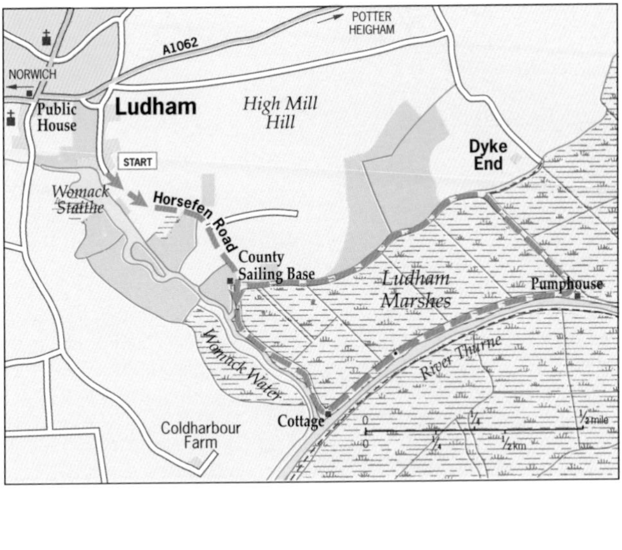

**What to look out for**

The dyke systems on the marshes have a rich animal and plant life. A special feature of the area is the Norfolk aeshna dragonfly which is only found on the Norfolk Broads and is now the symbol of the Broads Authority. Redshank and lapwing breed on the grazing marshes. The very tall marsh sow-thistle, also largely confined to the Norfolk Broads, is a feature of the marsh banks in late summer. The remains of an old pump mill stand in the marshes.

through a gate then turn left along another grassy track which is partly bordered by a wood on the right-hand side. In about ¼ mile the track bears right by a house and emerges to join the outward route by the 'County Sailing Base'. Retrace the route back to the start point.

**Grazing marshes**

The grazing marshes in Broadland have traditionally been grazed by cattle during the summer. The rich pastures were particularly good for fattening cattle, and animals were driven down on foot by drovers from as far away as Scotland. The marshes were drained by a system of dykes, and water was returned to the river by pumps – originally wind-powered, then steam driven and most recently fuelled by diesel. The older methods were the least efficient and consequently the grazing marshes would frequently flood in winter, providing a marvellous habitat for wildfowl.

In the 1960s and 1970s many of these old grazing marshes were ploughed up to be intensively farmed for cereals, but farmers are now being encouraged to return the land to the more traditional grazing practices. Hopefully, this will prevent the further pollution of the Broads and herald the return of its rich plant and animal life.

*A drainage channel across the marshland*

# Little Gidding

**WALK 41**
CAMBRIDGESHIRE
TL127817

A pleasant walk along country lanes around the charming and curious old settlement of Little Gidding.

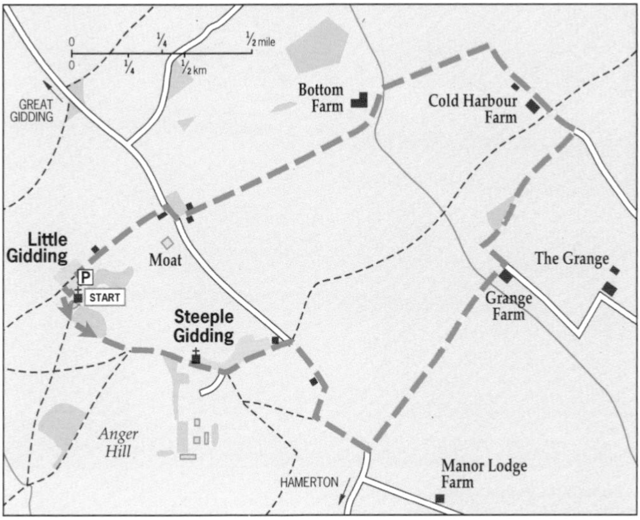


**Information**

The walk is about four miles long
Level, easy walking on footpaths and quiet lanes
No stiles
Refreshments at Little Gidding
Toilets at Little Gidding

START
Little Gidding is about 1 mile south-east of Great Gidding, which straddles the B660, near the A1 north of Sawtry. Take the narrow minor road to Little Gidding and watch for the right, signposted but marked 'No Through Road'. Go to the end of this lane and park in the car park.

DIRECTIONS
From the car park, first visit the delightful Church of St John the Evangelist. On emerging from the church, follow the sign for the Ferrar House Parlour. Turn left at the bridleway sign. Head diagonally left across the field to a line of trees about 100yds away, aiming to go round the back of them. Turn left beyond the trees and continue to a gate in the fence ahead. Go through this gate and follow the path up the slope, with the wood on your left.

*The Church at Steeple Gidding*

The steeple of the church at Steeple Gidding comes into view as you round the end of the wood, and this brings you to a proper track. Turn right down here towards Steeple Gidding.

Pass the church in Steeple Gidding, and follow the road round to the left, ignoring the footpath on your right at the turn. Turn right at the next T-junction, for a stretch of road walking – it is a quiet country road with wide grassy verges. The road zigzags and brings you to another T-junction; turn left here and walk along this country lane. All around are views of gently undulating fields, typical of this part of Cambridgeshire, on the edge of the fertile fens.

*The flat landscape of Little Gidding*

**What to look out for**

On the left of the side road leading down to the Little Gidding community, look for the remains of the original moated manor house in the field.

Follow the road as it turns left at a farm, then right and uphill slightly, to pass a coppice on the left. At the top of the hill the road bends left (the 'Public Byway' sign on the right leads to Aversley Wood if you have time for a diversion) along Bullock Road, an old drovers' road. Pass a footpath sign, a farm, and then a house, all on the left. About 100yds beyond the house, reach a sign on the left marked 'Public Footpath, Little Gidding 1 mile'.
Turn left along this path and head straight down towards the red building ahead of you, an old barn which was once part of Bottom Farm. Keep on the main path which skirts round to the left of the barn, and head straight towards some more buildings. Go through the yard in front of these storage buildings, to the gate which leads you on to the main road. Turn right, then first left, down the track which leads you back to Little Gidding.

**Little Gidding**
The buildings at Little Gidding form a community, originally a 17th-century experiment in community living founded by Nicholas Ferrar, a merchant who turned his back on the business world. Charles I once sheltered here, and as a result it was sacked by the Parliamentarians in 1647. The community later inspired the poet T S Eliot to write 'Little Gidding', as one of his *Four Quartets*.

# *Godmanchester and its Water Meadows*

This walk combines water meadows, wooded tracks, historic buildings, river craft and locks. For those interested in botany the path passes through a Site of Special Scientific Interest.

**WALK 42**
CAMBRIDGESHIRE
TL224709

**Information**

The walk is about three miles long
Easy, level walking
Virtually no road walking
Dogs should be kept under control in the SSSI, where walkers are asked to keep to the paths
Plenty of grassy riverside spots for picnics
The Olde Mill at the start of the walk provides food and has a garden and waterwheel; pubs in Godmanchester

START
Bromholme Lane is two miles south-west of Huntingdon on the A604 and a mile east of Brampton. Turn south on the road signposted to The Olde Mill public house. Park the car near the track leading to the reservoir.

DIRECTIONS
Take the marked track eastwards over the bridge, with Hinchingbrooke House in view to the north across the water meadows. Go under the railway bridge (high speed trains cross here) and through a kissing-gate on to Port Holme. Take the central path eastwards across this SSSI and through a second kissing-gate on to the banks of the River Ouse. This leads on to a good footpath which crosses four footbridges and several small islands before leading into Godmanchester. Cross the Chinese bridge and turn left past Queen Elizabeth's Grammar School. Follow the road for a couple of hundred yards to Mill Yard car park, then turn left again and cross the bridge opposite Island Hall.
Retrace your steps as far as Port Holme, take the left-hand path after the kissing-gate and follow the river bank as far as a small beach in a large loop of the river. (Avoid going straight on towards the railway as the path can be very overgrown.)
Veer off to the north-west where you will soon meet the original track near the railway bridge. A short walk will bring you back to Bromholme Lane.

**What to look out for**

When crossing Port Home meadows (SSSI) keep your eyes open for the rich assortment of wild flowers.
The land here has been farmed under a traditional haymaking/grazing regime which has given rise to its botanical diversity; look for yellow rattle, ragged robin and marsh orchids among the display.
Butterflies are numerous on sunny summer days, as are dragonflies and damselflies closer to the river.

**Godmanchester and Island Hall**
As you approach the small and attractive town of Godmanchester the diversity of architecture to be seen across the river is striking. This is The Causeway, now designated an Outstanding Conservation Area. Originally a Roman settlement, Godmanchester continued to prosper through the ages, but

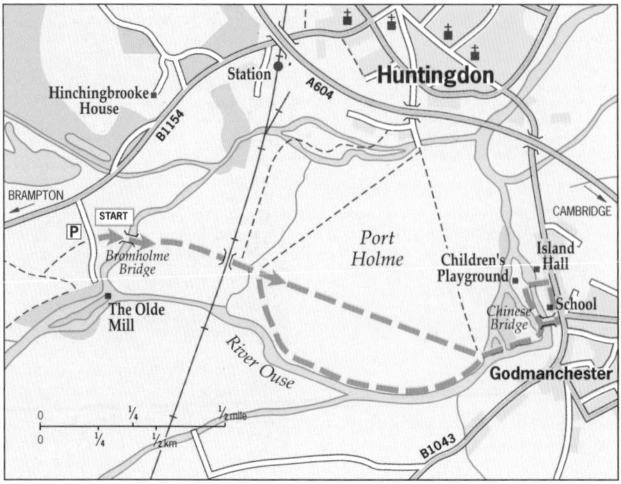


still maintains a village atmosphere with a population of just 3,000. Of particular interest are the Chinese bridge, a replica of the original dated 1827, and Island Hall, a large riverside mansion built in 1730 with well-maintained riverside grounds. It is open to the public on summer Sunday afternoons.

**Hinchingbrooke House**
Although not quite on the route of this walk, Hinchingbrooke House can be clearly seen to the north from Bromholme Lane and Port Holme meadows. Now a school, it belonged at one time to Oliver Cromwell's grandfather and both James I and Charles I are said to have been guests here. The house has limited opening to the public during the spring and summer. Cromwell has many connections with this part of Cambridgeshire. He attended school in nearby Huntingdon and was later Member of Parliament for the town.

*The Chinese Bridge at Godmanchester*

# *Ferry Meadows*

**WALK 43**
CAMBRIDGESHIRE
TL149975

Woods and meadowland, river and lakeside are all included in this pleasant walk on well-maintained paths, and there is a great deal of wildlife interest.

START
Ferry Meadows Country Park is situated in a bend of the River Nene just west of Peterborough. It is two miles east of the A1 Alwalton exit on the A605, just north of Orton Wistow. Follow country park signs and park in the large car park (charge on Bank Holidays and summer weekends).

DIRECTIONS
Start the walk at the visitor centre and follow the path skirting the bottom of Overton Lake eastwards to Ham Bridge.
Cross and turn right to reach Bluebell Bridge. Cross the river and turn first left opposite the golf course, up the wooded Riverside Walk and along the river edge (or take the higher Bluebell Walk which has a tarmac surface). Part-way along the path there are a few low steps to be climbed.
Follow the path left to Ferry Bridge where you cross back over the river into Gunwade Meadow.
Turn left and continue down Ferry Walk to Gunwade Lake; here turn right over the pontoon bridge. Proceed past the children's play area on the northern edge of Lynch Lake, turning first left along the path that will bring you back to the visitor centre.

**Ferry Meadows Country Park**
This country park contains over 1,200 acres of countryside, including three lakes. The presence of water is felt everywhere – the park is sited on the flood plain of the River Nene – and results in a wide variety of water and wetland conditions.
There is also archaeological interest, with the site of a 1,700 year old Roman farm, well and fishponds within the park and the site of a Roman fort within the golf course across the river.
Gunwade Lake, the largest of the three, is the site of the National Watersports Centre, which organises a wide variety of courses and activities.
Originally set up by Peterborough Development Corporation, the park is now run by the Nene Park Trust 'to provide in perpetuity enjoyment of countryside recreation for the people of Peterborough and visitors to the city'. The park has its own station on the Nene Valley Railway, a popular preserved steam line.

**What to look out for**

Three lakes provide roosting and feeding grounds for a wide variety of waterfowl. The sympathetic management of the land is further encouraging many species to nest in the woodland. Here, and in the protected grassland areas, primroses, cowslips and bluebells flourish in spring and you may be lucky enough to find southern marsh or common spotted orchids. Many species of butterfly and dragonfly have been identified here too.

**Information**

The walk is about two and a half miles long
Level, easy walking
No road walking
Lakeside beach and safe swimming area for young children; swimming strictly prohibited elsewhere
Information centre, café and toilets
Dogs should be kept under strict control
Seats and picnic tables around the lakes

*Gunwade Lake is the largest of three at Ferry Meadows*

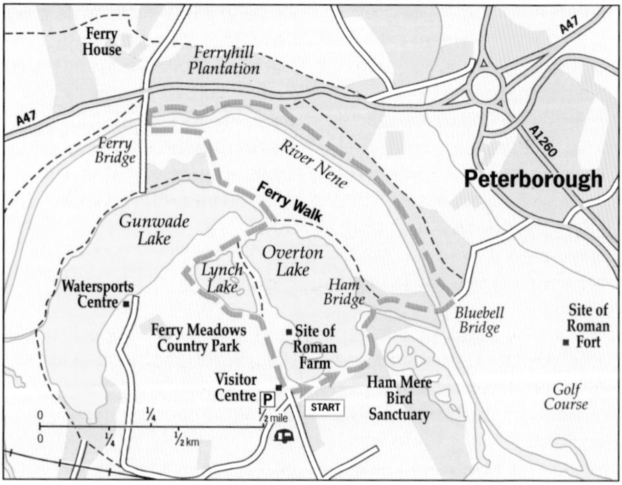


## The Nene Valley Basket Industry

Along the river edge, shortly before reaching Ferry Bridge, is a plantation of willows, or osiers, which once formed the basis of the local basket-making industry. In order to preserve the plantation, the trees are cut back every few years – taking over the role originally fulfilled when the willow pliable wands were harvested to be woven into strong baskets.

# Three Leicestershire Villages

**WALK 44**
LEICESTERSHIRE
SK690130

This is an adventurous and exacting walk. It visits three villages in a particularly attractive corner of Leicestershire and takes in a wide variety of countryside, from pasture to plough, and from green lane to cricket pitch.

**Information**

The walk is about four miles long
Easy walking
Virtually no road walking
A lot of stiles; possibly some electric fences to roll under
Dogs should be kept on leads
Pubs in all three villages, all serving food and welcoming children
Various picnic spots along the walk

START

The village of Gaddesby is just north-east of Leicester on the B674 (off the A607 from Leicester to Melton Mowbray). Park in the village and start the walk from its centre, by the church.

DIRECTIONS

Walk away from the church down Church Lane, turn right onto the road at the bottom and left down a tree-lined avenue, following the footpath sign, just past the Cheney Arms pub. Cross the river by the wooden bridge and cross the field to a gate ahead in the wire fence. Ignore the yellow arrow pointing left to the field corner and instead turn half-left and aim for half-way along the field boundary, where a little bridge crosses a brook.

Turn half-right in the next field and aim for the far corner, just down from which is a stile. Cross the next field to the clump of trees in the opposite left-hand corner. Climb both stiles and cross the next field to a stile a little way up the opposite hedge, then walk straight across the next field to a stile half-way up the opposite hedge.

Cross the next (bumpy) field to a stile by a gate, a few yards to the left of the modern twin barns. This gives on to an often very muddy track leading to the village of Barsby, coming out by the King William Inn. Walk down Main Street towards the church, and cross the road into Baggrave End and then Church Lane.

Take the path to the left and pass through the kissing-gate. Cross the field, past the pond, to a stile in the right-hand corner, then cross the next field to a double stile in the opposite corner. Walk down the field to a stile by a solitary tree and some gating, and on to an iron kissing-gate under a chestnut tree. Cross the drive, go through another kissing-gate, cross a field and then two bridges by the cricket ground. Turn left at the road. This is the village of Ashby Folville. Turn right at the Carington Arms and go up Highfield End. Ascend the flight of steps by the footpath sign, climb the stile, go straight across the field to the gate and turn left down the

**What to look out for**

The hedgerows are home to many small animals and birds. Look out for tufts of fur caught on low branches which will tell you where rabbits and even foxes pass through regularly.

*The church at Gaddesby (left)*

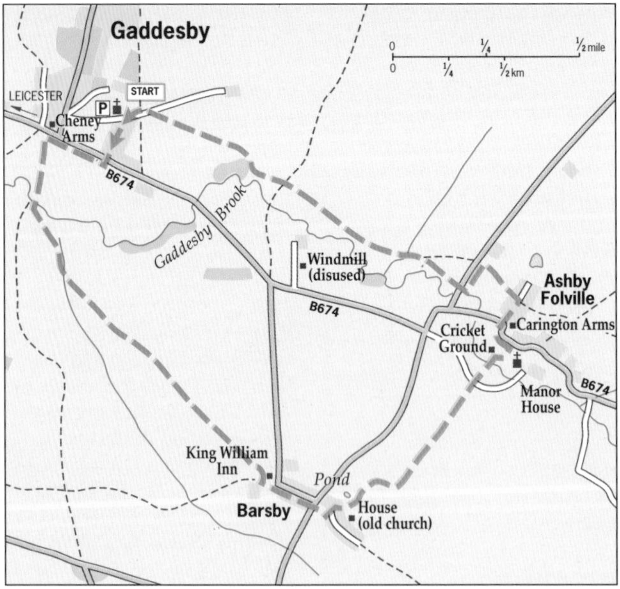


lane. Go through the gate on the right before the bridge and follow the path through the meadow. Gaddesby church spire is clearly visible ahead. Cross a footbridge and stile, go straight across the next field to a stile, and then cross the next two fields and one more stile. Cross another field and a stile marked by a red-tipped post, make for the right-hand corner and cross into the field. Follow the southern boundary beside the stream. Turn right at the farthest corner up the hedge line to the hill top, where a yellow marker shows the way across a stile, then walk through another field and cross a stream. Walk up to a gate near a brick building and climb the nearby stile. Turn left along the track back to Gaddesby church.

### The villages

Though time has not stood here, their character has remained largely unspoilt. Gaddesby has a particularly interesting church with fine medieval workmanship. In Barsby a house called Godson's Folly was originally built as a mortuary chapel.

# *Hartshill Hayes Country Park*

**WALK 45**
WARWICKSHIRE
SP307941

Starting with a section of the 'Centenary Way' footpath, this varied walk goes through Hartshill Hayes Country Park on the Atherstone Ridge. The scenery in this area includes farmland, open grassland and a large wood, and the route partly follows a disused railway line.

### START

Oldbury Cutting Picnic Area (free parking) is four miles north-west of Nuneaton, at a sharp bend in a lane north of Ansley Common.

### DIRECTIONS

From the bottom of the hill in the picnic area follow the waymarked 'Centenary Way' along the green embankment. Cross a farm track via two stiles and after about 125yds (muddy), turn left over a stile. Cross fields on a well-defined path, climbing two more stiles, to reach a large field to the east of Moorwood Farm. From the top left corner of the field bear right to the bottom corner and take the stile on the left signed 'Hartshill Hayes Country Park'. Cross a small field, climb two stiles in quick succession and

**Information**

The walk is three and a half miles long
Undulating ground, not generally steep, but muddy in places
A lot of stiles
Some lane walking
Dogs should be kept on leads through Moorwood Rare Breed Leisure Farm and under close control in the country park
Pub at Hartshill Green; no children's room
Grassy areas suitable for picnics at Oldbury Cutting and Hartshill Hayes Country Park
Toilets at Hartshill Hayes Country Park

*Bluebells in the country park*

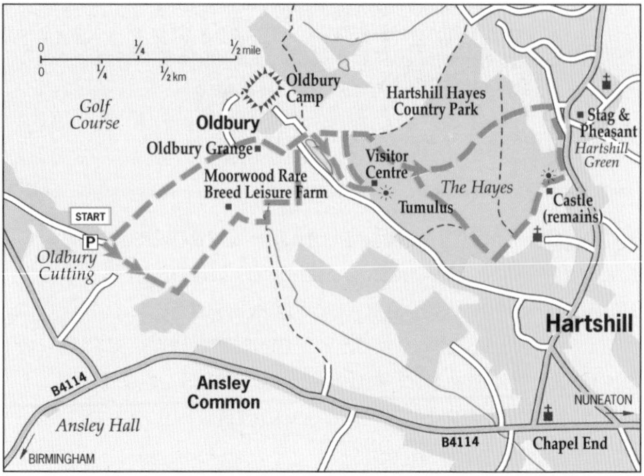


bear left, passing a path junction to a fenced way beside a narrow pool. At the end, bear right uphill on an enclosed path to a stile. Go over a rise in the field beyond, heading diagonally towards a red-roofed bungalow, to reach Oldbury Lane via a stile at the far corner, opposite an (unsigned) entrance to Hartshill Hayes Country Park. Passing through a kissing-gate into the Park, turn right and skirt a covered reservoir to join a path to the visitor centre. Return to the open hillside and descend to the right, beside a large wood, the Hayes, passing the adventure play area. The path enters the wood and skirts its lower edge, then swings inwards. At marker post 3 descend to the left. Ignore post 4 and follow the main path to the edge of the wood, where a causeway and steps lead to a road above. Turn right to Hartshill Green where the Stag and Pheasant pub overlooks the small green and a bus shelter commemorating the poet Michael Drayton. Climb Castle Road (footpath alongside) to a waymarked path on the right, opposite

*Common dog violet*

Abbey Cottage, and follow it past the ruins of Hartshill Castle. Keep within the edge of the woods to a cross-path from a kissing-gate and houses on the left. Turn right and proceed to a junction with a broader track, taking the middle track back to the open hillside.

To return to Oldbury Cutting, go out to Oldbury Lane, where you first entered the country park, and descend to the right, passing Oldbury Grange on the left and the entrance to Moorwood Rare Breed Leisure Farm.

**Hartshill Hayes Country Park**

The county council's 136 acres of open hilltop and woodland overlook the Anker valley, with views far across neighbouring Leicestershire to the rocky tors of Charnwood Forest. Facilities include a visitor centre and café, toilets and a car park (charge).

**Moorwood Rare Breed Leisure Farm**

The farm (admittance charge) offers visitors the chance to see around 30 rare breeds of farm animals. Spinning demonstrations are given, and there is a tea room with a children's play area.

**What to look out for**

From the path through Moorwood Rare Breed Leisure Farm many unusual breeds of farm animals can be seen in the fields. At Hartshill Green note the unusual dedication of a bus shelter to an Elizabethan poet – the locally-born Michael Drayton. The path back to the country park passes the rather scanty ruins of Hartshill Castle.

**WALK 46**
NOTTINGHAMSHIRE
SK532266

# The West Leake Hills

**Information**

The walk is about four miles long
Ascent and descent of hill are fairly gentle
No stiles
Pub (Star Inn) just to the south of the village at the crossroads; also pubs in nearby East Leake
The woodland section is among several good picnic places along the walk

This delightful walk goes up into the hills above West Leake village, where there are panoramic views over Nottingham and its surrounding countryside, returning through a landscape of woods and pastures.

**START**

West Leake is some ten miles south of Nottingham City Centre and is easily accessible from the A453, the A6006 or from the junction of the A6 and M1 (junction 24) at Kegworth. Park in the village and start the walk from the eastern end of West Leake.

**DIRECTIONS**

Where the road turns right out of the village there is a large field entrance with a bridleway marker. Enter the field and follow the track up the hill (Fox Hill). Almost immediately there are good

*Fields of rape above West Leake*

views, initially of the huge power station to the left, then into Leicestershire to the right and behind. Fine woodland soon takes the place of the power station on the left. Keep straight on when the track meets a farm lane, and straight on again past another little road coming in from the left.
When the lane eventually bends to the right, turn left, following the public bridleway sign along the ridge of Crow Wood Hill. Rushcliffe Golf Course is to the right.
Follow the path onto and along the edge of the golf course and continue, with the trees on your left, past an old red-brick barn on your right. As the golf course comes to an end, continue along the path, following the bridleway sign, through some trees to reach a gate. Go through the gate and, following the blue arrows, keep along the edge of the field, with the wood on the left (remarkable views right of Nottingham in the distance).
At the corner of the field turn left through a gate, follow the path along the left of the hedge and pass through a gate into the wood. Turn right along the track which almost immediately bends to the left, later descending between two arms of woodland. At the bottom turn left along the track to the barn, then right along the farm lane. Just before the line of trees ahead, turn left along a track which, after a while, becomes a path that leads along the edges of the fields and so back to your starting point at West Leake.

**What to look out for**

The view of the city of Nottingham from the hill on this walk is particularly impressive – it is not often that you see such a large city set in its surrounding countryside. The woods have a rich variety of flora, including masses of bluebells, particularly in the recently felled areas; lesser celandine and greater stitchwort add contrasting colour.

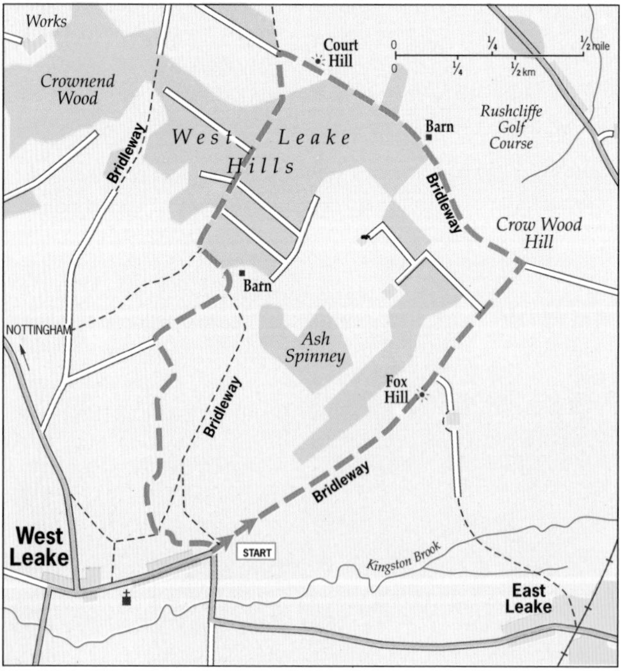


**Nottingham**
Nottingham is a city which has grown extensively in recent times and yet, at its heart, still manages to retain a little of the flavour of the days when it was a bustling county town famous for its Goose Fair and Castle. In fact it has a very long history and it was an important fortress from pre-Roman days until the late Middle Ages. Its many excellent museums and other attractions include the award-winning Brewhouse Yard Museum, the Lace Hall, a fascinating reminder of the Nottingham lace industry, and the hi-tech 'Tales of Robin Hood' in which visitors are transported back to Sherwood Forest in 'time cars'.

# The Canal at Brewood

This is a most enjoyable and easy walk with plenty of interest, the last stretch being along the Shropshire Union Canal. An atmosphere of peace and solitude prevails along most of the walk, which is ideal for lovers of wildlife.

**WALK 47**
STAFFORDSHIRE
SJ883086

**START**
The village of Brewood is eight miles north of Wolverhampton just off the A5 and the A449. Start the walk from the church of St Mary and St Chad in Church Road, a short distance from the main square. There is plenty of parking in the village.

**DIRECTIONS**
Walk to the church along Church Road, away from the centre of the village, and turn left into Dean Street. Cross the road opposite the church and take the alley immediately at the side of Dean Cottage. After 25yds turn left onto the track and then immediately right

*Walking at Brewood*

over a stile into the field. Follow the hedge on the left and cross a stile, then a small brick footbridge, then two stiles leading up to the road bridge over the canal.
Turn right to cross the bridge and follow the winding track for about ¼ mile. Turn left at the sign for the farm. After 100yds pass a handsome red brick farmhouse on your right and turn left over a stile, following 'Staffordshire Way' signpost. Follow the path through the pasture for about ½ mile, keeping to the line of trees on the left. Cross two stiles in short succession before reaching The Avenue. Turn left and continue to cross Avenue Bridge.
(To extend the walk at this point, follow the 'Staffordshire Way' sign, to cross The Avenue and go over a stile to

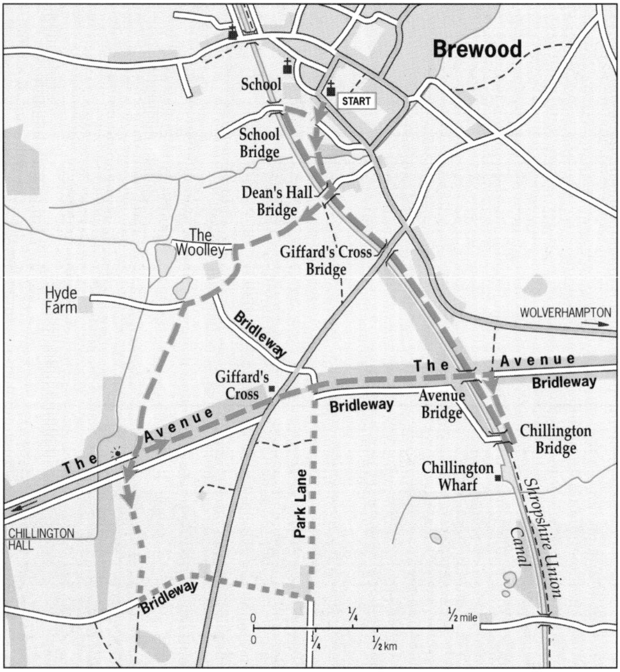


## Information

The walk is about four miles long

Level, easy ground, except for steep descent to canal towpath at Chillington Bridge

Several stiles

Dogs may be let off leads under supervision along the towpath

Various pubs in Brewood village

Parts of the towpath are suitable for picnics

cross the lane. Go through a kissing-gate and into a long pasture, keeping to the hedge line on the left. After about 500yds, cross the stile and turn left onto the footpath. Just past cottages, cross the road ahead (Park Lane) and continue forwards up the lane, following it round to the left by a group of houses and continuing for about ½ mile.

When Brewood church comes into view, turn right down the bridlepath through a gateway just before the lane turns to the left again. Walk through woods for about 500yds and cross Avenue Bridge.)

Bear right along a path leading to the field alongside the canal.

Follow the line of the canal along the field and at the far end turn right into the track leading over canal bridge. Proceed with great care down a steep path at the left-hand side of the bridge to reach the towpath. Turn right along the towpath, passing under Avenue Bridge and two road bridges (the second was crossed at the beginning of the walk). Just before the next bridge, follow a pathway up to the right to come up onto the track by the school and walk the short distance back to the village, retracing your steps to the church.

## What to look out for

Avenue Bridge is a particularly handsome structure, designed to be in keeping with Chillington Hall and Park. The canal was cut particularly deep at this point so as to be kept out of the view of the Giffard family. Giffard's Cross is a short distance from Avenue Bridge. It is also named after the Sir John Giffard who, it is said, shot an escaped panther there with a crossbow in 1513. The panther had originally been sent from Africa as a gift.

### Chillington Hall

Chillington has been the home of the Giffard family since 1178. The present house was built by Sir John Soane in 1786 and the park was designed by that most famous of landscapers, 'Capability' Brown. Both are open to the public on Thursday afternoons between May and September.

# Castleton and Cave Dale

This is an easy exploration of the best of Derbyshire's limestone country, centred on the busy tourist village of Castleton, with its famous caves and castle. The walk climbs up the rocky gorge of Cave Dale, then descends steeply back to the village.

**WALK 48**
DERBYSHIRE
SK149829

**Information**

The walk is two miles long
Involves some steep sections
Several gates, stiles and cattle grids
Dogs should be kept on leads at all times
Pubs and cafés in Castleton
Picnic places in Cave Dale
Toilets at car park

*The view from Peveril Castle, high above Castleton*

**START**
Castleton stands at the head of the Hope Valley on the A625 Sheffield to Chapel-en-le-Frith road. Park in the large village car park (pay-and-display) in Cross Street.

**DIRECTIONS**
From the car park, turn left along Cross Street, passing the Town Ditch on the left. In a few yards, at The Castle pub, turn right (Castle Street). Passing the church on the left, enter the Market Place. Turn left to pass the war memorial into Bargate, then in 50yds turn right, signposted 'Limestone Way'. Cross a wooded stile where the rock walls narrow, and

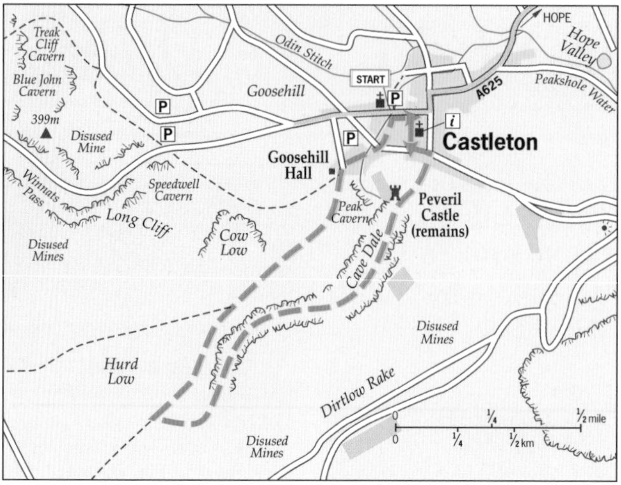


start the climb up through the dale (Peveril Castle stands high on its precipitous crag above you to the right). Follow this path to a metal gate near the head of the dale, where the gradient eases. Now keep a dry stone wall on your right and later pass through a metal gate. At the next metal gate, turn sharp right into a walled green lane which leads over the hill. (Cave Dale is now visible to the right, and on reaching the crest of the hill, the face of the 'Shivering Mountain' of Mam Tor is on the left.)

Pass through an old metal gate and keep ahead, descending more steeply now. At the foot of the hill pass through a gate onto a walled lane, with Goosehill Hall on your left, to re-enter Castleton at Goosehill Bridge. Afterwards keep left to walk down the footpath beside Peakshole Water, which issues from the huge mouth of Peak Cavern. On reaching the main road, turn right into Cross Street, with the car park almost opposite.

**What to look out for**

The grassy slopes of the Derbyshire Dales are rich in flowers, including early purple orchid, cowslip, bird's-foot trefoil and common rock-rose. On some of the steeper slopes, particularly below crags, is the rare limestone polypody fern. Butterflies include orange tip, green hairstreak and common blue. The woods are home to chaffinches, willow warblers, wood warblers, spotted flycatchers, and great spotted and green woodpeckers.

**Caves and crags**

Castleton is at the heart of an area where streams sink suddenly beneath the porous white limestone rock into the spectacular caves which have been formed by this water erosion over the years. Many of the caves are open to the public. Peak Cavern (open Easter to October), in the village, has the largest cave entrance in Britain and once housed a community of rope makers.

Speedwell Cavern, at the foot of the Winnats Pass, is entered by boat on an underground canal cut by lead miners; the Treak Cliff and Blue John Caverns in the hills to the west, have the best displays of the rare semi-precious stone, Blue John, which is not found anywhere else in the world. Blue John and Speedwell Caverns open all year; Peak Cavern open Easter to October.

The craggy gorges of Cave Dale and the Winnats Pass are thought to have been formed when swift currents of meltwater from Ice Age glaciers cut through the 300 million-year-old reef limestone.

**Peveril Castle**

Originally built by William Peveril, son of William the Conqueror, Peveril Castle (English Heritage) occupies a commanding site overlooking the village. In ruins now, the castle is reached by a steep, zig-zag path from a corner of the village square and is open all year.

*Wood warbler*

# WALK 49
NOTTINGHAMSHIRE
SK643647

# *Rufford Country Park and Abbey*

### Information

The walk is about one and a half miles long
Level and easy going
No road walking
No stiles
Dogs should be kept on leads
Refreshments available at the Mill (north end of the lake) and the Stable Block (at the south)
Various excellent picnic sites in the Park, near the car parks at the southern and northern end, and near the lake
Toilets at the Mill and the Craft Centre

This is a pleasant and easy walk around the lake at Rufford Country Park, on the edge of Sherwood Forest, and includes a visit to Rufford Abbey and Craft Centre.

**START**

Rufford Country Park is three miles south of Ollerton and 16 miles north of Nottingham on the A614. It is well signposted. It can also be reached with ease from Mansfield via the A6075 or B6030. Start the walk from the main car park (there may be a charge). There is also a car park near the Mill at the north end of the Park.

**DIRECTIONS**

From the north-west corner of the main car park, head north following signs 'Ice House'. Here there is a choice of routes. Either continue straight on, looping right-handed after a while to arrive at the side of the lake, or turn right at the Ice House, signed 'Rufford Lake', walk across the Broad Ride and turn left along the edge of the lake. There are picnic sites adjacent to both routes. Whichever route you choose, continue round the lake past the Mill, cross the footbridge and then turn right to continue through the very attractive woodland. Later bear right to cross three footbridges and then turn left to visit the Abbey and craft centre before returning to the car park.

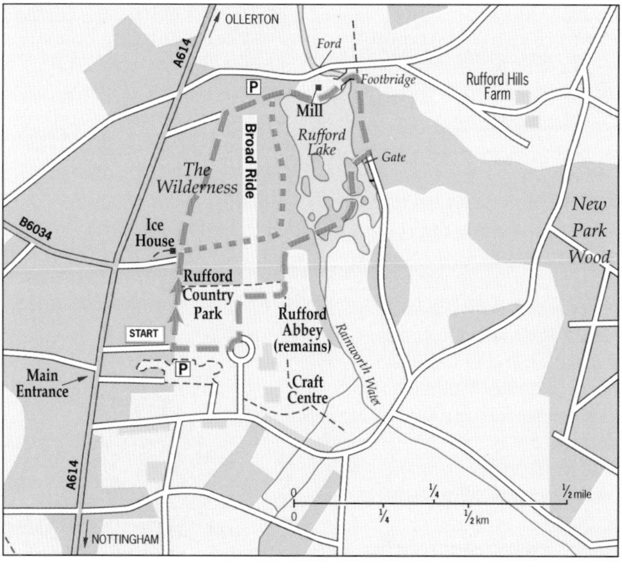


**Rufford Abbey**

Rufford has a history which goes back to well before the Norman Conquest when it was the property of Ulf the Saxon, but after the invasion it was given by the new King William to his nephew Gilbert le Gaunt. It was his grandson, the Earl of Lincoln, who founded a religious order here with Cistercian monks from Rievaulx Abbey in Yorkshire.

*Rufford Abbey, at the heart of the country park*

The Abbey of Rufford itself dates from 1147.
The estate passed into the Savile family at the Dissolution, and remained in their hands until 1938 – it now belongs to the county council – and there are still the remains of the Elizabethan house.

**What to look out for**

Rufford Lake is a nature reserve, and there is a special bird sanctuary at its southern end. Many different sorts of waterfowl can be seen on and around the lake, including Canada goose, mute swan, mallard, pochard and tufted duck. Great crested grebe, moorhen, coot and grey heron are among the other types of waterbird to be seen here.
The park has a flock of rare Mouflon sheep, which look almost like a small breed of deer, especially when, in the autumn, the rams charge each other and lock horns.

**The Craft Centre**

The Craft Centre includes a shop selling pottery, jewellery, textiles, glass, woodwork, leatherwork and metalwork, while the Gallery holds regular exhibitions. There are also lectures and craft demonstrations. Nearby are an arboretum, formal gardens, sculpture exhibition, orangery, restaurants and bookshop.

*Mallard*

# *Kirkby on Bain and Haltham*

**WALK 50**
LINCOLNSHIRE
TF240627

A delightful walk between the villages of Kirkby on Bain and Haltham, taking in pastureland, views of an attractive water mill and a stretch of the River Bain.

**START**
Kirkby on Bain is six miles south of Horncastle, just off the A153. Park carefully and considerately in the village and start the walk from the Ebrington Arms.

**DIRECTIONS**
Turn left along the pavement opposite the Ebrington Arms and follow the road round until turning left through a kissing-gate, opposite the village shop.

**Information**

The walk is about two miles long
Level, easy ground
A lot of stiles
Pubs in Kirkby on Bain and Haltham, both welcome walkers and children and serve food
Various picnic places along the walk

*The Horncastle Canal and bridge near Kirkby on Bain*

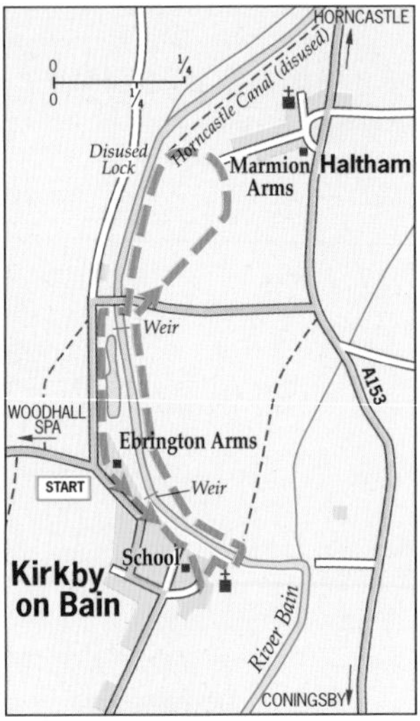

Kingfisher

## What to look out for

The River Bain attracts a good deal of wildlife, and it is fairly common to see grey herons in the vicinity. There is also a chance of seeing the sudden blue flash of the shy and elusive kingfisher as it flies low over the water.

Follow the path until it emerges at the end of a road joining from the right. Turn left then right here, down a path past the primary school, then left at the end to go through a churchyard. Do not cross the stile at the end of the path. Instead, cross the bridge over the river and turn left over a stile.

Follow the river bank, crossing another stile, and soon after the schoolyard on the opposite side of the river, branch right, away from the river, following the yellow arrow. Cross another stile and go along the edge of the field, with the mill on your left, and up onto the bank alongside the river. Climb the stile by the ridge at the end of the bank, and cross the road and the stile opposite.

Walk right-handed across the field towards the farm in the distance. Cross the dyke and follow the field round to the left, then proceed to cross a stile to the left of the red-brick house.

Walk up the road to the bend. Turn right here for the short distance to the village of Haltham.

Past the Marmion Arms, continue straight on at the bend in the road, following the footpath sign. The path swings round to the left and crosses a bridge and stile. Continue to the river. Do not cross the bridge, but turn left along the bank to proceed across a series of three stiles. Turn right at the road, over the bridge, left at the junction and so back to the start point.

### The Horncastle Canal

At the point where the walk returns to the river for the final time, the route turns left along the bank at a disused lock. The River Bain was canalised, opening in 1802 to provide a link from Horncastle to the River Witham, south of Tattershall, which in turn linked with the North Sea at the Humber Estuary to the north and the Wash to the south.

The canal owners fought a prolonged battle in the 1850s in an attempt to prevent the railway coming to Horncastle, but they lost and the canal's business began to decline. It carried its last cargo in 1878.

*The Marmion Arms in Haltham village*

# Evesham – River and Town

This is an easy walk in the Avon valley, linking Twyford Country Centre, with its many attractions, and Evesham, a lovely town with lots of historic buildings and attractive riverside parkland.

**WALK 51**
HEREFORD & WORCESTER
SP043465

**START**
Twyford Country Centre is nearly two miles north of Evesham and 200 yards beyond the bypass. Admittance and parking are free. At the car park, a map of the centre and surrounding country includes walks marked by the county council's Countryside Service.

**DIRECTIONS**
From the car park follow the track past the children's play area. Go through a gate and descend. Keep straight on past orchards on the right (Please do not pick fruit or collect windfalls) and down the steps to the river bank.
Turn right along the river. Downstream, The Bridge Inn stands on the far bank and a ferry sometimes crosses to it. Opposite the inn, climb a stile to a meadow and continue under the bypass, through or over 3 fences and a footbridge to the next field.
(Here you can shorten the walk by climbing a stile by the metal gate to the right at the far right corner and turning right along the track. Continue at * below.)
The main walk continues to reach Evesham by skirting around the marshy area to leave the field by a metal kissing-gate hidden in the hedgerow ahead, then follows the path under the Worcester-Oxford railway line to join an unmetalled track. Where the track swings right at the end of the chain-link fence, take a path into bushes and go through a metal gate.
Continue over a slipway and past moorings (with care – narrow unfenced path by the side of the river) to an old mill at the edge of the town.
At the road, turn left and proceed along it to a junction. Keep ahead to Bridge Street and turn right to the half-timbered Round House, or Booth Hall, at the top. Bear left into the Market Place and pass through the Norman Gate to the Abbey Precinct. To return to Twyford, go back to the mill by the river and follow the road to a junction. Keep ahead along Common Road and under a railway arch.
*Continue past the stile mentioned on the short-cut above and walk left of a hedge

*The banks of the Avon*

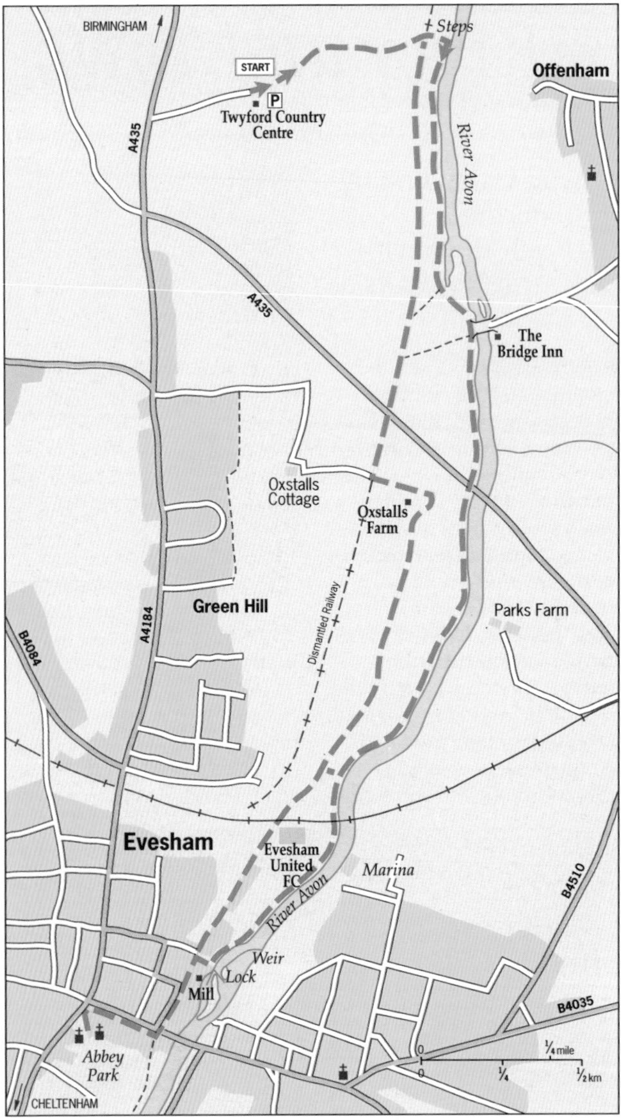

## Information

The walk is five miles long, with a shorter option of three and three quarter miles
Level, easy ground
No road walking, except in Evesham
Several stiles
Café and refreshment kiosk at Twyford Country Centre; pubs and cafés at Evesham
Grassy areas suitable for picnics at Twyford and Evesham, and along river bank

to Oxstalls Farm. Skirt the buildings to the right and, on the far side, turn right along a field margin beyond a hedge. At the field corner bear left to the farm gate. Carefully cross the bypass to the former railway, signed 'Footpath', and cross the stile. Continue until the track from Twyford is reached and return to the Centre.

**Twyford Country Centre**
The site includes a garden centre, farm shop, wildlife and falconry centre, crafts centre, cane centre, natural health and beauty shop, conservatory centre, country café and children's play area.

**Evesham**
In the Abbey precinct, occupying a beautiful site above the Avon, two parish churches stand almost side by side. Nearby is the 110ft-high Bell Tower, added to the Abbey only a few years before the Dissolution of the Monasteries.

## What to look out for

In summer the River Avon is lively and active, with fishermen lining the bank and holiday cruisers and narrowboats going to and fro. There are wildfowl on the water and thistles in the riverside meadows attract goldfinches in the autumn.

# A Walk on the Malvern Foothills

**WALK 52**
HEREFORD & WORCESTER
SO766471

This is a moderately strenuous walk offering dramatic views from the Malverns, and a brace of pretty villages.

### Information

The walk is about seven miles long
Undulating terrain, with a couple of steepish slopes
Lots of stiles and gates to negotiate
Can be muddy in winter
Dogs should be kept on leads
Pubs in Great Malvern and Mathon

**START**
The walk starts in North Malvern: park with care on the B4232, close to the Lamb Inn.

**DIRECTIONS**
Opposite The Lamb, a road descends to a junction. Cross over and follow the sign for the West Malvern Outdoor Education Centre. Continue on this road, which becomes a track, through the activity centre to Birches Farm. As you enter the farmyard turn left through the second gate, with fields on the right and trees on the left. Pass through two gates aross three fields, heading towards some houses. Leave the third field via a gate, and go between houses to a lane.
Turn right and continue to Croft Farm. Go straight through the farmyard, keeping left, to reach a stile. Go over, cross a short field to another stile, and enter a sloping field.
Continue down to reach a track. Turn right and

*Looking east at Croft Farm*

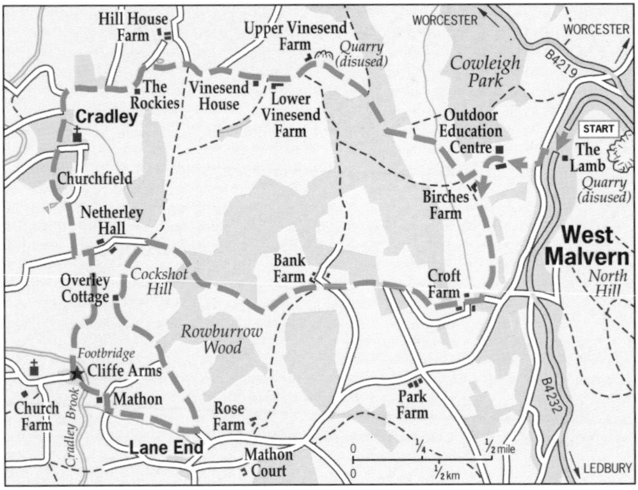


continue for a few yards before veering off left diagonally down towards woodland. Look for a path among the trees, follow it to a stile and turn right on to a lane. Continue, to pass Banks Farm. Footpath signs abound, but keep to the main track as it skirts left of a pond, leads through a gate, and rises gently.

Shortly, the track curves right towards woodland. Stay on the same track through the woods until, where it descends and drifts left, a sign directs you to turn right on to a narrow, rising path. Soon this plunges to a stile.

Descend Cockshot Hill. Where it flattens bear left across the grass. Turn left on a track going south-east: to keep this line head for a cottage, passing through a gate just before. Follow the track past the cottage and through a gate, and head straight on to pass through another gate into a field. Follow the left margin and pass through a small gate in the top left hand corner, turning immediately right onto an overgrown track. Eventually pass another cottage and after 400 yards, reach another. Immediately before it, turn right over a stile into a field, and cross several more fields to reach a road. Turn right and continue into Mathon. Turn right beyond the Cliffe Arms onto a path, and cross a footbridge to reach a field. Head straight across this to a stile, then continue across a field, a stile and more fields to reach a gate at a track. Go through, and bear left into Cradley.

Pass the church, right, and go straight through Cradley, continuing up a slight rise before the road bears sharp right. After Buryfields on the left, a narrow lane goes right. Take this, and at a T-junction turn right. Follow this lane to Upper Vinesend Farm. Just before the farm turn right onto a gated track, which rises and narrows steeply to woodland.

At the fork bear left, descending steeply. Cross fields going straight down, and turn left to cross over a stream. Turn right towards Birches Farm, but just before it turn left over the second stile, half-way up the field. Climb straight up, towards a permanent caravan, and cross two more stiles by trees to reach the lane by the OE Centre. Turn left to retrace your steps up to Malvern.

### What to look out for

The church in Cradley contains an unusual Saxon frieze, which is worth seeking out. The church is reached through an attractive lychgate.

**Malverns**

The Malvern Hills form a dramatic ridge, criss-crossed with paths, with marvellous views over the surrounding countryside. They are also famous for the purity of their water.

*Above Cockshot Hill*

# Llangattock Circuit

From the attractive village of Llangattock, this is an enjoyable walk along a section of the Monmouthshire and Brecon Canal, usually busy with pleasure boats in the summer. The return is through woodland and fields, with good views of the Black Mountains.

**WALK 53**
POWYS
SO212177

**Information**

The walk is two and a quarter miles long
Easy walking
Several stiles
Pubs at start end of walk
Toilets in recreation area near start

**START**
From Crickhowell cross the old bridge spanning the Usk, turn left and then immediately right along a minor road leading into Llangattock village. Cars may be left in Park Drive opposite the Horse Shoe Inn adjoining a recreation area.

**DIRECTIONS**
Facing the Horse Shoe Inn, turn left and then shortly go right over a bridge and past old stone cottages to reach Llangattock church. After visiting the church continue along the road and bear left at the next junction.
Go through a metal kissing-gate on the right and walk up through the field, making for the top right hand corner. Cross a stile and turn immediately left under a canal bridge, along the towpath of the Monmouthshire and Brecon Canal.
On the other bank you will

*Moorings at Llangattock Wharf*

pass Llangattock Wharf, which now provides moorings for the Llangattock Boat Club, and a block of old lime kilns.

Walk on, passing beneath stone bridges and overhanging trees. When you pass beneath bridge 112 (you will need to pass the bridges then look back to see their numbers) go over a stile on the left and continue down a broad track.

On reaching a bend cross a stile on the right and follow the path through a larch wood. Cross a stile at the end of the wood and keep straight on following a line of telegraph poles in the middle of a field. Look out for a footpath sign on the left beside a metal kissing-gate. Go through it and follow a lane back to the start.

Primrose

**Llangattock Church**
Dedicated to St Cattwg, this church was founded in the 6th century but rebuilt in the 12th. Inside are a set of stocks and a whipping post.

**Monmouthshire and Brecon Canal**
Constructed between 1794 and 1800 this canal was used for transporting coal, lime and agricultural produce between Newport and Brecon. It was also connected by various tram roads to local ironworks and carried iron ore and finished products. Commercial use of the canal came to a close with the building of railways, but today it is a very popular leisure amenity, navigable for 32 miles through the Brecon Beacons National Park.

**Llangattock Wharf**
This wharf was at the end of a tram road which descended from the limestone escarpment on Mynydd Llangattock. Limestone was brought here to be burnt in the lime kilns, then the extracted lime was taken by barge to Brecon and sold for agricultural purposes.

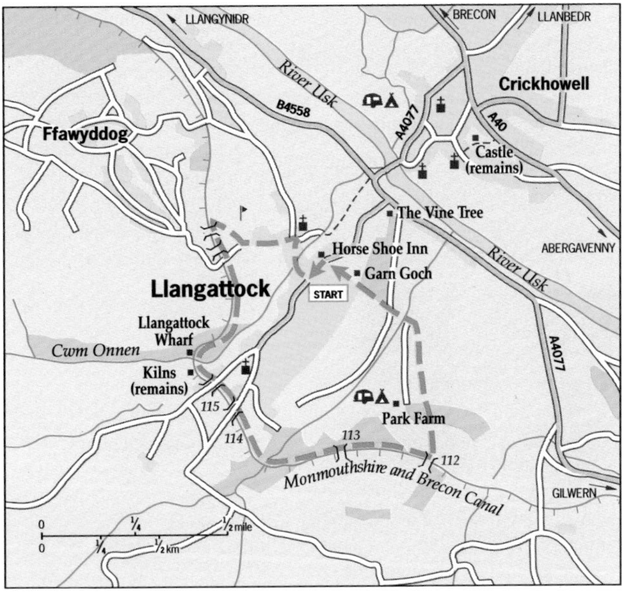


**What to look out for**

Grey herons and kingfishers are often seen along the canal, and mallards with their accompanying brood are also an essential part of the canal scene. Primroses and lesser celandines grow along the canal bank in spring.

**Garn Goch**
A low mound in the recreation field at Llangattock carries a plaque which identifies it as a burial mound, most probably of Neolithic date (4000-2500BC).

The stone chamber with its capstone is an Ancient Monument site.

# *Cefn On Park and Ridgeway Walk*

From an enclosed woodland garden with rhododendrons and azaleas, the route climbs up to a ridgeway walk, with spectacular views south over Cardiff and the Severn, and northwards to the Valleys and the Brecon Beacons.

**WALK 54**
SOUTH GLAMORGAN
ST179837

**Information**

The walk is six miles long
Several stiles and gates
One fairly steep section – stout shoes are advisable in wet weather
Cefn On Park is open daily from 7.30am to sunset – times are posted in the car park
Toilets near the park entrance
Picnic area near the pond

*Cefn On Park seen from Craig Llysfaen*

**START**
From Cardiff, take the A469 towards Caerphilly, and turn right, signposted 'Cefn Onn 1 Mile', along Capelgwilym Road. Turn left to the car park, just before the underpass.

**DIRECTIONS**
From the car park head straight for the pond (to the left, uphill, is an open field and picnic area). Retrace your steps, and half-way down the main path between the railings and double gates, turn sharp left through a black iron wicket gate.

Turn left onto the scenic path above the railway cutting. Continue past the entrance to the mile-long Caerphilly railway tunnel, which was opened in 1871. At the next black wicket gate turn sharp left; cross the stream and sweep uphill to the right – an interesting Victorian brick ventilation shaft appears above the tunnel. At the next style, turn left (noting the spring on the right), and walk uphill. Before the field at the top take the steep, narrow limestone-chip path to the right, zig-zagging up the Carboniferous limestone ridge to the waypost, marked 'Rhymney Valley Ridgeway Walk' (blue waymarker). Turn right and continue to Cefn Onn Farm. Cross a stile, a metalled road and another stile, and continue along the fence to a third stile. Continue along the fence and emerge into woodland, eventually descending to an open field on the left. Cross a stile and turn sharp right, down into the valley to a river, crossing a stile and a wooden bridge. Walk up a gully through the forest. Do not cross the next bridge on your right, but instead turn sharp left uphill, and after a few yards take a

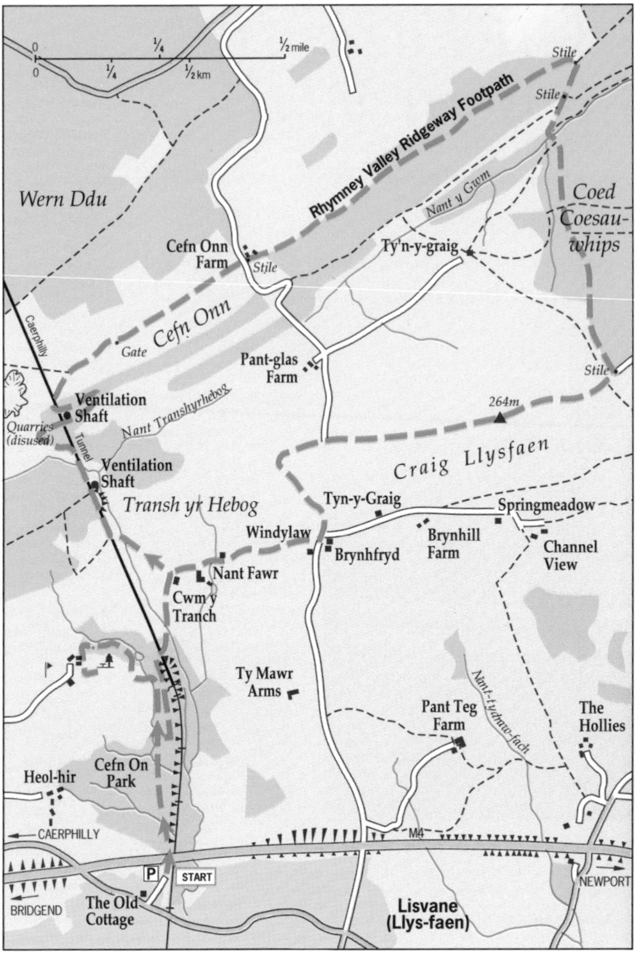


right-hand fork. Continue on and over a stile at the end of the path, turning right onto the bridleway which runs along Craig Llysfaen ridge, with exceptional views of the Gwent Wentlooge Levels, Cardiff, the Severn, and south-west England.
Keep on this track past a weather station, to the box gate at the end. Turn left down a steep narrow lane. Just after a road comes in from the left, turn right through a recessed gate, marked 'Cwm y Tranch' (yellow waymarker). At the end of the brick wall, go back through the black metal wicket gate and retrace your steps to the car park.

**Cefn Onn Park**
The park is particularly spectacular in April and May, when the azaleas and rhododendrons are in full bloom.

**Rhymney Valley Ridgeway Walk**
This waymarked walk encircling the Rhymney Valley offers spectacular panoramas from Somerset to the Brecon Beacons. Look out for the 13th-century Caerphilly Castle, and Pen y Fan, the highest mountain in south Wales. Many of these ridge paths are ancient; some were used by the Romans to avoid the densely forested valleys, while others are old pilgrim routes.

*Cefn On Park*

## What to look out for

Cefn Onn blossoms with spring flowers, and rhododendrons and azaleas flower in profusion here from April to May. Look out for grey squirrels, jays, robins and tree creepers foraging for insects. On the hillside, look out for wild garlic, bluebells and primroses.

**WALK 55**
DYFED
SN667193

# Carreg Cennen Castle

The main object of this pleasant, easy walk is to visit the ruins of Carreg Cennen Castle which is situated in this wild and remote corner of the Brecon Beacons National Park.

### What to look out for

Kestrels and ravens nest in the cliffs below the castle. The kestrel is a fascinating bird to watch for it can hover motionless, with just the tips of its wings moving to keep it still while it searches for prey. Buzzards may also be seen circling overhead: listen for their mewing call.

**START**
Leave the A483 at Ffairfach, just before Llandeilo and follow the road for two and a half miles to the village of Trap. From here a lane leads up to a car park just below the castle.

**DIRECTIONS**
From the car park follow the lane towards the castle, stopping at the farm to pay your admission fee. After exploring this romantic fortress, go back down to access path and follow a broad track leading down into the Cennen Valley, crossing a wooded slope and descending gently to the valley bottom. Turn right here and follow a path beside the River Cennen. Soon the ruined castle will come into view, dramatically silhouetted against the sky on its limestone crag.
Go over a stile on the left, descend some steps and continue beside the river passing below the castle crag. The track in due coursejoins a lane which is followed past Pantyffynnont farm and uphill to a T-junction. Here turn right and walk back along the road for a short distance to return to the car park.

**Carreg Cennen Castle**
Perched on the top of a 130ft limestone crag, Carreg Cennen is said to be one of the most romantic castles in Wales.
According to tradition it was originally built for Urien – one of King Arthur's knights – but the present building dates from the time of Richard II.
It is a fascinating place to explore, particularly the vaulted passage cut through solid rock that leads for about 150ft inside the cliff to a well. The steps leading to the vault can be found in the left-hand corner of the inner ward – it is a good idea to take a torch along with you, for exploring.

During the Wars of the Roses, the castle was captured by Lancastrian supporters who later had to surrender to the command of Edward IV. In 1462 five hundred men

*Carreg Cennen overlooks the village of Trapp*

## Information

The walk is two miles long
Very easy, with a short climb up to the castle and one other ascent
Little road walking at beginning and end on quiet lanes
Picnic site at car park
Pub in the village of Trap
Toilets at car park

equipped with picks and crowbars were employed to make the castle uninhabitable and were paid the grand sum of £28 for their work.

**Owain of the Red Hand**
It is said that in a cavern below the castle Sir John Goch, also known as Owain of the Red Hand, is doomed to sleep for a thousand years, and that when this 14th-century Welsh hero and his fifty-one companions awake there will be peace all over the world.

*Carreg Cennen, perched high on its lofty crag*

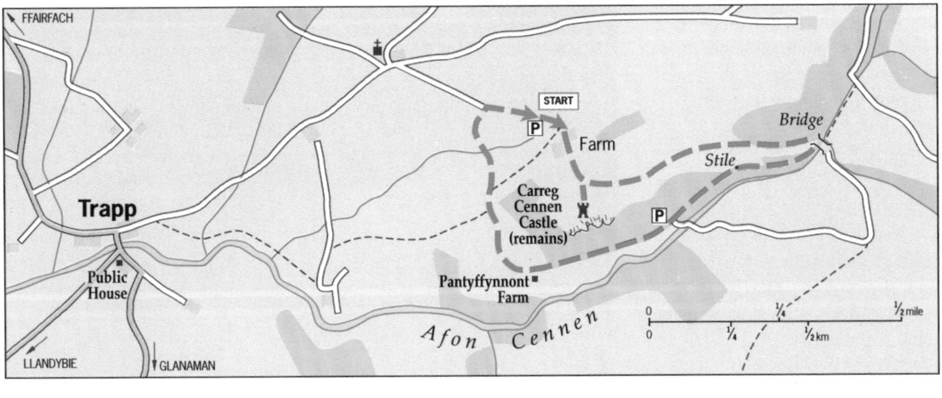

# *A Ramble Around Nevern*

**WALK 56**
DYFED
SN084400

This pleasant walk takes in the historic church of St Brynach and its curiosities, and passes through a beautiful, peaceful countryside following riverside and woodland paths.

**Information**

The walk is three miles long
A gentle walk along well defined paths and tracks
A few stiles to cross
Pub in village is called the Trewern Arms
Toilets by village school

**START**

Leave the A487 at Velindre to follow the B4582 down to the pretty riverside hamlet of Nevern. Park carefully on the roadside by Nevern Church.

**DIRECTIONS**

From the main gate of Nevern Church turn right to follow a footpath between a stream and the churchyard wall. Turn left by a cottage to cross a small footbridge over the stream and then continue along a stony track. On meeting a road turn right. Go uphill for about 100yds and at a bend keep straight on to follow a path signposted 'The Pilgrim's Cross'. After about 50yds reach the cross, carved on the rock face to your right. The path continues, soon levelling out, and is well shaded by overhanging trees. Go over a stile and proceed through a pleasant wooded valley. Keeping the fence on your left, cross a stile and walk on through the trees. Now following a ledge cut into the hillside, ascend some natural rock steps to reach a stile. Cross a field and then go left through a metal gate. Continue down a stony track for a few yards towards a building and look out for a path descending on the right. This goes down to a little footbridge spanning a stream. Keep straight on across a concrete drive, passing to the left of a garage and then to the right of a cottage. Continue through the trees just above the river. After passing a derelict cottage the path rises gently. On reaching Pont Newydd farmhouse, turn left to follow a rutted track. Shortly you will cross a stone bridge (Pont Newydd), after which the track ascends slightly. On joining a surfaced lane keep straight on to pass Llangwynmair Manor hotel. Just past the derelict farm buildings turn left up a footpath and go through a

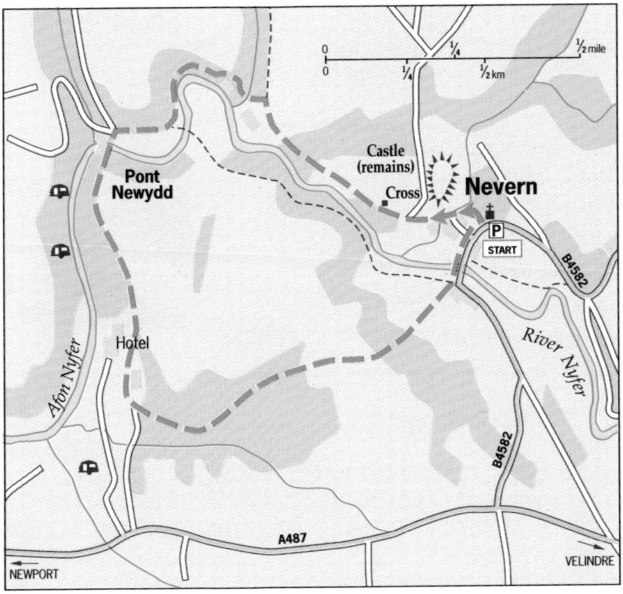

*The attractive old bridge leading into Nevern village*

gate, beneath a tunnel of trees and through woods alive with birdsong. On reaching three gateways take the middle path, soon walking between high banks with wild flowers. Go over a stile and through a field, cross another stile and turn left along a road to go over a stone bridge and return to the church.

**Nevern Church**

Founded in the 6th century by St Brynach, Nevern church has a squat battlemented tower which once provided the community with a refuge from marauding sea rovers. It is approached through an avenue of ancient yew trees. One is known as 'the bleeding yew' because blood-red sap oozes out of a broken branch – and, it is said, will do so until a Welshman re-occupies the castle on the hill above. In the churchyard stands a beautiful 10th-century Celtic cross. According to legend, the first cuckoo of spring is supposed to arrive in Nevern on St Brynach's day (7 April) and perch on the stone.

*Ramsons*

**What to look out for**

It is a good walk for observing wild flowers – and for picking blackberries in late summer. Bluebells and ramsons grow in the woods, and rabbits and squirrels are much in evidence. You can look out for trout and salmon in the River Nyfer, but the fishing is private.

# Twm Sion Catti's Cave

Well shaded for a hot day, this walk is set in wild and dramatic scenery, making a complete circuit of a wooded hill above the confluence of the Tywi and the Doethie.

**WALK 57**
POWYS
SN788471

**START**
The walk starts at the RSPB car park at Ystradffyn, just past the church. From Llandovery take the minor road north to Rhandirmwyn and head towards the Llyn Brianne Reservoir.

**DIRECTIONS**
Go through a little gate at the end of the car park and follow a board walk across a marshy area. At the end of the board walk follow the path to the right down through the trees towards the river, soon reaching a pleasant riverside glade with seats.
Follow the path up and down steps around the hillside above the river, which now flows noisily through a rocky gorge. The path leads up to a junction where a flat boulder makes a convenient seat.
(It is possible to avoid the steep climb to the cave by continuing directions at * below.)
The path leads directly upwards to Twm Sion Catti's Cave, climbing steeply and threading its way between and over moss-covered boulders. Look out for an arrow scratched into the rock ahead of you – pointing left at a spot where you could easily follow a false trail. The cave is now directly above and a slippery squeeze – on all fours – will get you inside. Return then to the main track.
*Continue around the hillside – down steps and around rocky corners to pass through the final section of the rocky gorge. The sound of the river fades as you round the hill and the track surface becomes less rocky and more grassy, leading through the ferns and trees. Eventually return to the board walk and retrace your steps to the car park.

*Garden warbler*

**What to look out for**

Over 40 species of birds breed in these woods, and between April and July look out for pied flycatchers, redstarts and wood warblers. A wealth of non-flowering plants include mosses and lichens on tree trunks, and ferns such as lady fern and polypody on the ground.

**Ystradffyn**
This chapel, dedicated to St Paulinus, stands beside the ancient road to Strata Florida Abbey, to which it once belonged. It stands on the three-way boundary of the

## Information

The walk is two miles long
Well-maintained track with some ascent, particularly up to the cave; take care when the rocks are wet and slippery; the remainder follows an easy gradient
No stiles
Dogs should be kept on leads
Pub in Rhandirmwyn serves bar snacks
Picnic place beside river near beginning of walk

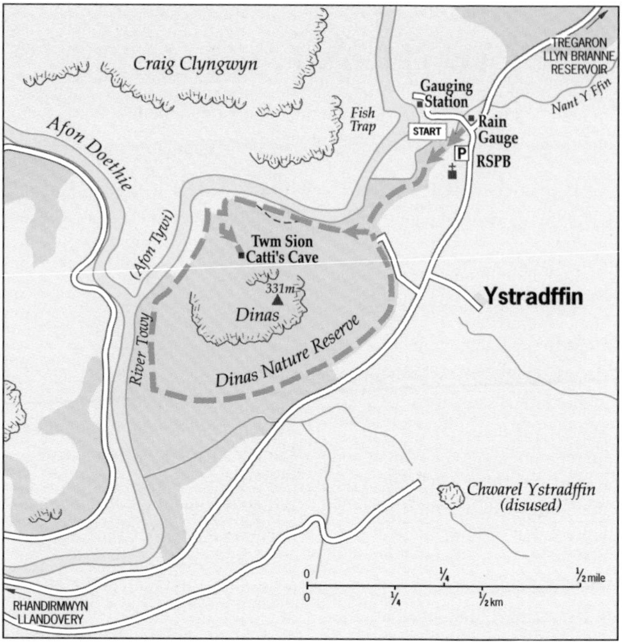


old counties of Cardiganshire, Carmarthenshire and Breconshire.

**Dinas Nature Reserve**
This reserve, acquired by the RSPB in 1968, is a good example of a Welsh sessile oak wood and is home to the red kite. Some 90 species of bird are recorded in the reserve each year, and over 40 species regularly breed here during spring and early summer; these include pied flycatchers, redstarts and wood warblers, all migrant visitors to Britain.
The centrepiece of the Nature Reserve is the conical hill of Dinas, but though its name suggests the existence of a fortress on the summit, there is no real evidence of one.

**Twm Sion Catti's Cave**
Born at Tregaron in 1530, Twm Sion Catti (real name Thomas Jones), lives on in legend as a highwayman and a practical joker – often referred to as the Welsh Robin Hood.
Popularly believed to be one of his hiding places, the cave is really just a hollow formed by a large rock leaning against the face of another one. Inside, hundreds of names have been scratched and carved with varying skill on every available rock surface. This defacing has been going on for centuries – some dates back to 1839.

*Historic graffiti in the cave*

# A Walk Around Hay-on-Wye

## WALK 58
POWYS
SO230422

This walk is a mixture of town and countryside around the fascinating old market town of Hay-on-Wye. The town has an interesting history and is famous for its numerous book shops which attract visitors from all over the world.

### Information

The walk is one and a quarter miles long
No stiles
Easy, level walking all the way
Plenty of pubs and cafés in the town
Picnic tables and riverside seats on the route
Toilets in the town

**START**
The starting point for the walk is a large car park near Hay-on-Wye Craft Centre and Information Centre on the south side of town.

**DIRECTIONS**
Leave the car park, cross the road and turn left along the pavement. Shortly, turn right down Back Fold Lane to pass below part of the Tudor mansion adjoining Hay Castle. The lane snakes around old buildings and meets Castle Street. Turn right and shortly stop to look up at the front of Hay Castle. Now bear left and then left again and go down to the Clock Tower. Cross the road and turn right along the pavement, then left by the Three Tuns – 'the Last Free House in Wales'. Follow the pavement down Bridge Street and just before the bridge go right by a footpath signed 'Bailey Footpath and Picnic Area'. Pass a couple of picnic tables on the right and follow the path around to the left, passing under the road bridge before turning left along a path running parallel with the River Wye.
Look out for a path on the left which goes under an old railway bridge and continue beside a stone wall. Go through a gate and then another gate on the left to enter the churchyard of St Mary's parish church. Turn left along the pavement, cross the road and go through a metal kissing-gate to follow a path beside a dingle. Cross a little bridge and continue along the path, over another footbridge and meet a road. Turn left along a pavement and pass the Swan Hotel and Hay Cinema Book Shop. Cross the road and follow the pavement down Peterchurch Road (signposted) and return to the car park at the start.

**Hay Castle**
The remnants of Hay Castle, consisting of a gateway and a

*Robin*

### What to look out for

Overlooking Hay-on-Wye are some superb hanging woodlands, comprising mainly sessile oaks. Redstarts and pied flycatchers are sometimes seen in spring and summer. Woodland flowers to look out for include wood sorrel and wood spurge.

tower, are linked to a handsome Jacobean mansion with tall chimney stacks and gables. The house was badly damaged in a fire some years ago and is gradually being rebuilt. It is not open to the public.

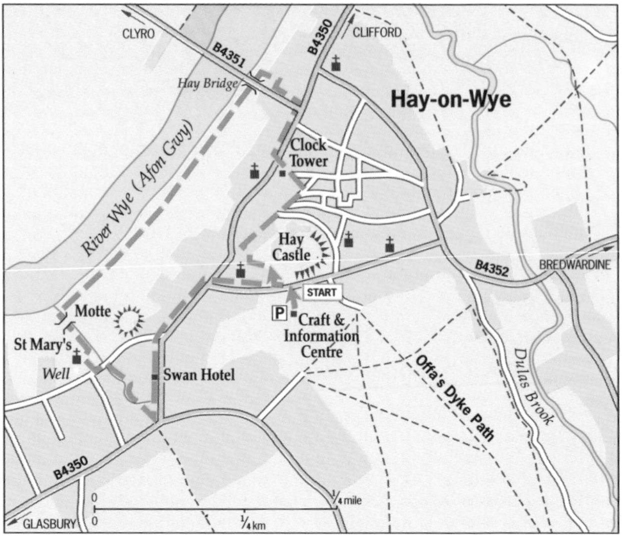


**Old Railway**

The old railway was originally a tram road, built in 1818 to link the canal at Brecon to Talgarth, Hay and Eardisley in Herefordshire. It was later developed into a railway.

**Effigy of Mol Walbee**

Inside the church is a mutilated effigy which is reputed to be that of Maude de Valerie otherwise known as Mol Walbee. She was the wife of the wicked Norman Lord William de Braose and came to a sad end, being starved to death by King John in Windsor Castle.

**The King Of Hay**

Richard Booth's first empire was as the owner of the world's largest second-hand book shop. He then decided that, as Hay was in neither England nor Wales, it must be a kingdom of its own and he is now well established as the self-styled 'King of Hay'.

*The Cinema Book Shop, one of many*

# *Upper Arley - River, Woods and Reservoirs*

From the delightful little Severnside village of Upper Arley, the walk follows a lovely path downstream, before climbing to circle Trimpley Reservoir and lagoon, high above the river, and returning through woods and farmland.

**WALK 59**
HEREFORD & WORCESTER
SO766802

**Information**

The walk is three and a half miles long
Clear paths and bridleways; some hills
Virtually no road walking
Dogs should be kept on leads in the sheep pasture beside Trimpley Reservoir
A few stiles
Pub on each side of the river at Upper Arley, with gardens but no children's rooms; bar meals served; tearoom in village
Plenty of open grassland at Trimpley Reservoir, suitable for picnic

### START

Upper Arley lies beside the River Severn, three and a half miles north of Bewdley. It is accessible via a lane from Shatterford on the A442 Kidderminster-Bridgnorth road.

Alternatively, cars can be parked free at Kidderminster, Bewdley or Bridgnorth stations and the village reached by steam train on the Severn Valley Railway. At Upper Arley there are public pay car parks on each side of the river. Start from the pedestrian-only river bridge across the Severn.

### DIRECTIONS

From the eastern end of the long metal footbridge head south (downstream). At a large house ('Worrall's Grove'), leave the waymarked Worcestershire Way, keeping to the riverside path. Pass under Victoria Bridge, beneath which there is a stile to cross. After about 200yds, another stile leads into a sheep pasture. A notice board gives information about Trimpley Reservoir.

Skirt the trees bordering the river, cross a railed footbridge and climb to the left to reach the reservoir. Bear right along its bank and left at the end, before dropping down to the smaller lagoon and walking anti-clockwise round it to the stile and gate leading into woodland on the far side.

Cross the Severn Valley Railway (with care!) and ignore a left-turn, but higher up fork left, and soon bear left along a broader track to the end of a surfaced lane by the waterworks' entrance. Enter the Arley Estate opposite and follow the bridleway through

**What to look out for**

At Upper Arley note the jetties used by the former chain ferry. Early in the walk there are signs indicating the Worcestershire Way, an official 36-mile walking route from Kinver to the Malvern Hills. The riverside path goes under the splendid Victoria Bridge of 1861. The Trimpley Reservoir, built in the 1960s to supplement Birmingham's Elan Valley water supply, gives fine views west across the vast Wyre Forest. From the farmland towards the end of the walk look left for the Shropshire Giants, Titterstone Clee Hill and Brown Clee Hill. Much of the walk is within sight – and sound – of the steam trains on the Severn Valley Railway.

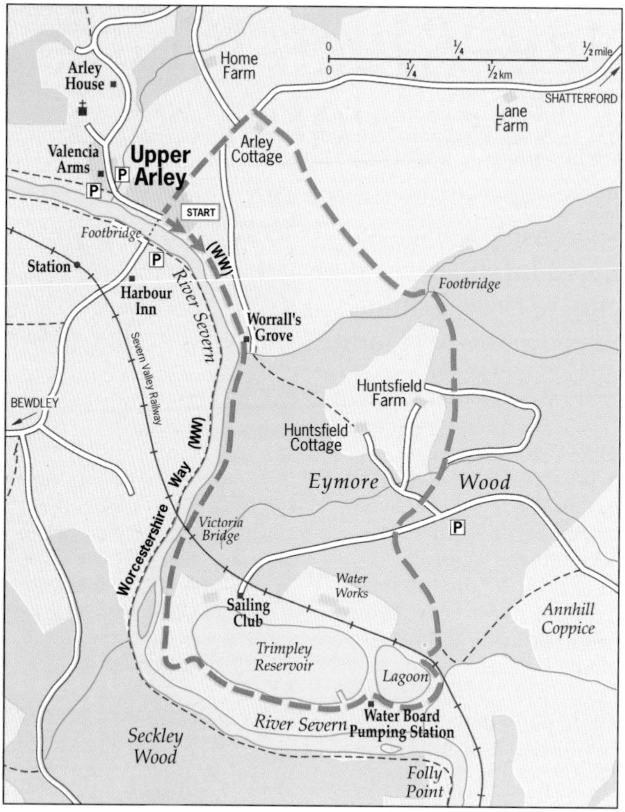


Wild Thyme

Eymore Wood. It descends, crosses the Worcestershire Way, and climbs steadily through mature forest to a hilltop crossways. Take the track ahead, descending through tall, straight pines to a bridge over a stream. The way soon rises out of the woods and crosses high farmland to a lane. Turn left and descend to Upper Arley.

**Upper Arley**

The little village is beautifully set beside the broad River Severn. The Valencia Arms, in Frenchman's Street, took its name from the courtesy title of the eldest son of Lord Mountnorris, Lord of the Manor. Next door, protruding into the road, stands the battlemented Arley Tower, built in 1842 by the then Lord Mountnorris. Its purpose was to block the view from the house of Mr Sam Willcox, who had refused to sell his home to his lordship. No planning permission was required in those days!
The street climbs to St Peter's Church, which houses the tomb of a crusader, believed to be the unfortunate Sir Walter de Balun. He joined the Eighth Crusade in 1270, but never reached the Holy Land, dying of injuries received in a tournament on his wedding day.

*The River Severn at Upper Arley*

**WALK 60**
SHROPSHIRE
SO457899

# A Traditional Working Farm

**Information**

The walk is just under three miles long
Mostly waymarked; gentle hills
Some quiet lane walking
Dogs should be kept on leads in pastures
A lot of stiles to cross
Refreshments, including meals, at Acton Scott Working Farm Museum café
Picnic areas at museum

This walk begins at the Acton Scott Working Farm Museum and passes through the gentle hills and pastures of Ape Dale, in the Shropshire Hills Area of Outstanding Natural Beauty.

## START

Acton Scott Working Farm Museum is two and a half miles south of Church Stretton and three quarters of a mile east of the A49(T) Shrewsbury-Hereford road at Marshbrook. Parking is free for farm visitors, who are welcome to leave their cars while walking local footpaths.

## DIRECTIONS

From the waymarked stile in the corner of the car park cross to a stile at the far corner of the field. Enter woodland and descend along its edge to a stile on the left. Turn right through a field to a corner stile with two waymarks.

*Horse-power at Acton Scott Farm*

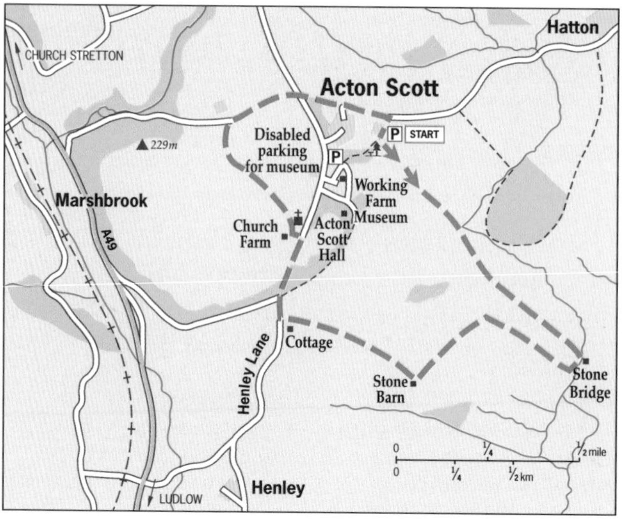


Follow the right-hand arrow over a large field and continue for about ½ mile to a stile at the bottom right, with a fine view ahead to Wenlock Edge.

Descend the next field, cross a double stile and continue to the bottom left corner. Turn right for a few yards, then left on to a track. The way swings right along a dismantled railway for about 75yds to a right-hand gate. Bear right here and join an old bridleway bordered by trees. Swing left at the top of the field and continue along the upper field-edge and through a gateway, heading towards a stone barn.

Just before the barn turn right through a gate and follow a hedge over a rise and down the other side, to where a track continues to a cottage on Henley Lane. Turn right and climb to the church.

From a gate at the far right corner of the churchyard follow the right-hand hedge, then veer down to a waymark post under an oak. Descend to a stile by a gate, climb the field beyond to a solitary oak and bear right to a gate on a lane. The museum is to the right, beyond crossroads.

**Acton Scott Working Farm Museum**

The museum is managed by Shropshire County Council on 23 acres of land belonging to the neighbouring Hall. Work as it would have been done in the pre-tractor age goes on daily in the fields and outbuildings. Various crafts are demonstrated, including those of dairymaid, wheelwright, blacksmith and farrier. The farm is open from April to November; closed Mondays except Bank Holidays.

**Parish Church of St Margaret**

Though the date 1722 can just be made out over the south porch, there has been a church here since 1291 and the building was restored in the early 19th century. A brass plate to Elizabeth Mytton (died 1571) shows her with her husband and eleven children. From the footpath leaving the north-west corner of the churchyard there is a magnificent panorama of the Long Mynd and Ragleth Hill.

*The wheelwright's workshop*

**What to look out for**

Many wild flowers can be found in the meadows, where the occasional hare may be seen. In summer there are crops, such as wheat, barley and oilseed rape in some of the fields – lively young cattle in some of the others, perhaps.

# Parson's Bridge

**WALK 61**
DYFED
SN753791

This is a varied route providing several points of interest in a wild and spectacular part of Wales.

**Information**

The walk is four miles long
A strenuous walk,
with several ascents and
a taxing descent to
Parson's Bridge
A lot of stiles
Pub in Ponterwyd
Good picnic spot by a pool
towards end of walk

START
Ysbyty Cynfyn is on the A4120 about midway between Devil's Bridge and Ponterwyd. Parking is available just in front of the church.

DIRECTIONS
Walk beside the church wall to go through a small metal gate, then continue along a wide track. Soon you will be looking down into a valley and the track in due course descends a wooded slope in a series of zig-zags to reach the metal Parson's Bridge, spanning a deep gorge.
On the far side, turn left to follow a track beside a fence leading up to a wooded slope. Two stiles are crossed and you then follow the edge of a field, keeping a fence on your left. Go over another stile and then continue along the top side of the field along a

*The view from the stone circle near Yspytty Cynyfan*

## What to look out for

The red kite has its last British stronghold in this part of Wales. Watch the skies for this graceful bird which has long wings and a deeply forked tail. It sometimes shares the skies with buzzards, which are much more commonly seen.

broad track. After crossing another stile, head diagonally up to the right to a ruined building, and then continue to join a gravel track. Bear left along the track, which joins a tarmac road beyond Llwyn Teifi Farm.

Continue for some distance, ignoring track on left, then go over a stile on the left and down to a little footbridge spanning a stream. Head up through a field to a farm. Bear right and follow the road into the hamlet of Ystumtuen. Follow the road to the right, cross a bridge and on reaching a stone bungalow go through a gate on the right and walk past an old mine to follow a track up the right-hand side of a little valley.

A pool comes into view ahead of you (a good spot for a picnic), beyond which go over a stile in a fence and continue up to the top of the pass. Cross another stile and continue, with the fence on your right, to subsequently re-cross the fence via another stile.

On joining a track keep straight on (a detour to the left leads to a small stone circle). Follow a signposted path down a slope to a stile and then go straight across a field to another stile. From here the path leads steeply down a wooded slope to Parson's Bridge. Retrace your steps back to the start.

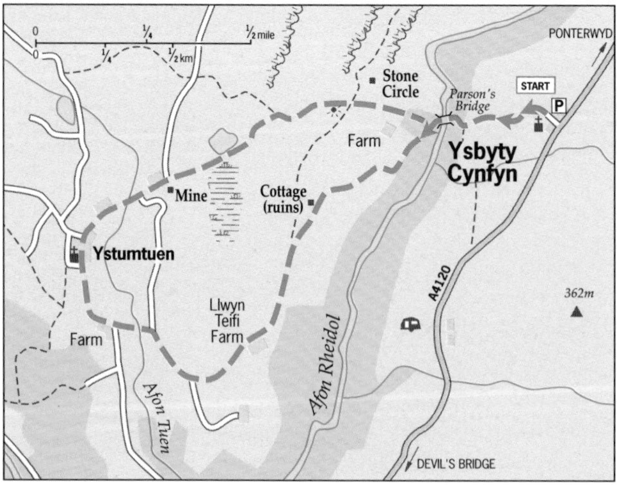


### Ysbyty Cynfyn Church

Four large prehistoric standing stones in the churchyard wall provide evidence that this was once a pagan site, Christianised by the establishment of a church, probably in the 6th century. The churchyard contains a sad inscription on a stone opposite the church porch, recording the death of quadruplets, all within six days of their birth. Their father died of typhus a month later.

*Ox-eye daisy*

### Parson's Bridge

The first bridge here was built for the benefit of a parson who came from Llanbadarn Fawr, near Aberystwyth, to conduct the services at Ysbyty Cynfyn. One day the rickety old bridge collapsed and he fell to his death. Today's bridge is a metal structure and quite sound.

# *The Spectacular Waterfall of Pistyll Rhaeadr*

Though short this walk encompasses both the tranquil and powerful aspects of nature, passing through quiet sheep pastures to reach an awe-inspiring waterfall.

**WALK 62**
CLWYD
SJ075295

**START**
Llanrhaeadr-ym-Mochnant lies on the B4580 between Oswestry and Llanfyllin; from the village follow a four-mile cul-de-sac signposted 'Waterfall'. Either park in rough lay-bys 200yds or so before reaching the road end, or in Tan-y-pistyll farmyard (small charge).

**DIRECTIONS**
From just outside the gated entrance to Tan-y-pistyll, take a narrow path uphill to pass through the left-hand of two small gates. Continue to the edge of the wood then turn right on to a broader path. Go through a narrow gate and continue past weirdly exposed tree roots to open country, crossing a ladder stile by a wide gate. Continue up the valley, ignoring a public footpath which ascends steeply left, to where a track slants down from high on the left. Veer right to follow this track down to the stream. Cross the narrow stream on stepping stones and then, beyond a gate, slant rightwards up a green track, soon merging with a broad track which joins from the left. Follow the broad track around the hillside, descending gently (magnificent views of the distant waterfall) to its gated junction with the surfaced approach lane. Here the two routes diverge.
For the shorter walk, turn right and follow the lane back to the start point in under ½ mile.
For the extended route, turn

*The highest waterfall in Wales*

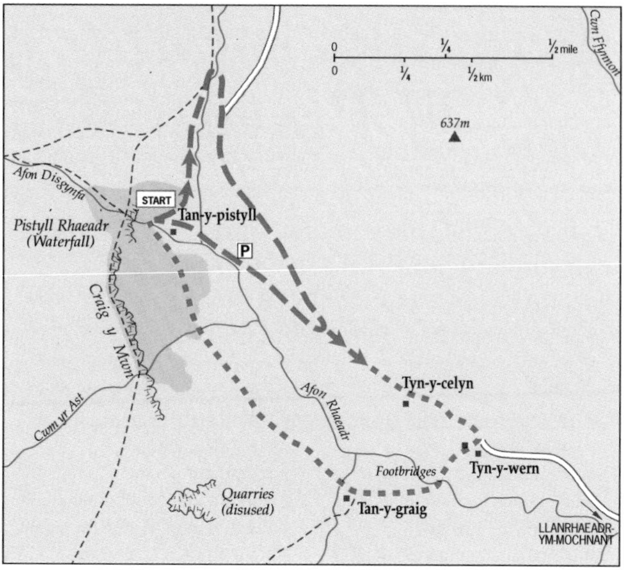


left and follow the lane for a little under ½ mile. Take an initially surfaced track leading down to the right. Go past Tyn-y-wern farmyard and through a gate. Continue along the track over two footbridges to Tan-y-graig (home to inquisitive sheep dogs). Avoid the farmyard itself by veering slightly right on a track leading to a gate in 100yds.

Beyond the gate the track forks into three. Take the left-hand, uphill fork for 100yds then bear right across the hillside along an obvious slatey path. Beyond mine ruins the path runs alongside a fence with fine views into the valley.

Ignore a stile and yellow arrow on the right and continue straight on, entering woodland at a stile. Within an area of mature trees, the path bends right to the stream and crosses it below the spectacular waterfall by an iron footbridge. The car park is reached soon after.

### Information

The walk is one and a half miles long, with an optional extension of another mile
Mostly good tracks but with a short section of uneven ground
Less than half a mile of road walking on a dead-end lane
Dogs must be kept on leads
A few stiles; stepping stones across stream
Picnic sites by rocky streams near the start and finish
Café with outside seating and view of waterfalls at the car park
Toilets at the start point

**Pistyll Rhaeadr**
The Afon Disgynfa drops almost vertically down a cliff barrier into a pool then spouts beneath a natural rock arch into the lower fall. At 245ft high, the 'Spouting Waterfall' is the highest in Wales. The cliff barrier is a geological feature of the last ice age, having been formed about 10,000 years ago by glacial action.

*Dandelion*

**Bishop William Morgan**
Bishop Morgan began translating the Bible into Welsh in 1578 while living at Llanrhaeadr-ym-Mochnant, the village in the valley below the waterfall. His bible played a central role in the survival of the Welsh language.

### What to look out for

This is sheep-farming country so, depending on the season, you will see lambs with their mothers, or sheep dogs at work gathering sheep for dipping or shearing. Among the woodland in the river valley below the waterfall you might see a dipper or hear a great spotted woodpecker. More common bird species include coal and marsh tits.

# Clocaenog Forest at Bod Petrual

**WALK 63**
CLWYD
SJ036511

This is a gentle pine forest walk with a delightful prelude and finale through mixed woodland and around a lake inhabited by ducks. Information boards and displays set out in a restored gamekeeper's cottage add to the interest.

### Information

The short walk is less than a mile long, the full walk about three miles
Good paths or tracks throughout
Almost no road walking
No stiles
No pub or refreshments
Picnic tables near the start point and by the lakeside
Toilets near parking area

### START

Bod Petrual (or Petryal) lies about 400 yards off the B5105, about seven miles south-west of Ruthin, on a narrow lane signposted to Melin-y-wîg. There is a large parking area.

### DIRECTIONS

From the parking area, go past the Forestry Commission information board (leaflets available here from the honesty box) on a path soon merging with a good track. Follow the track to a white cottage, the ground floor of which is now a visitor centre. From the back door of the cottage (that is, the entry not the exit door), veer left across the clearing to enter the dark forest on a good path. After passing between stone gateposts, follow the path to the left, then 20yds later swing right on to a broad path bedded with pine needles. The path soon narrows and becomes stony as it descends gradually into the little valley of the River Clwyd, and curves to the right. The river, here merely a trickling stream, can be glimpsed through trees or reached from several points by a short detour.

The path soon merges into a broad, slatey track which leads in 50yds to the surfaced approach lane. Here the two routes diverge:

(a) for the short route turn right and walk along the lane for 100yds to the lake. Turn right and follow the lakeside path back to the picnic and parking area.

(b) For the longer walk, go 50yds left along the lane then turn right onto a broad forestry track. After about a mile the track reaches the forest edge then curves right back into the depths. Ignore the track which veers left and continue straight on, along

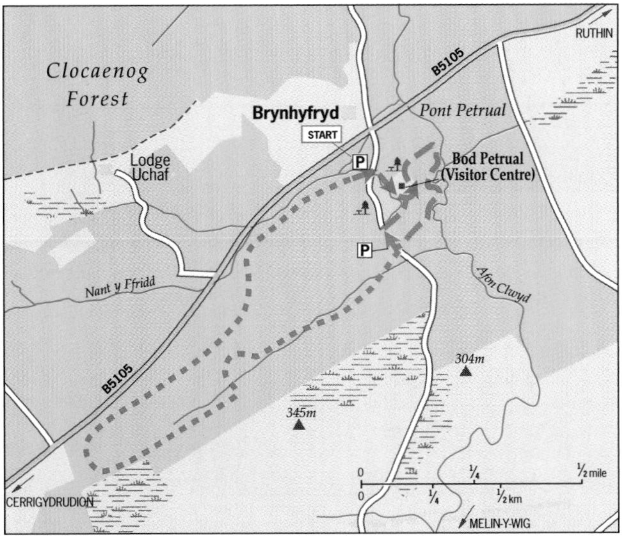

*The lake and Cocaenog Forest*

the obvious track which leads back to the approach lane. Turn right to explore the roadside lake before returning to the parking and picnic area.

**Clocaenog Forest**

Clocaenog Forest was established in the 1930s, at a time when the need to produce timber as cheaply and quickly as possible superseded any aesthetic appreciation of these uplands – hence the monotonous rows of Sitka and Norway spruce. The trees are now mature and ready for felling, so subsequent planting will be in accordance with the present more enlightened attitude to forestry.

The area has undergone several stages of planting and felling since the natural forests were first cleared by settlers during the Neolithic period, some 3,000 years ago. Information boards in the Bod Petrual visitor centre explain fully the evolving Clocaenog landscape (open daily during holiday seasons).

**What to look out for**

You are more likely to hear than see birds of prey in the forest. Bold, inquisitive blue tits and chaffinches may join you at the picnic tables, and mallard on the lake will paddle over at the first rustle of a sandwich bag. Though the sunless forest floor cannot support much growth, the borders of the tracks display a variety of hardy wild plants.

*Woodpigeon*

# *Beddgelert and the Aberglaslyn Gorge*

This walk follows the progress of a river as it slides quietly through green pastures then thunders down a rock gorge. A disused railway tunnel and a legendary dog add adventure and intrigue. Less energetic walkers can enjoy the more peaceful river scenery of a shorter walk from the village.

**WALK 64**
GWYNEDD
SH590481

### Information

The full walk is just over three miles long; the short walk just over a mile
Easy, level walking on the short route; the long route includes a rough, rocky section
Almost no road walking
A torch is useful in the long tunnel
No stiles
Dogs must be kept on leads on the short walk
Several pubs in Beddgelert
Many excellent riverside picnic sites
Benches on the path to Gelert's Grave
Toilets near start of walk

### START

The village of Beddgelert is 15 miles south-east of Caernarfon, at the junction of the A4085 and A498. From the junction, at the little hump-back bridge, take the road towards Porthmadog. After about 200 yards you will see signs for a large car park on the right.

### DIRECTIONS

Return to the hump-back bridge, then follow the narrow lane on the right to its end. Cross the footbridge at the river confluence then turn right to follow the riverside path downstream to an iron bridge in about ½ mile. This is where the two routes diverge. (For the short walk via Gelert's Grave, cross the bridge then turn right to follow the path upstream: directions continue at * below). For the extended walk through the Aberglaslyn Gorge, do not cross the river at the iron bridge but continue downstream along a broad track (the bed of the dismantled Welsh Highland Railway), passing through two short tunnels.

When about 50yds from the entrance to a long tunnel, descend to the riverbank and follow the exciting path through the gorge until overlooking a road bridge.

Turn sharp left and follow steps uphill through woods to where the path levels.

Beyond a gate the tunnel track will be seen on the left. Go through the 350yd tunnel to rejoin the approach track and follow it to the iron bridge.

*Continue upstream and at the second gate Gelert's Grave can be seen beneath a large tree on the left, but to protect

### What to look out for

As you follow the progress of the river, watch out for grey wagtails and dippers, both of which perch on boulders in the fast-flowing water. Moss and ferns grow in profusion in the gorge, and beside the water – look out for polypody fern, hard fern and oak fern in particular.

grazing land continue a little further until a signed slate path leads back left over pastures to the fenced grave. Return to the riverside and continue upstream along the gravel and slate path. Go through a final gate to arrive in the lane by the toilets.

**Gelert's Grave**
An inscription at Gelert's Grave tells the tragic tale of a faithful hound fatally misjudged by his master. The story is entirely within the tradition of poignant Welsh legends, in which this part of Snowdonia – closely associated with Arthur and Merlin – is especially rich. One does not enquire too deeply about factual support for these enthralling tales.

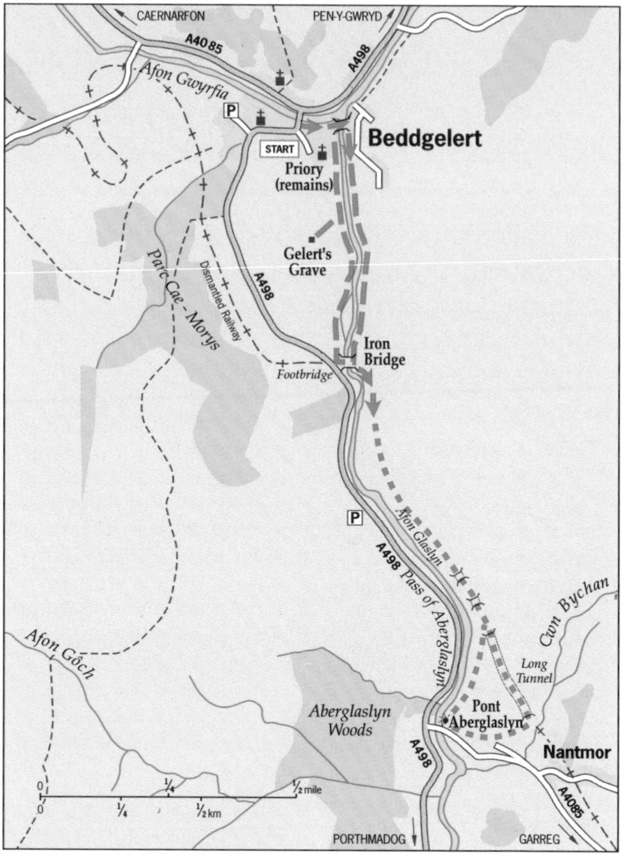


*Yellow pimpernel*

*The rocky bed of the River Glaslyn*

**Welsh Highland Railway**
This narrow-gauge railway carried passengers and goods between Caernarfon and Porthmadog until its closure 1937. Recent attempts to resurrect the dismantled line as a tourist attraction have so far been resisted.

# Newborough Forest and Llanddwyn Island

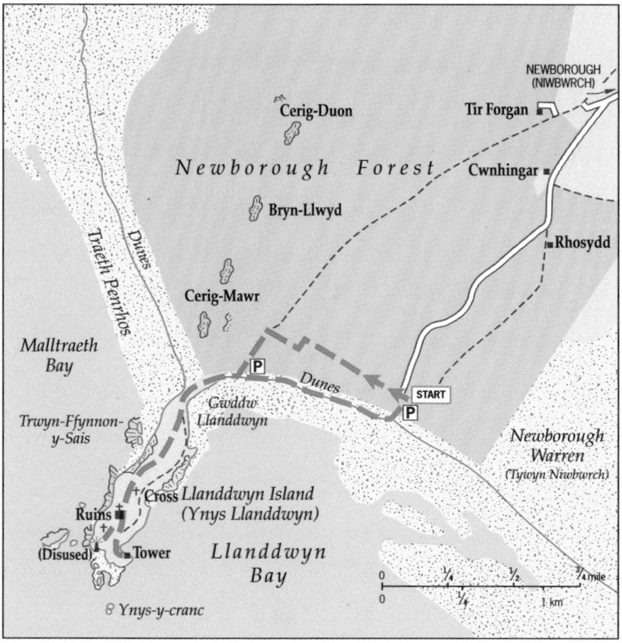


**WALK 65**
ANGLESEY
SH406634

This varied coastal walk contrasts the dark pine forest with the dazzling glare of a sandy beach, with an old lighthouse and lots of sea birds to observe along the way.

**START**

Newborough (Niwbwrch) lies near the southern tip of Anglesey, on the A4080 about 12 miles south-west of Bangor. At the crossroads in the village centre, take the minor road signposted 'Traeth/ Beach' and 'Lladdwyn' to a large car park (small fee).

**DIRECTIONS**

Take the broad forestry track from near the car park entrance and follow it westwards, parallel to the beach, for a little over ½ mile. Turn left at a T-junction of tracks to arrive at a car park. A path on the right now leads through a depression between trees (sometimes deeply drifted with sand) and out onto the wide sweep of the sandy beach. Follow the curve of the beach to the right and cross the neck of sand – briefly impassable only during the highest tides – onto Llanddwyn Island. Pass the information board and continue along a broad path, passing a ruined church, to the southern tip of the island (there are several lovely beaches to the right off this path).

After viewing the disused lighthouse (no entry) and other relics, return along the same path, or via detouring paths on the east side of the island, to the connecting neck. (Note that some of the rocky prominences of the tip of the island are cut off by the rising tide.)

Veer right onto the beautiful sweep of dune-backed beach and walk along it for about ¾ mile to the gap in the dunes which leads back to the car park.

**Newborough**

The 'New Borough' was initially inhabited by reluctant villagers evicted from the site of the proposed Beaumaris Castle by Edward I. In attempting to cultivate the land, they succeeded only in exposing their homes and land to the inexorable drift of windblown sand. Marram grass was planted to stabilise the dunes, which then became home to the rabbits which at one time provided the villagers with their major source of income. Half the huge dune area of Newborough Warren has since been planted with Corsican pine, managed by the Forestry Commission.

**Llanddwyn Island**

There are several constructions on the southern half of the island, including a stubby marker tower which predates the disused lighthouse. The ruined abbey, of 15th-century origin, stands on the site of the 5th-century chapel of St Dwynwen, the Welsh patron saint of lovers. St Dwynwen is commemorated by the nearby Latin cross; the nearer Celtic cross is of recent origin. The row of cottages near the little harbour were once the homes of pilots employed to guide boats through the treacherous entrance to the Menai Straits.

**What to look out for**

Oystercatchers, with their distinctive black and white plumage and long, red beaks, can be seen around Llanddwyn Island, while colonies of shags occupy the smaller islands offshore. Other seabirds lay eggs among the thin scrub which covers the ancient rocks of the island, so avoid straying from the paths. These rocks are of pre-Cambrian origin – over 600 million years old.

**Information**

The walk is three and a half miles long
Good paths and forestry tracks
No road walking
No stiles
Dogs should be kept on leads on Llanddwyn Island to protect nesting birds
No pub or café
Idyllic picnic places in secluded bays on Llanddwyn Island
Toilets at the start point

*The sandbar link to Llanddwyn Island*

# South Stack and Holyhead Mountain

## WALK 66
ANGLESEY
SH211819

**Information**

The walk is three miles long
Rough ground on the (avoidable) final ascent to Holyhead Mountain; otherwise generally good paths and tracks
Very little road walking on a dead-end lane
One stile
Café/shop (seasonal) near start
Picnic possibilities on Holyhead Mountain
Ice cream van often parked above lighthouse steps

Though of modest length, this walk takes in the site of an Iron Age settlement, a rocky summit, winding lighthouse steps with unequalled cliff scenery and an RSPB observatory with telescopes trained on nesting sea birds.

**START**
Follow the A5 through Holyhead, almost to the ferry terminal, then turn left onto the harbour front (Prince of Wales Road). Take the second left, signposted 'South Stack', then turn right at a T-junction. Follow this lane for about one and a half miles then turn right, also signposted. There is a large car park on the left after another half mile.

**DIRECTIONS**
Cross the stile almost opposite the car park entrance to arrive at the Iron Age hut circles within 100yds. After exploring these, return to the lane and turn right, passing the café, and climb the hill to reach a small car park. Turn right here to follow a stony path inland, later merging with a surfaced lane. Pass the old radio relay station (to avoid the climb to the top of Holyhead Mountain, continue at * below). Where the lane veers left towards the new radio station, head towards the hump of Holyhead Mountain on the main track.
Continue for a while until another path merges from the right, then fork right and ascend steps. Where the path crests the skyline, turn right to ascend a steep path to the triangulation point and remains of a Roman lookout tower at the summit of Holyhead Mountain.
Retrace your route back to the old radio station, * then take the narrow path which passes on the right side of the fenced compound to a disused lookout tower with views of South Stack Lighthouse far below. Continue along the

**What to look out for**

On a fine day the mountains of Snowdonia can be seen from the summit of Holyhead Mountain; in exceptionally clear conditions Ireland can also be seen. Below and to the east look out for car ferries plying across the Irish Sea between the port of Holyhead and Dublin or Dun Laoghaire.
During the nesting season (February to July) the South Stack sea cliffs are vibrant with bird life – puffins, fulmars, razorbills and guillemots among them; and choughs are present throughout the year.
At other times you may see rock climbers creeping slowly up the 400ft high vertical cliffs.

The view from South Stack

### The Iron Age Settlement of Cytiau'r Gwyddelod

The circular stone bases of more than a dozen Iron Age huts can be clearly seen here. When in use, the huts had conical roofs supported by a central pole, and in some of the circles you can still see evidence of hearths. When raids were imminent, the settlers sought refuge within the stone fortifications built on nearby Holyhead Mountain.

Puffins

path, descending to the road ahead.
(South Stack Lighthouse is now automatic, so access is prohibited. However, it is worth descending at least halfway down the winding steps for tremendous views of sea cliffs and the birds which nest precariously on their ledges. Return to the top of the steps.)
Follow the lane to the café car park then take the path leading down to Ellin's Tower observatory, perched on the cliff edge. Either return to the café and turn right along the lane, or follow a broad path leading directly back to the car park.

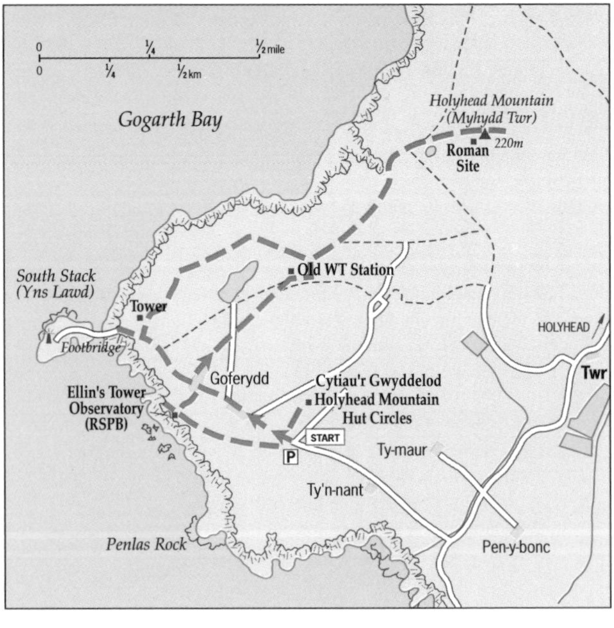

# Castles Above the Plain

*Beeston Castle stands in a dramatic setting above the Cheshire Plain*

Two fairy-tale castles, perched on high sandstone crags, are the highlights of this easy stroll around the well-wooded Peckforton Hills. From the ramparts of Beeston Castle the views are outstanding, extending across the fertile patchwork of fields of the Cheshire Plain.

**WALK 67**
CHESHIRE
SJ540591

**START**
Beeston is about two miles west of the A49 from Bunbury. The walk starts from the car park of Beeston Castle.

**DIRECTIONS**
From the car park (or after visiting the castle) turn right along the lane following a wall round to the right. Soon, by a second car park, join a narrow footpath signposted 'Sandstone Trail' and continue to a stile.
Turn left and descend through a conifer plantation to another stile by a cottage. Turn right into the field by the cottage and go half-left across this field, crossing a footbridge and a stile.
After another 25-30yds, cross another stile and turn right, ascending to the top of the field, heading for another stile. At the stile, turn right into a lane and just past a cottage on the

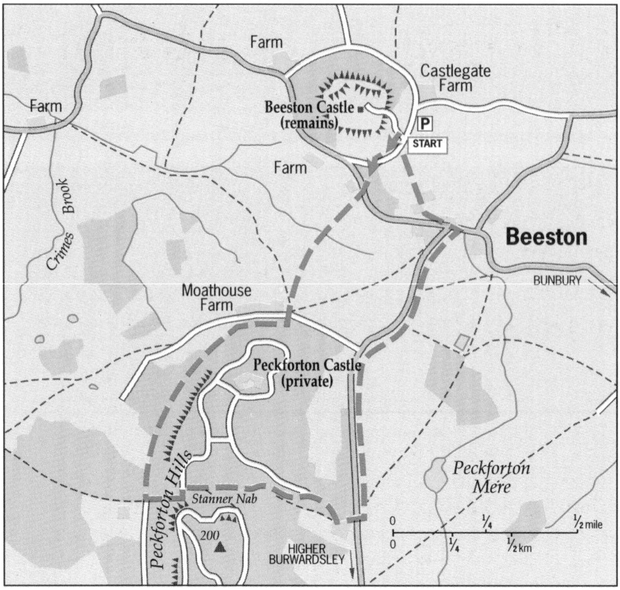


## Information

The walk is three miles long
Easy walking
Some road walking on a country lane
Several stiles
Dogs should be kept on leads
Refreshments available at Beeston Castle and the Pheasant Inn at Higher Burwardsley

right, turn left through a gate and into the trees. This woodland track skirts the grounds of Peckforton Castle (private). After a gate, a path crosses from the right. Turn left and follow the signposted path straight ahead up the hill.

Keep left through the trees, then turn right. Continue to follow the high walls which enclose the Peckforton Castle estate, to reach the pinnacled gatehouse of the Castle Lodge.

From the Lodge turn left and follow the lane for about a mile to return to the village of Beeston and the start point.

**Beeston Castle**

Built by Randulph de Blundeville, Earl of Chester, on his return from the Crusades in 1220, Beeston Castle stands on a commanding red sandstone knoll some 500 feet high, lookingout over the levels of the Cheshire Plain.

The castle, an English Heritage property today, played an important part during the Civil War, when it was finally besieged. The castle was 'slighted' by Parliamentary forces after the Battle of Rowton Moor. There are tales of hidden treasure in the Upper Bailey well, and there is a small museum in the castle grounds.

**Peckforton Castle**

This is a mock medieval castle, built in 1844 by Antony Salvin for Lord Tollemache, and is not open to the public.

## What to look out for

Chestnut trees, thought to have been introduced to Britain by the Romans, are a feature of the woodlands which surround Peckforton Castle. Sessile oaks and other trees clothe the slopes of the Peckforton Hills, which rise steeply out of the Cheshire Plain. They were formerly part of the Royal hunting ground of Delamere Forest. The woodland harbours wood sorrel, ground ivy and early purple orchids in spring.

The hills are of red sandstone, laid down during the Triassic period about 200 million years ago. The views from the hills extend across eight counties, from the Pennines in the east to the Welsh hills in the west.

# *Bradfield Dale*

**WALK 68**
SOUTH YORKSHIRE
SK262920

The route links the twin villages of High and Low Bradfield, idyllically set in a steep Pennine valley. Fine views of the surrounding moors, an interesting church and the story of the worst dam-burst disaster in British history make this a walk to remember.

**START**
Low Bradfield is off the B6077, about seven miles west of the centre of Sheffield. The walk starts from the car park on the western side of the village recreation ground.

**DIRECTIONS**
From the car park turn right, following the narrow path signed 'Path to High Bradfield', parallel to the stream on your right and a wall on your left. Turn right at the second footbridge, and up a steep flight of stone steps. At the top cross a track and climb five more steps. Keep ahead between a fence and a wall to reach the road.
Turn left along the road which leads up and alongside the wall of the Agden Reservoir. When the road curves round to the right, follow the footpath signed 'Bailey Hill', which winds steeply up to the right by the side of a plantation. Continue to climb up steeply until you reach a path junction by a stile on the right. Directly ahead and partly overgrown by trees is Bailey Hill, a Norman motte and bailey castle (no access).
Turn right over the stile and follow the path across to the churchyard, entering through two gates. Walk through the churchyard to the main gate, with the Watch House on your left. Keep forward into Towngate and into the hilltop village of High Bradfield.
Now turn right into Woodfall Lane, signed 'Low Bradfield and Dungworth'. Soon after the lane bends to the left, turn left at a stone stile following public footpath signed 'Low Bradfield'. Keep to the edge of

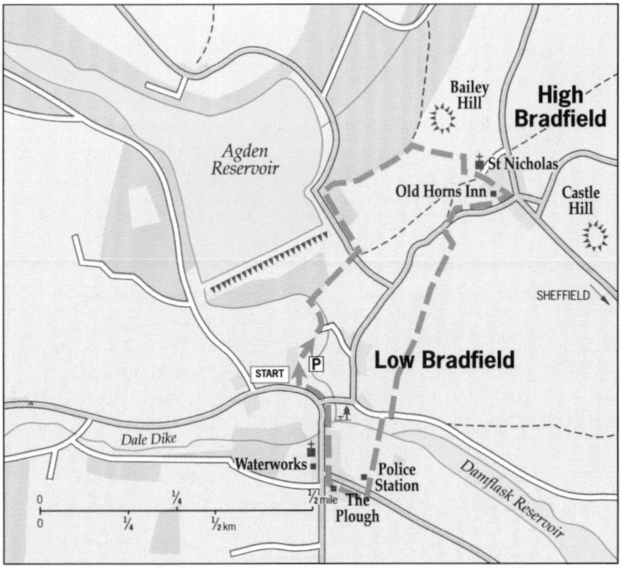


**What to look out for**

Despite their usual retiring nature, weasels are seen fairly regularly in the area, feeding among the stone walls. Watch for agitated meadow pipits perched on the stones.
Foxes are sometimes observed crossing the open moors, which are the haunt also of red grouse.
The reservoirs harbour waterbirds in autumn and winter.

the field by a stone wall, and follow it as it curves right. Continue across several walls and stiles to cross the fields, keeping a line of electricity poles 20yds to your right, and later descend another uneven flight of stone steps onto a lane (care needed) near the upper end of the Damflask Reservoir.

Cross the footbridge over the River Loxley almost opposite the steps, and continue along School Lane, which leads via a walled path to another lane, emerging by the police station. Turn right here back towards the village, and right again at The Plough pub into Mill Lee Road for the return to the car park.

**St Nicholas Church, High Bradfield**

This lovely parish church built mainly in the 15th century has fine views across the green, reservoir-filled dale to the moorlands beyond. The Gothic-style Watch House on the edge of the churchyard was built in the days when body snatching was rife.

**The Bursting Dam Disaster**

Just after midnight on 11 March 1864, the newly-completed Dale Dike Reservoir west of Low Bradfield burst its walls following a landslip. About 700 million gallons of water surged down Bradfield Dale and on as far as the outskirts of Sheffield. A mill at Low Bradfield was swept away and a total of 244 people died. Another 20,000 were made homeless.

**Information**

The walk is two miles long
Mostly easy lane and field walking, with one steep climb
Several stone squeeze-stiles
Dogs should be kept on leads
Pubs in Low and High Bradfield

*The parish church of St Nicholas*

**WALK 69**
WEST YORKSHIRE
SE212269

# Oakwell Hall

### Information

The walk is just under two miles long
Mainly easy walking
Information centre at car park
Café and exhibition areas in converted farm buildings by the Hall
Picnic area with play area between the car park and the Hall
Toilets at the car park (with baby changing room) and at the Hall

*Large bindweed*

Though close to the roaring traffic of the M62, this walk enters a different world – of an Elizabethan stone and timber country house with a lovely walled garden, amidst the open spaces and pleasant footpaths of a modern country park.

**START**

There is a large, free car park on the A652 between Bradford and Dewsbury, reached from the M62 (junction 26) via the A58.

**DIRECTIONS**

From the Country Park entrance and car park, take the wide track ahead beyond the Information Centre, by the wooden gate.

This path crosses a broad field (part of a reclaimed colliery) and leads steeply down to a bridge over Oakwell Beck.

Cross, and walk up the steps towards the garden in front of Oakwell Hall with its little statue of a ram.

Unless you are going into the hall, take the path to the left of the house, alongside the walled garden behind the hall and past the wildlife garden.

Continue past the arboretum to reach the old railway, and go up a fenced path back to the old railway bridge.

Turn right along the footpath alongside the old railway cutting (avoid the horse track). After 50yds climb steps, at the top of which is a seat with a fine view across Oakwell Hall and Country Park and the Spen Valley, with the tall television mast on Emley Moor a notable landmark.

The path soon descends past birch trees. At a cross roads take the narrow path

### What to look out for

The Tudor/Jacobean style herb garden by the Hall entrance contains a variety of culinary and medicinal herbs, while the old walled garden has been laid out in formal style, with old roses and other plants and shrubs of the period.
There are lots of interesting things to see in the woods, scrub and grassland of the country park. Woodland birds are common among the oaks and silver birches, and waterside plants flourish along the streams. A nature trail leaflet is availible.

*Oakwell Hall, set at the centre of a delightful country park*

descending to the right, parallel with the stream, past oak and birch woods, soon crossing a wooden footbridge to the woods.

Keep on the main path, but soon take a crossing path to the right, which leads to another footbridge over the stream, then cross the bridleway (watch out for galloping horses). Cross the field ahead on the pathway, but keep inside the next field wall before bearing left into a picnic area, and up a stone ramp into the car park.

Keep straight ahead towards Oakwell Hall and Visitor Centre. Return along the path in front of the Hall, taking the steps down to Oakwell Beck and back along the same route to return to the car park.

**Oakwell Hall**

The Hall, which has been faithfully refurnished in period style, began as a mid 15th-century timber yeoman's house which was later encased in stone by a prosperous local landowner, John Batt – look for the date over the door. The house has remained largely unchanged for 350 years.

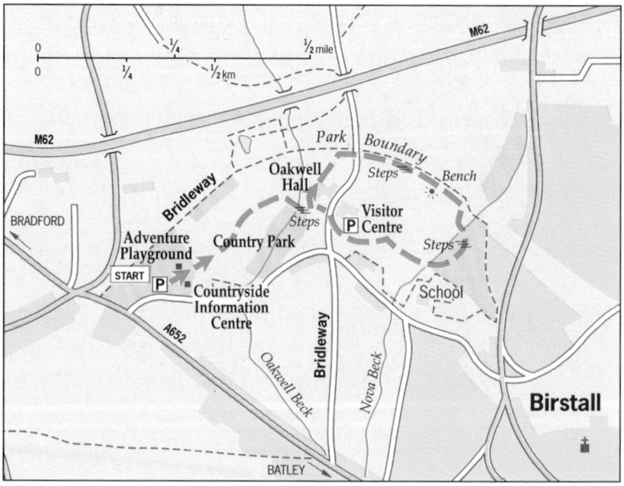

# Three Pyramids at Castle Howard

**WALK 70**
NORTH YORKSHIRE
SE727677

From the village of Welburn this walk visits some of the more unusual buildings on the Castle Howard Estate.

**Information**

The walk is about four and a half miles long
Some sections may be muddy
Several stiles
Pub in Welburn; café and other facilities for visitors at Castle Howard

### START

Welburn is off the A64, south-west of Malton. Park carefully at the roadside by Chestnut Avenue in Welburn.

### DIRECTIONS

Take the bridleway, where the houses begin, and continue for ¼ mile to a field entrance. Turn left along a track, with a hedge on the right, and descend to a gate. Pass through, and follow the path through woodland. At a fork, bear right to cross a stile, then go uphill to the Four Faces. Continue straight ahead for 400yds to see the Pyramid in Pretty Wood. Return to the Four Faces and turn right, to follow the track for ½ mile.

Where it bends right to a gate, you can see beyond to the Great Pyramid, the dome of Castle Howard, and the Mausoleum. Descend to a road; turn left and immediately right down a track to the bridge, for great views of Castle Howard and the bridge.

*The fountain at Castle Howard*

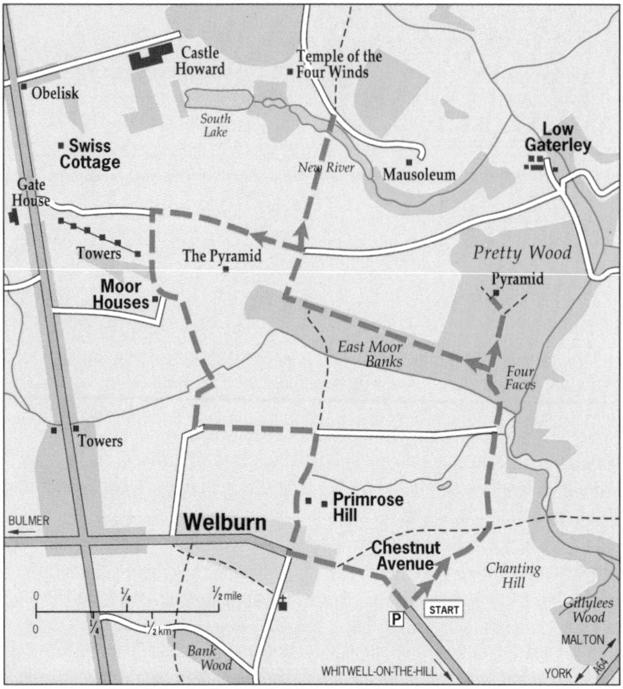


### What to look out for

Castle Howard's landscape is designed to resemble an Italian painting. Notice the Great Pyramid's eight stone lanterns, the Temple's fine urns, and the openings in the bridge's balustrade that match the shape of the mausoleum, with its 20 columns.

Return to the road and turn right, passing the Pyramid. Another pyramid is seen ahead, above a gateway. Take a signed track to the left, past a ruined tower, and follow another sign diagonally left downhill across the field (no obvious path) to the end of a small wood, and cross a stile in the trees. Head towards a corrugated iron barn – may be muddy. Follow the hedge round to the left by farm buildings and cross a stile

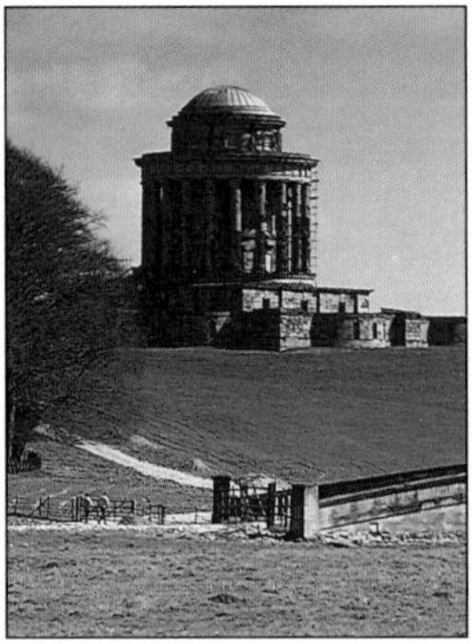

Turn right (arrowed), with a hedge to your right, towards Welburn church spire.

Go over two more stiles to reach and cross a third, set in a wire mesh fence. Bear right around the field edge until the fence turns right, then follow right around the edge of the field to a track. Turn left along the track, and continue for ¼ mile to a junction of tracks by an oak tree. Turn right here towards Welburn, and continue to meet a lane. Go straight on, and at the main road turn left, to return to the start point.

**Castle Howard**

The great 18th-century palace of Castle Howard was designed by Sir John Vanbrugh, and is familiar from its starring television roles in *Brideshead Revisited* and *The Buccaneers*.

The grounds are also magnificent, with a number of family memorials, including the Great Pyramid. The Pyramid Gate was built in 1719, and both the Pyramid in Pretty Wood and the Four Faces some time before 1727.

The Temple of the Four Winds, near the bridge, is on the former main street of Henderskelfe village, demolished when the castle was built. The Ruined Tower, a folly, is part of Vanbrugh's medieval-style estate wall.

The Mausoleum is a masterpiece by Vanbrugh's young assistant, Nicholas Hawksmoor. The castle is open from March to October.

*The Mausoleum*

# WALK 71
NORTH YORKSHIRE
SE797841

# Pickering Castle

Pickering's romantic 12th-century castle provides the focal point for this walk on the edge of the North York Moors National Park; additional attractions which can be combined with the walk include a steam-hauled trip on the North Yorkshire Moors Railway or a visit to the delightful Beck Isle Folk Museum.

## Information

The walk is two miles long
Relatively easy, but some stony woodland paths, with uphill sections
Several stiles
Dogs not permitted in Pickering Castle
Cafés and pubs in Pickering; tea shop by the castle entrance
Informal picnic area by the castle walls, and a really delightful streamside picnic area in front of Beck Isle Museum
Toilets in Pickering and by the castle car park

## START

The walk starts at the crossroads and bridge below Pickering Station. There are plenty of well signed car parks in Pickering and at the castle, but all can be busy on summer weekends.

## DIRECTIONS

Cross the bridge to the Beck Isle Museum and picnic area, then go through gate along the track to the left of the museum (marked 'Riding Stables'). Go through a gate to the left and along the broad, grassy track past the stables. Soon the path veers right to continue beside the beck and over a stile – ignore a concrete footbridge on the right.

Turn left, away from the beck, over rough pasture towards a wood ahead. Enter the wood by another stile, crossing a track into a caravan site, before following a narrow path between trees to exit at a stile.

Bear half-right across a ridged field, and at the top go through the right hand of two field gates onto a stony track.

Follow the track by woods, crossing a stile beside a gate (waymarked) and a farmhouse (now a pottery). The way narrows between hedges to a metal gate, then a second gate, before curving right over an open field towards cottages.

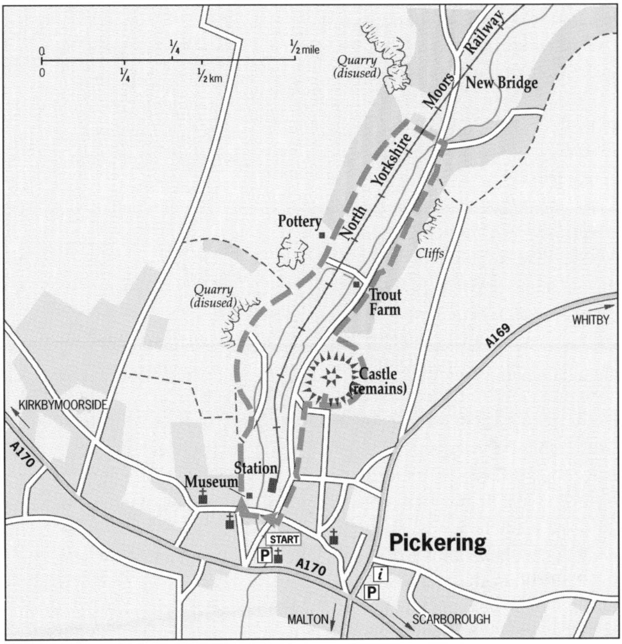

*The ruins of Pickering Castle*

Turn right through the gate by these cottages (waymarked) and right again to a path leading to a pedestrian gate across the railway line (look out for trains) and a footbridge over the stream. Follow the path to the road.

Cross the road and bear right to a path into the woods, which climbs the embankment parallel to the road. It soon joins a broader path from the left, passing limestone cliffs on the left. At a fork keep left, joining another track parallel to the road, and avoiding a path bearing right to the road. Keep to this path, with more cliffs on your right, to reach another fork. Bear right here to join the road with care, and cross to the other side. Pass a trout farm on the beck. Turn left for 250yds to a wooden barrier and footpath sign, taking a path on the opposite side of the road.

Follow an old wall away from road up an incline by the edge of the wood. Where the wall ends go left for 10yds, then right to where paths split below the castle walls. Head right then left up to the castle walls, circling left to the main entrance, then bearing right down steps. Turn left down Castle Road to return to Pickering centre.

**What to look out for**

The woods include oak, ash, rowan and whitebeam, with wood anemones and yellow pimpernel on the ground below.

**Pickering Castle**

Enjoying a superb position on a limestone bluff overlooking the town, Pickering Castle (English Heritage) dates from Norman times. It is said that most kings of England between 1100 and 1400 visited the Castle, mainly to hunt in local forests. It is open daily in summer; closed Mondays in winter.

**Beck Isle Museum**

Collections of domestic bygones, including a room of children's toys, old shops, farm implements and a moorland kitchen bring the past to life in this fascinating museum. It is open daily from Easter to October.

# Swinsty

**WALK 72**
NORTH YORKSHIRE
SE187537

A lovely lakeland and woodland walk, with picnic areas, attractive waterside paths, two dams, views and reflections.

START
The Swinsty and Fewston Reservoirs are south of the A59 about ten miles west of Harrogate. Turn off southwards for Fewston village just west of the A59/B6451 junction. There is a well-screened Yorkshire Water car park (free) on the Fewston–Timble road just to the west of Fewston Embankment. There is an alternative car park and picnic site on the minor road to the south of Fewston.

DIRECTIONS
From the car park take the track which runs through the wood immediately opposite the information board, closed to cars by a single wooden barrier. This becomes a broad, stone track through a dense coniferous plantation (Swinsty Moor Plantation) with fire breaks. After just over ½ mile this emerges opposite Swinsty Hall.

Turn left alongside the overgrown garden wall to the rear of the hall, down to the track at the side of Swinsty Reservoir, and turn right towards the dam. Cross the dam and follow the reservoir road past the lodge for nearly ¼ mile, then bear left along a woodland path which goes close to the reservoir side. At a gate this path joins the lane. Turn

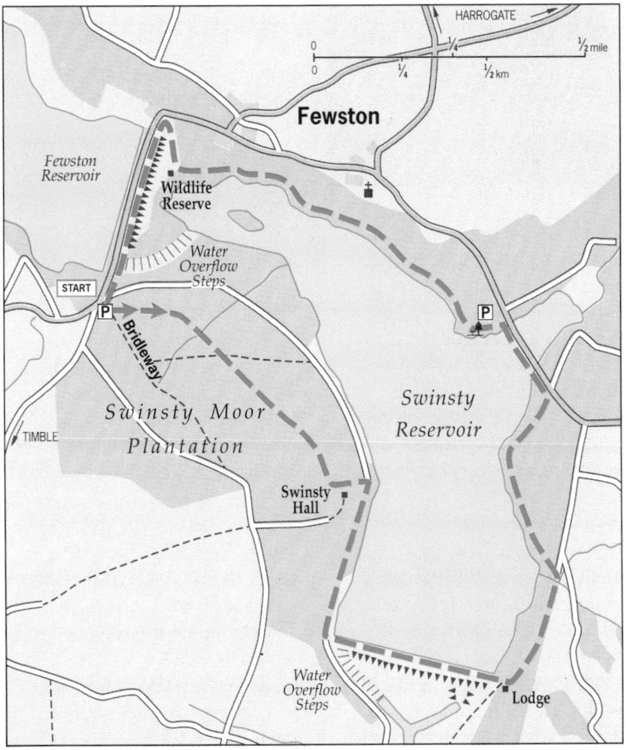


**Information**

The walk is just over three miles long
Level walking, except for logged slope up to Fewston Reservoir Road; half a mile of rough track at start of walk
No stiles
Dogs must be kept under control
Timble Inn about three quarters of a mile from the start/finish of the walk serves food and light refreshments; it has a family room
Picnic areas at the start of the walk and on east side of reservoir
Toilets and small information point at start of walk

*The reservoir from afar (above), and (below ) about as close as you can get!*

left along the lane, crossing over the bridge which spans the eastern arm of the reservoir.

At the far side, a path leads back into the woodland by a car park and attractive picnic site. Keep ahead along the water's edge, following a beautiful path through woods at the reservoir side (fine views through the trees). This eventually emerges in open grassland past a small wildfowl reserve and climbs the embankment of the Fewston Dam to a gate.

Turn left into the Fewston Embankment road, keeping along the pavement to the end of the dam, to reach the car park 100yds beyond the end of the dam.

**Swinsty Reservoir**

In 1876 the construction of the great dam across the little River Washburn created Swinsty Reservoir to supply the city of Leeds with fresh water. It is one of a chain of reservoirs – Thrushcross, Fewston, Swinsty and Lindley – and many billions of cubic metres of water come through it each day.

Some of the water in Swinsty has been collected in the valley, but much comes from as far away as the River Laver Leighton Reservoir at Masham, about 20 miles away.

**What to look out for**

Though this is an area of commercial woodland, the variety of trees is not confined to the usual coniferous spruce, larch and pine, but also includes rowan, sycamore, willow, alder and beech – and the edge of the woods has lots of wild flowers. Large-scale reservoir works include two dams and outflows.

Both woodland and lakeland birds can be seen, including finches, blue tits, wood pigeons, woodpeckers, mallard and teal.

**Swinsty Hall**

This beautiful Elizabethan house dates back to 1570. An old Dales legend maintains that the hall was built from the ill-gotten gains of a once poor London weaver called Robinson. It is said that, during the Great Plague, Robinson stole gold from the plague victims.

In fact, there is not a shred of truth in this story, and the truth is more prosaic: the mansion was actually built by one Ralph Wood, a local landowner, for his newly married son, Francis.

Today, the remains are so overgrown that it is easy to miss all together.

# *Wycoller Village, the Beck and the Moors*

This pleasant walk rises gently from a beautiful village in a wooded valley and touches the fringes of open moorland (best avoided in cold, wet weather though). The walk is strong on both heritage and views.

**WALK 73**
LANCASHIRE
SD926395

**Information**

The walk is three and a half miles long
There is a gradual climb to the moors
A few stiles
Dogs should be on leads through farms and fields
Café, museum and picnic site at Wycoller

**START**

There is access to Wycoller from Colne or Laneshaw Bridge on the A6068 – both approaches being signposted. The roads are narrow and access to Wycoller itself is restricted to locals and disabled visitors. Everyone else must park 600 yards from the village at the Trawden Road Car Park.

**DIRECTIONS**

Follow a tarmac path parallel to the narrow road to reach Wycoller. Go straight through the village passing in turn the café, cottages, bridges (cross the beck here), Wycoller Hall, the museum, toilets, duckpond and picnic/play area.

Walk along the track with Wycoller Beck on the right, heading uphill very gently. At a signpost for Dean House Farm bear left, crossing the beck, and soon pass Parson Lee Farm on the right. Stay by the beck, below the farmyard, going through the gate or crossing adjacent stile.

Continue uphill rather more steeply along a grassy track, where dogs should be kept on leads.

On reaching a drystone wall,

*The ruins of Wycoller Hall*

**What to look out for**

Three types of stone bridge – arched, clapper and clam are encountered. Look for moorland birds such as meadow pippits and golden plovers, as well as woodland and meadow wildlife at lower elevations. On the higher parts there are views of Pendle Hill, famous for its stories of witchcraft. The excellent small museum, with its various handlooms and old agricultural implements, also has countryside information.

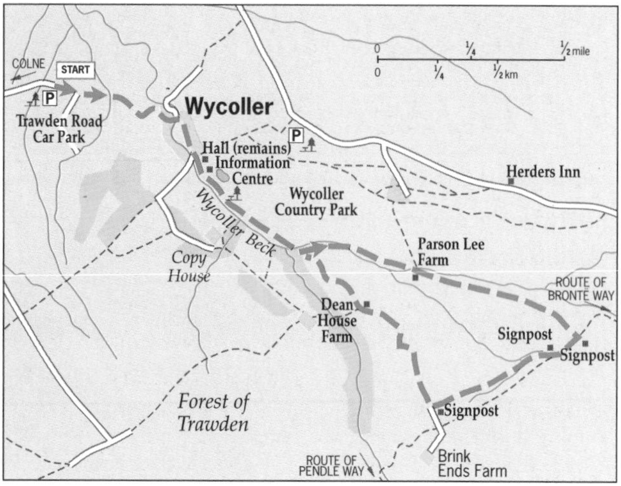


cross a stile by a gate and turn right at sign for Brontë Way and Pendle Way. Go downhill a short way on a good track, then branch to the right along a less clear rushy track where there is a signpost for Wycoller. Follow the track through two gates, then cross a wooden step-stile on the right. There is another signpost for Wycoller.

Walk downhill through a field, following a fence, a wall, another fence and another wall. Go through gate (or cross the adjacent stile, rather awkward), then go through another gate into the yard of Dean House Farm. Look for yellow marker arrows and follow the access track away from the farm, downhill to a gate near Wycoller Beck. Simply retrace your steps through Wycoller and return to the car park.

## Wycoller

This was a small handloom weaving village dating from the 16th and 17th centuries, pre-dating the larger mill towns nearby.

When plans to flood the valley for a new reservoir were announced, all the inhabitants were evacuated, but when the plan was shelved they did not return and the village fell into ruins. It became a noted beauty spot and was subsequently restored and the surrounding area became a country park. The Brontë Way and Pendle Way both pass through the village.

## Wycoller Hall

The building dates from the 16th century and was considerably extended by Squire Cunliffe in the hopes of attracting a wealthy wife. His real passion, though, was cockfighting and he died bankrupt.

The Hall once stood three stories high, though the ruins suggest there were only two. Charlotte Brontë used the Hall and its setting in her famous novel *Jane Eyre*, where it featured as 'Ferndean Manor'. Note the enormous stone fireplace, curious keyhole-shaped wig powdering cupboard and stone mullioned windows.

*The old stone bridge over the beck*

# *Lever Park, Rivington Reservoir and Rivington Barns*

## WALK 74
LANCASHIRE
SD629139

### Information

The walk is three miles long
There is a short ascent which can be muddy
No stiles
There is a café, information centre and play area at the start of the walk
Plenty of places for picnics
Toilets at start point

This is a walk for any season, although autumn, with all its glorious colours, is perhaps the best time to explore the woodland tracks around Lever Park. There is an information centre which gives an insight into the wildlife and historical interest of the area.

START
There is no direct access to Lever Park from the nearby M61. Make an approach from Horwich or Chorley, following signposts for Great House Barn, where there is a car park.

DIRECTIONS
From Great House Barn, follow a track towards the wooded shores of Rivington Reservoir. Turn left to follow a wide path which runs roughly parallel to the reservoir shore and continue to the ruined folly known as The Castle.
Walk away from the 'front door' of the castle along the most prominent track. This is quite broad and is lined with oak and sycamore. The track leads to a road, but just before reaching it, turn left along a lesser track. Now cross straight over the road. (To cut the walk short, follow a footpath parallel to the road, which leads straight back to Great House Barn.)

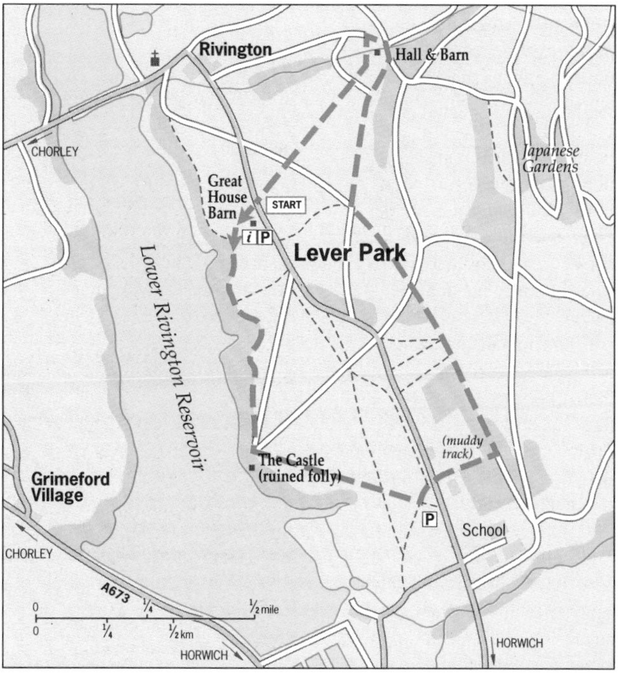

*Looking across the peaceful waters of Rivington Reservoir*

A narrow path, which can be very muddy, climbs gently uphill from the road. It is lined with holly at first, then bends to the left as it levels out in
a wood.
On reaching a wide track turn left, continue to a crossroads of tracks and keep forward. At the next junction, turn right and follow a track gently uphill. Later, start walking downhill and keep left to follow a fenced track out of the wood.
Rivington Hall comes into view ahead. Keep to the right of the Hall, then turn left around Rivington Hall Barn. Walk downhill and cross a bridge over a pond.
A narrow road with speed ramps (Hall Drive) leads straight through a beech avenue to return to Great House Barn.

**The Reservoirs**
There are five reservoirs near Rivington and three more at Roddlesworth, all are connected to the same system which pipes water mainly to Liverpool. Construction of the reservoirs began in 1847, but the work wasn't completed until 1875. The total capacity of the system is 4 million gallons.

**Lord Leverhulme**
William Lever was born in Bolton in 1851. He entered his father's wholesale grocery business and expanded it considerably.
In 1884, Lever ordered soap from manufacturers and stamped it 'Sunlight Soap' at a time when few brand names were in use. He later moved into soap manufacture, built the village of Port Sunlight and became a leading industrialist. He died in 1925.

**Lever Park**
Lord Leverhulme bought most of the Rivington Estate and developed it as a home and parkland. The two ancient cruck barns were converted into refreshment rooms and a Japanese Garden was established on the higher slopes. The Castle – a copy of Liverpool Castle – was built overlooking Rivington Reservoir. The park was opened to the public in 1904 and is now managed as a country park.

**What to look out for**

Visit the information centre first, which offers a fine range of books and leaflets about Lever Park and the West Pennines moors. A small exhibition details the history and wildlife of the park. The information centre is in Great House Barn – a building supported by an enormous oaken cruck-frame. Rivington Hall Barn is a similar structure; both barns have been rebuilt, but the cruck-frames are original. There is a wide variety of birds to see in the woods, including treecreepers, tits and chaffinches.

# Hest Bank, Morecambe Bay and the Lancaster Canal

**WALK 75**
LANCASHIRE
SO468665

This walk features contrasting scenes, from the open shores of Morecambe Bay to the enclosed towpath of the Lancaster Canal, with plenty of water and wildlife.

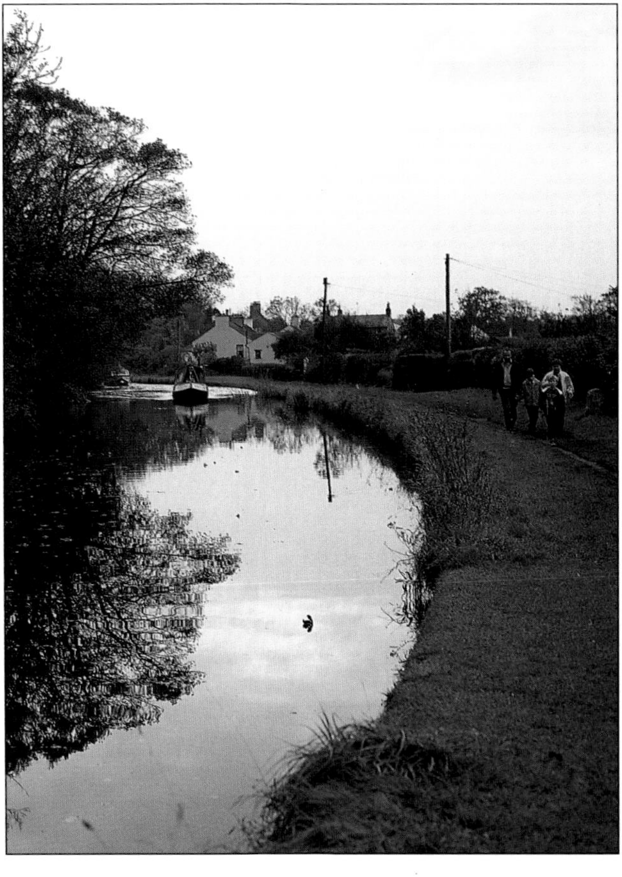

START
Hest Bank is on the A5105 between Morecambe and Carnforth. Look out for the Post Office, then immediately go over a level crossing to reach the car park on the shore.

DIRECTIONS
Follow the shore road which quickly becomes a gravel track for about 200yds, then pass to the left of a fence and keep to a line between the level saltmarsh and a steep slope of hawthorn scrub. (If walking out on the saltmarsh, keep well away from the dangerous mud flats and tidal channels of Morecambe Bay.) Continue, staying near the edge of the saltmarsh, to eventually go through a narrow stile in a wall, by a sign 'All dogs must be on a leash'. Walk gently uphill and enjoy the extensive views. Walk down the field to a tiny yellow gate where a stile leads into a small field containing a few caravans. Pass Jumbo Rock and keep to the left of Red Bank Farm and cross a high, narrow stone step-stile. A minor road leads along the shore, passing a toilet block and a row of houses. Avoid walking on the road by following a grassy bank on a parallel route overlooking the marshes. Where the road veers inland, continue on, to pass a row of houses. On reaching some

*A stretch of the canal*

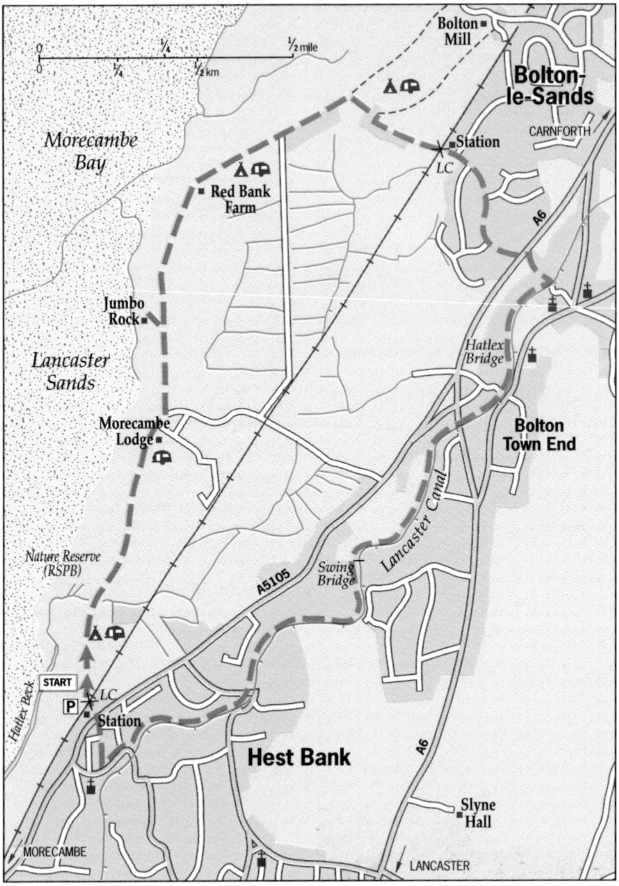


## Information

The walk is nearly four miles long
Mostly level ground with half a mile of road walking
A few stiles
Dogs must be kept on leads through first field beyond salt marshes – see directions text
Restaurants at Boulton-le-Sands
Seating at a few points along the route
Areas suitable for picnics along the shore
Toilets near car park at the start

seats overlooking the bay, turn inland and proceed to Bolton-le-Sands, past a caravan site, climbing over a rise and going over a level crossing before reaching a pavement. Cross the A6 road (pedestrian crossing nearby) and head straight up a minor road to reach a canal bridge. Do not cross the bridge, but turn right and use a stile to get on to the towpath. Pass a wide bridge carrying a busy road; next is a low-level swing bridge; then a small stone bridge; and finally another small stone bridge with boats and barges moored on either side.

There is a signpost beyond the bridge which gives various canal destinations. One arm points to the shore at Hest Bank. Walk straight down Station Road, passing the shops, then cross the road at a pelican crossing. Use the level crossing to return to the car park.

### The Lancaster Canal

The canal from Preston to Tewitfield was opened in 1797. By 1819 it had been extended to Kendal, but the northern section is now derelict. Traffic along the canal declined with the construction of a railway on a parallel route. Today the canal is used purely for leisure.

## What to look out for

Many species of gulls, waders and wildfowl can be spotted around the shores of Morecambe Bay, with ducks to be seen on the Lancaster Canal. An information board at the start of the walk gives more information. Take binoculars to look across the bay to the Lakeland Fells – there is a view indicator at the start to help identify them. The canal towpath is kept clear of vegetation, but many wild plants flourish alongside garden boundaries. Look out for canalside milestones.

# Bolton Priory

**WALK 76**
NORTH YORKSHIRE
SE071539

This is a walk with lots of variety – a ruined 12th-century priory, riverside areas with a footbridge, stepping stones, stretches of sand and pretty woodland paths with fine views. It is also relatively sheltered, making it an ideal winter walk.

**Information**

The walk is about two and a half miles long
Mainly on woodland or riverside paths, with two short but easy climbs and a section high above the river
No road walking
A few stiles
Refreshment facilities in Bolton Abbey village; cafeteria, restaurant, snacks and ice cream at Cavendish Pavilion (seasonal)
Extensive grassy picnic areas by the priory footbridge and along riverside
Toilets at Bolton Abbey car park and Cavendish Pavilion

**START**
Bolton Abbey village can be reached from Skipton (six miles west) on the A59, turning north at Bolton Bridge along the B6160, or from Ilkley via the A65, joining the B6160 at Addingham. There is a large, well signed car park (charge) at Bolton Bridge.

**DIRECTIONS**
From the top end of the car park, pass the Information Board, turning right into the village. Cross the B6160 (very busy at times) to the hole in the wall opposite, which is the footpath into the Bolton Abbey Estate.
Go down the steps towards the riverside and head towards the wooden footbridge and stepping stones. Cross the bridge (the stepping stones should be avoided unless river is very low) and ascend the hillside to reach a higher level path through the woods.
Keep on the main path through the woods, eventually descending to a stile and rounding the hillside to join the lane from Storiths. Keep ahead to cross the stream at Pickles Gill by the footbridge to the right (or stepping stones ahead). Turn left alongside the stream to a stile which leads to the riverside path and then a second stile to cross the wooden bridge at the Cavendish Pavilion.
(The walk can be extended at this point into the Strid Wood Nature Trails; free map available at entrance.)

*The priory, seen across the river*

From the Cavendish Pavilion, go back along the riverside past the parking areas, following the curve of the river to the right where, on the hillside, a narrow path leads to steps and a stile then meets the road by the Cavendish Memorial. Keep left along the path parallel to the road and go through a gate to the entrance of Bolton Priory Church.

Maintain your direction along the church drive, past the rectory, taking the stile left to a path over the field, rejoining the path to the hole in the wall for the village centre.

**Bolton Priory**

The priory was founded by a group of Augustinian canons, who moved here from Embsay, near Skipton, around 1154. The church (still in use) and most of the ruins date from the 12th to the 15th century, the newest part being Prior Moone's western tower which was never completed. The roof is a very recent addition. Bolton Hall was converted from the former gatehouse in the 18th century; the rectory was once a grammar school, endowed by the 17th-century scientist, Robert Boyle (of Boyle's Law fame).

**The Legend of the White Doe of Rylstone**

During Elizabethan times an abortive rising against the Queen spelled disaster for the Nortons of nearby Rylstone Hall, resulting in imprisonment or death for most of the family. A surviving sister, Emily, would walk six miles across the moors to visit her brother's grave in Bolton Priory churchyard, taking with her the little white doe that had been a gift from her brother. Long after her death the white doe would still be seen wandering around the gravestones.

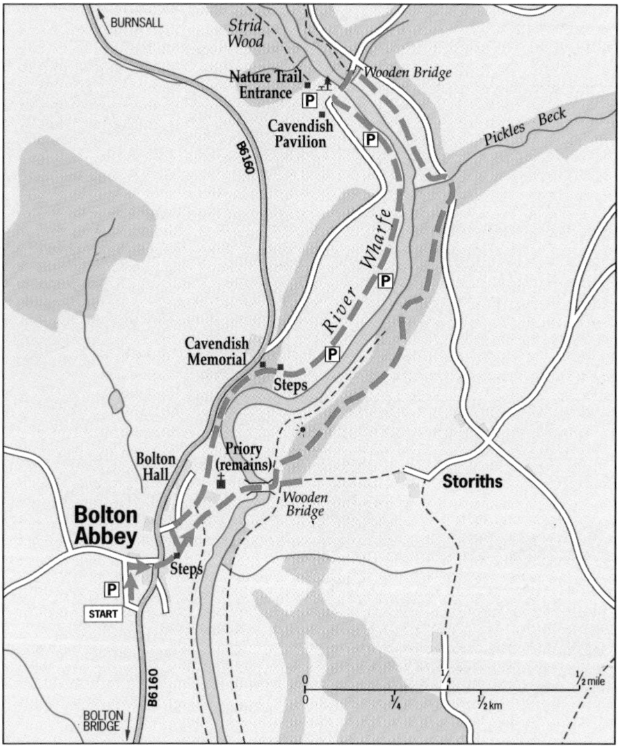


**What to look out for**

Trout can often be seen from the footbridge by the priory, and birdlife includes mallard, dippers and grey wagtails along the river, blue tits and chaffinches in the woods.

*Song thrush*

# Tarn Hows

**WALK 77**
CUMBRIA
SD322998

Tarn Hows is one of Lakeland's pearls. Its beauty is legendary: still waters reflecting tall stands of firs and larches and rocky islets topped by pines.

**Information**

The walk is just under two and a half miles long
Steep and stony path at first, then level around the lake
A few wicket gates
No refreshment facilities nearby
Picnics are possible anywhere, but the grassy slopes and headlands along the south shore are ideal

**START**
The walk starts from Glen Mary Bridge on the A593 between Skelwith Bridge and Coniston. There is a small car parking area among the trees on the east side of the road, just south of Glen Mary Bridge and Yew Tree Tarn – look out for National Trust signs 'Tom Gill' and 'Glen Mary' next to the pull-in.

**DIRECTIONS**
From the car park, cross the stream by the footbridge and turn right, along a stony path. Continue uphill on this path, through oak woodland with the tumbling gill to your right. The path bends round to the left. Several paths appear and disappear up the slope and it is not always easy to follow the right one, but this is not critical; keep heading up with the cleft of the gill just to your right. Eventually the path leads to a wicket gate. After this the ground begins to level off. The series of waterfalls is the Glen Mary Falls. Continue uphill with the stream still on your right. Soon the trees end and the path leads out on to the lake shore. Turn right along the wide track and go through the gate, then simply keep to the smaller gravelled path above the lake shore. The south side of the lake has open grassy places; these give way to birch groves and conifers in Rose Castle Plantation on the east side, whilst the north and west sides are heavily wooded with ornamental plantings of tall conifers. Keep to the main path. (For a challenging detour, a path to the right leads to the ridge of Tom Heights. This is the peak to the west of the lake and offers spectacular panoramic views.) The main path soon leaves the shore, but if you want to explore the marshy inlets there are side-paths which link up eventually with the main path again. Continue along the main path to the starting place just before the gill and the gate, then turn right to follow the path back through the wood.

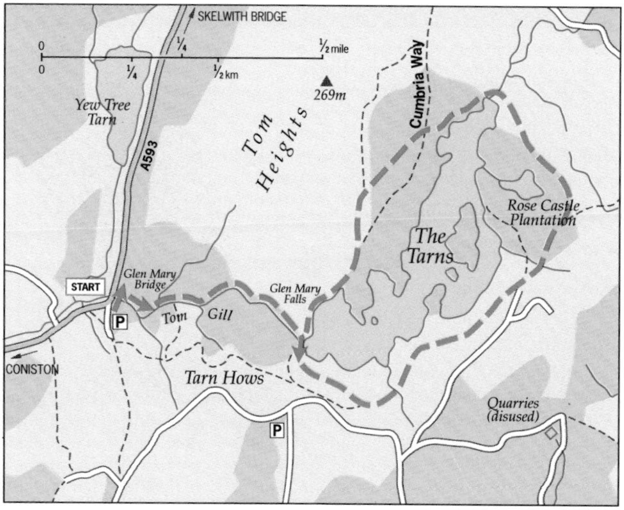


**Old Trees, New Trees**
The trees of the Lakeland

*Tarn Hows from Sawrey viewpoint*

valleys were once an important resource, managed in coppices and cut down to their bases every ten years or so to provide crops of sturdy poles. The poles were then used either to make bobbins in local factories or to make charcoal, the fuel needed to smelt iron. Although they were coppiced regularly the trees were never removed or killed. Trees have stood on this spot for at least 8,000 years. Some, such as the small-leaved limes which grow among the oaks close to the gill, are rare and are only found in ancient woods. The impressive stands of conifers around Tarn Hows were planted in Victorian times and have added greatly to the drama of the place.

### What to look out for

The pedunculate oak of southern England is replaced in the Lake District by the sessile oak. If you look carefully at the leaves you will see that they taper at the base and have a long stalk, unlike the southern oak which has lobes and a short stalk. Three species of bird – wood warbler, pied flycatcher and redstart – are summer breeding visitors to these woods.

# Discovering Ullswater

This delightful lakeside walk follows a rocky, undulating path through woods and pastures set below a craggy fellside. The path rounds several picturesque promontories before descending to a landing stage in the Howtown inlet, from where the lake steamer returns you to the start.

**WALK 78**
CUMBRIA
NY390169

**Information**

The walk is seven miles long
Boots and basic agility are required for the rough paths
Provisions and toilets in Glenridding
Perfect picnic spots on the rocky lakeside

*The 'Lady of the Lake'*

**START**
Glenridding village is on the A592, midway between Penrith and Windermere. Park in the public car park (charge) by the pier, and check return sailing times from Howtown before you set off. Lake steamers operate from Easter to October, but may be cancelled in rough weather (Glenridding Pier, tel: 017684 82229).

**DIRECTIONS**
Take the lakeside path south from the car park exit. Cross the main road and climb some steps to a path which, despite one more crossing, continues to parallel the road through trees. On pavements now, continue through Patterdale: 100yds beyond the church, turn left on the track to Side Farm.

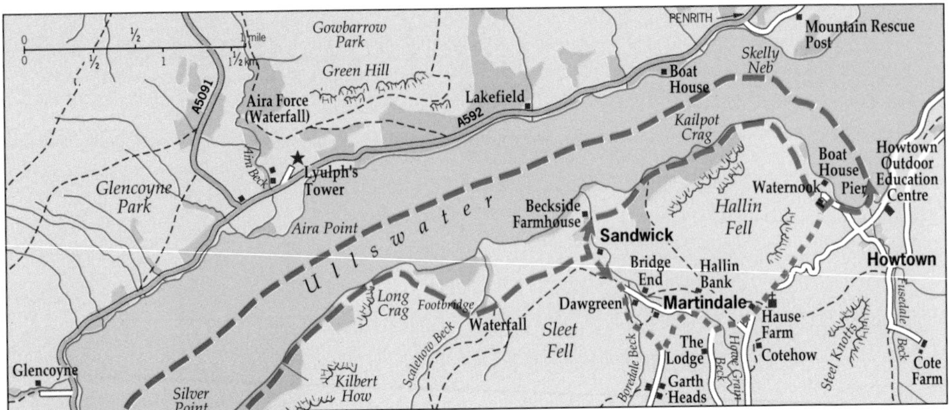


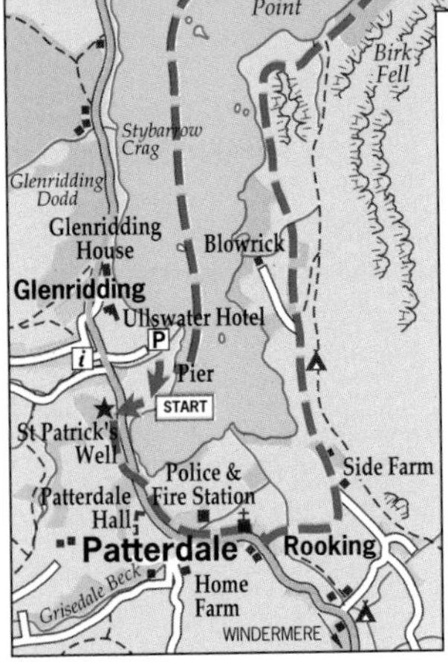


Turn left in the farmyard, signposted 'Lakeside path to Sandwick and Howtown', and follow a track beneath the rock-studded and bracken-clad fell. Ignore gated tracks forking left and lesser trails bearing off right.

Soon the track degenerates into a rough bridleway and brings a thrilling, sudden view of the lake before dipping and rising to Silver Point – an excellent picnic spot.

The rocky path undulates through woodland pitched steeply above the shore before veering away from the lake to bring a distant view to the right of Scalehow Force, an impressive waterfall in spate. Soon after, the path meets a lane: follow this down to the left, into the hamlet of Sandwick. (For an alternative route here, see * below.)

Faced by several gates at the lane end, take the furthest right and cross the beck, heading back to the lake shore. Beyond several field gates, the path creeps over bony tree roots in Hallinhag Wood to emerge at Geordie's Crag, another fine viewpoint. Children can be supervised as they explore the landward-facing rocks here, but keep them away from a dangerous slope overlooking the lake.

Continue circling Hallin Fell until 50yds beyond Waternook. Turn left here through a wall gate and descend steps to the shore of Howtown inlet. Follow the lakeside path and cross the footbridge to Howtown Pier, to catch the steamer back to Glenridding.

*Alternatively, turn right in Sandwick and follow the lane towards Martindale House and Boredale. At the junction turn sharp left, back towards Hallin Fell. Continue and keep left, to pass Martindale church on the right. Turn left just after the church onto a grassy track, to meet the main route at the wall gate.

**What to look out for**

Spared the bustle of Windermere, and flanked by attractive fells, Ullswater is the more peaceful and picturesque of the two largest stretches of water in the Lake District. The two steamers, *Lady of the Lake* and *Raven*, were built more than a hundred years ago and converted to run on diesel oil in the 1930s.

# Castle Eden Walkway

## WALK 79
CLEVELAND
NZ402243

An old railway line has been converted into more than a walkway and nature trail, and is a small paradise for children, with play areas, picnic sites and even a model railway.

### Information

The walk is about two and a half miles long
Mainly level, easy walking with one steep slope which can be avoided
Excellent for dogs
Countryside Warden service available at most times
Picnic sites but no refreshment facilities
Toilets close by (may be closed)

**START**
The walk starts at the car park of the Station House Visitor Centre at Thorpe Thewles, signed off the main A177 Stockton to Durham road.

**DIRECTIONS**
From the car park take the wooden gate at the exit, cross the hollow and walk up the steps on the other side to the station platform by the Visitor Centre. Turn right and follow the Castle Eden Walkway – a surfaced path along the old railway trackbed – for a little over ¾ mile, passing the entrance to the Nature Reserve.
Just past the third bridge turn left, go up the steps and at the top turn left again, crossing the bridge.
The path, signed 'Circular Route', enters a field and follows the field edge, curving round between a small group of trees before bending right to cross the fields. Continue to the right of more trees,

*The Station House centre*

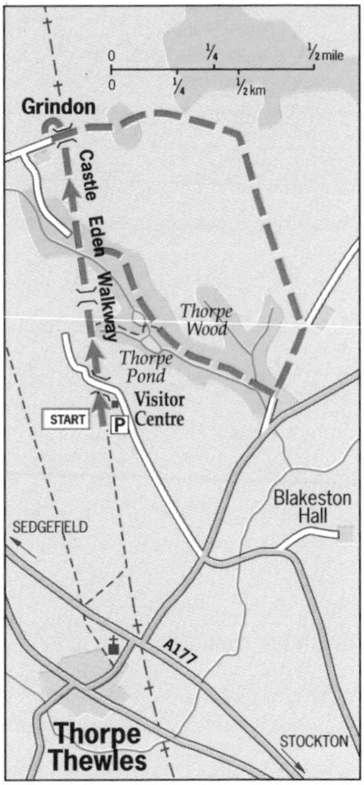


*On the route of the walkway.*

passing a sign 'Footpath Loop'. The path now descends alongside a hedge where the two tracks converge. Turn right, descending slightly, then turn right again opposite garage buildings to go through a wooden gate and enter Thorpe Wood (Nature Trail).

Continue along a surfaced path and pass Thorpe Pond. Where the path forks, keep straight ahead (or bear left to rejoin the railway path at an earlier point, avoiding the steep climb to come). Before a gate take a right fork up some steps and a short steep slope. Continue straight ahead past another gate. After a few yards the path bends left before going through a kissing-gate to rejoin the old trackbed. Turn left to return to the station and car park.

**What to look out for**

The railway embankments contain a wide range of butterfly species. Birdlife to be seen and heard includes mistle thrushes, coal and great tits, treecreepers, willow warblers, cuckoos, woodpeckers and birds of prey. Thorpe Pond has great crested newts, frogs, toads and dragonflies.
Wood anemones and bluebells (not for picking) flourish in the wood in spring, and giant bellflowers are at their best in July.

*Frog*

# Stanhope

**WALK 80**
CO DURHAM
NY995393

Weardale is one of the most attractive of the North Pennine valleys, criss-crossed by drystone walls, swathed in flower-rich meadows and pastures, and dotted all over with barns and farm cottages. Once the land of the Prince Bishops and heart of the lead-mining industry, this hotch-potch of history has turned a walk around the village of Stanhope into an adventure.

**START**
Stanhope is five miles west of Wolsingham on the A689. Park at the Durham Dales Centre, off the main road and just to the west of the Market Place.

**DIRECTIONS**
From the Centre turn left, along the pavement to the Market Place. Cross the road towards the Pack Horse Inn and bear left, down Butts Crescent. Before the river, turn left down The Butts beside a terrace of cottages, then cross a level crossing.

(Trains are few here, but take care.)
Follow the path across a pasture, away from the river, to a wicket gate. Go through the wicket gate and past some tall beech trees with a barn away to the right.
Cross the next field and go through another wicket gate, then over a sports field to meet the river and another level crossing. After the gates and crossing, follow the path over a meadow, with the river to your right. This leads to another wicket gate and out on to a side road.
Turn right along this quiet little road and cross a bridge over the river, then another bridge over the railway, and turn right along a metalled

*Below, stepping stones over the Wear, and left, St Thomas's Churchyard at Stanhope*

track through a caravan park. At the end of the caravan park, beyond some old cottages, continue straight on, over a stile and along a woodland path with the river down to your right.

After the wood the path bears right, downhill and beside a wall. Turn left at the end of the wall and follow the path between a fence and a row of trees, over the crossing, then beside tennis courts and another fence with meadows to the left.

Go over a stile and past the buildings of Unthank Mill, with the river now beside you on the right. Follow the riverside track, past a bridge (which can be used as an alternative route across the river if it is in flood) and on to the ford, crossing via the impressive stepping stones. Walk up the road and turn right just after the playing field, following a metalled track with the walls of Castle Park on the left and the river on the right. On reaching The Butts, turn left to return to the Market Place and Durham Dales Centre.

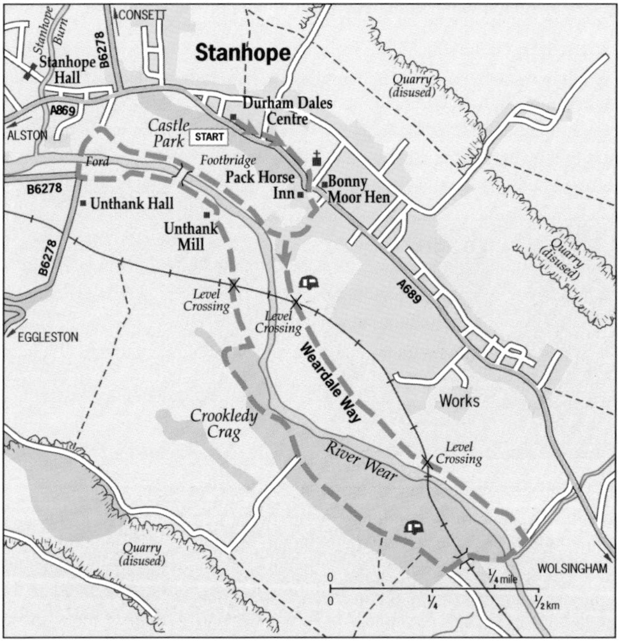


## What to look out for

There are some interesting buildings along the walk, including Stanhope Hall and Unthank Mill. The Butts was the archery range, dating back to the days when practice was compulsory. The Bonny Moor Hen still has the cellar where poachers were imprisoned. Woodland flowers along the walk include primroses, bluebells and cowslips, at their best in May.

### The Battle of Stanhope

In the early of the 19th century many of the Pennine lead-mining towns resembled the wild west; the law was not always easy to enforce and local villains were often treated as heroes.

The story goes that one night in 1818, a gang of miners were caught poaching on the Bishop of Durham's land. They were brought to Stanhope and imprisoned overnight in the cellar of what was then called the Black Bull Inn. However, a rescue party of miners attacked the keepers and there was a brief and bloody fight. In the struggle, the miners got clean away.

The Bonny Moor Hen, on the site of the Black Bull, is named after the red grouse that the miners were poaching.

## Information

The walk is just over four miles long

Mainly level, but with a descent in the town and an ascent up the wooded bank beyond

Several wicket gates

Stepping stone crossing of the river best undertaken in dry conditions; can be avoided by using the bridge downstream

Stanhope has a full range of facilities and places to eat

# Hadrian's Wall

**WALK 81**
NORTHUMBERLAND
NY713666

This walk, though fairly short, takes in a spectacular section of Hadrian's Wall, with splendid views stretching away to the east over Windshields Crag, its highest point. We return along the Roman Military Way.

**START**
The starting point of the walk is 14 miles west of Hexham. From the B6318 'Military Road' take the unclassified road, signposted 'Whiteside', leading north, opposite the Milecastle Inn. In one mile reach the Northumberland National Park car park by the lake at the reclaimed Cawfields Quarry Picnic Site.

**DIRECTIONS**
Leave the car park on the path alongside the lake, heading east, with Hadrian's Wall rising up on the ridge ahead. (The water may look inviting on a warm day, but heed the warning notices – it is not safe to swim.)
Turn right after the first kissing-gate, go through

*At Cawfields Crag*

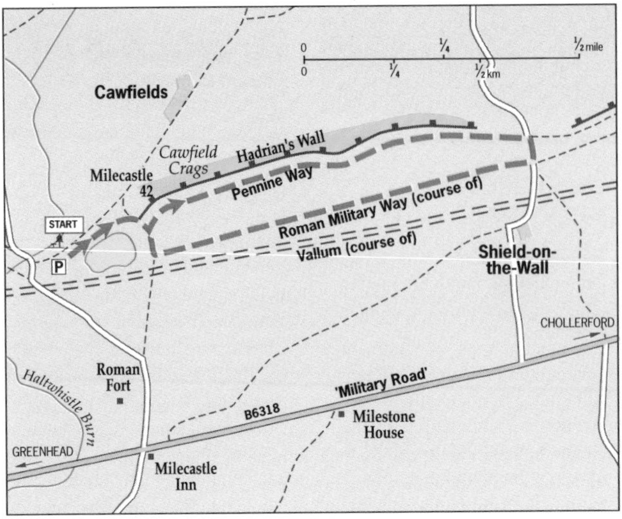


## Information

The walk is just under two miles long
Good grassy paths; steepish climb and descent alongside the wall, but gentler return route
A few stiles and kissing-gates
Dogs must be kept on leads
Pub three quarters of a mile from the start serves bar meals
Picnic site near the car park and several good spots along the route

another and join the Pennine Way as it bears left uphill beside the wall. Milecastle 42 lies at the foot of the slope, and the highest point of the walk comes after a short steep pull 500yds later.

Descend, keeping near the wall. Go through a kissing-gate, and turn right on to a tarmac road. In a few yards cross a stile over the wall on the right. Go straight across the field and over the ladder stile opposite, then follow the straight green path, the course of the Roman Military Way. This heads directly towards a small pointed hill, the other side of which is the face of the quarry.

At its foot, turn right and continue, to rejoin the outward route at the gate below the Milecastle. From there go back past the lake to the car park.

### An Outpost of the Empire

The remarkable construction of a defensive wall from coast to coast, built by the Romans under the rule of Hadrian, has a world-wide reputation. The part within Northumberland National Park, utilising the natural defences of the crags of the Whin Sill, is the most dramatic and best preserved. On all sides there are wide open views of a wild countryside which is not very different now from how it must have looked in those days.

It speaks volumes for the military authority and the organisation of the Roman Empire that such a 'boundary wall' could be conceived and implemented over many decades, then garrisoned and defended for nearly 400 years at such a distance from the seat of power in Rome.

*Heather flowers*

## What to look out for

In the summer months the rocky ground produces a fine display of flowers; thyme and common rock-rose are a particular feature. There are also wild chives, possibly introduced by the Romans as a culinary herb.

Meadow pipits are among the few small birds that thrive in this harsh terrain. Among livestock, tough breeds like black Galloway cattle and Scottish Blackface sheep predominate, well able to cope with hard winters and sparse grazing.

# Balcary Cliff Tops

**WALK 82**
DUMFRIES & GALLOWAY
NX821495

This is an invigorating walk across the cliff tops of the Solway coastline, an area rich in ornithological interest. The views take in the beautiful Galloway Hills, an offshore island and the distant peaks of the Lake District. Care must be taken on the cliffs.

### START

Balcary Bay is part of Auchencairn Bay on the Solway Firth and lies about two miles south-east of the Galloway village of Auchencairn, on the A711 Dumfries to Kirkcudbright road. Start the walk from the car park opposite the Balcary Bay Hotel.

### DIRECTIONS

Follow the road from the car park round past the holiday homes to the left and take the signposted track for Balcary Point and Rascarrel. Turn left after passing through the wooden kissing-gate near the house and walk along the edge of the field to another kissing-gate which takes you through a small copse along a gravel path. Continue through the copse and fork right where you can see a derelict lifeboat station below on the left. Proceed through bracken and gorse to Balcary Point, where there are excellent views of the huge, sharp rocks and the dramatic seascapes beyond.

Follow the path through the metal kissing-gate, down from Lot's Wife to Rascarrel Bay (about a mile) with a dry-stone wall on the right. Continue down to and along the shoreline across stones. Walk behind the holiday homes at Rascarrel Bay and take the path to the right, passing through two wooden kissing-gates, parallel to Rascarrel Moss Plantation. At Loch Mackie pass through another kissing-gate and turn right, following the edge of the field with a wall on your right. Continue alongside the wall (the path here can be very muddy). Pass through a gate next to a derelict farm cottage and continue along a farm track (with fine views of the Galloway Hills of Bengairn and Screel).

Return to the car park down the farm track, past a house on the right.

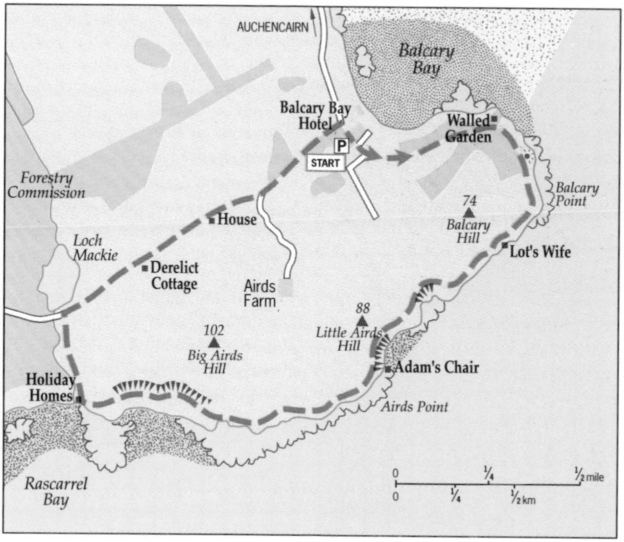


### Information

The walk is three and a half miles long
Hilly, and very muddy in places
No stiles, but several kissing-gates
Hotel at Balcary Bay

## What to look out for

From the cliffs above Balcary Point there is a superb view out to Hestan Island, to Auchencairn Bay and even across the Solway Firth to the peaks of the Lake District. The area, part of a Site of Special Scientific Interest, is noted for its colonies of sea birds. Look out for cormorants, razorbills, kittiwakes, fulmar and guillemots around the Balcary Heughs. Hestan Island has breeding Arctic terns, as well as oystercatchers, rock pipits and ringed plover; all are present between May and July. Loch Mackie, fringed by willow carr, birch and reeds, supports a host of colourful dragonflies between May and September.

*Black-headed gull*

### Smugglers' Haunts

The Balcary Bay hotel was built by Manx smugglers in the year 1625 as a trysting-place for freebooters. It was the headquarters of the smuggling syndicate of Clark, Crain and Quirk, and was raided by Customs Inspector General Reid in 1777. A private house until 1948, it then became a hotel, and still has secret underground chambers with walls five feet thick and doors opening onto the sea. Along the coast is Adam's Chair, a natural rock seat which was once the haunt of a notorious smuggler who used a lantern up here to guide smugglers' vessels to shore.

### Hestan Island

This island, now a wildlife sanctuary, is accessible only at low tide and has caves once used as hiding-places for contraband whisky and brandy.

The island was immortalised as 'Isle Rathan' by Samuel Rutherford Crockett in his novel *The Raiders*. Once worked by copper-miners, it is also the site of a manor-house built in the 14th century for Edward Balliol.

*The cliffs at Balcary*

# WALK 83
DUMFRIES & GALLOWAY
NY192668

# *The River Annan*

### Information

The walk is three and a half miles long
Level, easy ground
About three quarters of a mile of road walking
A few stiles
Blue Bell Inn serves snacks, but does not allow children
Plenty of cafés and ice-cream shops in Annan
Picnic area near car park

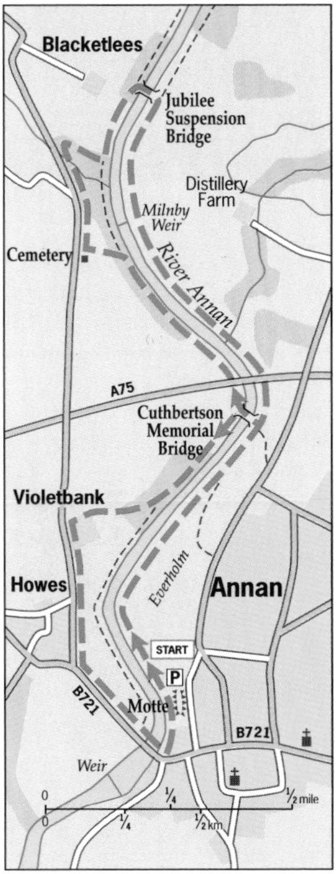


This is an easy and very popular walk along the wooded banks of the River Annan. The river is noted for its wildlife and for the number of deciduous trees which line its banks.

**START**
Annan is off the A75 Gretna to Stranraer road, 17 miles north-west of Carlisle, and the same distance from Dumfries. The walk starts from the Everholm car park, just outside the town, next to the Motte.

**DIRECTIONS**
Follow the riverside path on the edge of the Everholm playing fields. Go through the gate at the end of the path, where it becomes a rough track. Follow the track, pass through a kissing-gate and continue down to the Cuthbertson Memorial Bridge. Cross the footbridge and turn right. Proceed along the riverbank passing under the road bridge until you come to a footbridge.
Turn left up the steps onto a path which leads to the cemetery. There is a seat about 50yds from the steps. Cross the metal stile into the cemetery. Go straight ahead across the cemetery to the left side of the gatehouse. Turn right at the main gate along quiet Brydekirk Road, through a wood and turn right at the old bridge. Go down to the river again, turn left and follow the path at edge of the field to reach Jubilee Suspension Bridge. Cross and turn right to continue back along the river. Cross a stile at the edge of the field. Cross Cuthbertson Bridge again and turn left along the river, later taking the track up to Violetbank on the Brydekirk road.
Turn left and follow the road to the outskirts of Annan. Turn left immediately after the Blue Bell Inn to return to the car park.

**The Everholm**
The nearest thing that Annan has to a public park is The Everholm playing field and sports complex. The athletics track was opened by Steve Ovett, who lives nearby, and the centre has hosted a number of international athletics meetings.
The complex also has a rugby pitch, gym and conditioning room, outdoor table-tennis (during the summer) and a putting-green. There is a trim-track with a number of wooden exercise aids, such as monkey bars and leap-frog.

**The Annan Bridges**
The metal Cuthbertson Bridge, recently upgraded, was built as a memorial to Captain William Graham Cuthbertson and to the men

*Beside the River Annan*

and women of Annan who gave their lives during World War II. It provides an ideal point from which to watch the bird life on and around the river.

The Jubilee Suspension Bridge is an even finer vantage point, providing a panoramic view to the north, taking in the small wooded islet which splits the Annan in two and is known by the locals as 'Rabbit Island'.

**What to look out for**

The River Annan is noted for the number of grey herons which roost nearby. They can often be spotted perched on top of Milnby Weir between the two footbridges. Red-breasted mergansers and goosanders are also common along the river from April to July, and you may see the occasional kingfisher. The wooded stretch near what used to be Milnby Weir has one of the district's biggest rookeries.

The Motte is Annan's only 'ancient monument', now overgrown with deciduous trees, which historians say was the site of a castle built by the ancestors of Robert the Bruce.

*Yellow loosestrife*

# Harestanes Visitor Centre, Jedburgh

This is a satisfying walk through mature woodlands and along the quiet River Teviot and is one of four colour-coded walks ranging from one to four miles in length. The attractions include a dovecote, a clock tower and a fine visitor centre.

**WALK 84**
BORDERS
NT649247

**Information**

The walk is two and a half miles long
No road walking
A few stiles
Shop and tearoom at visitor centre

**START**
The Harestanes Visitor Centre is at Monteviot, three miles north of Jedburgh at the junction of the A68 and B6400. Start at the courtyard at the rear of centre.

**DIRECTIONS**
This walk is the one marked with blue waymarkers and is called 'The Doocot Walk'. Follow the path alongside the entrance drive past estate sawmills. Turn right at the top of the drive, through mixed woodland, past the old cricket pavilion towards the footbridge. Turn right and cross the footbridge over the Marble Burn. Continue until the paths divide, turning left and keeping to the path near the edge of the wood. At the

*At the Woodland Centre*

tarmac drive enter the woodland opposite by bearing left when crossing the drive. Turn right and follow a track across a stile and along the edge of the field. To your right along this path you will see the clock tower of the old stables. On reaching the woodland at the riverside, turn left and follow the path past the Doocot and over the old mill lade to the viewing platform on the River Teviot (view of Monteviot Suspension Bridge). Retrace your steps to the Marble Burn and go straight on, passing the pond on your right. The path then leaves the track and leads down to the burn. Turn right to walk alongside the tarmac track towards the Visitor Centre (look out for traffic near buildings). At the road junction turn right to return to the start point.

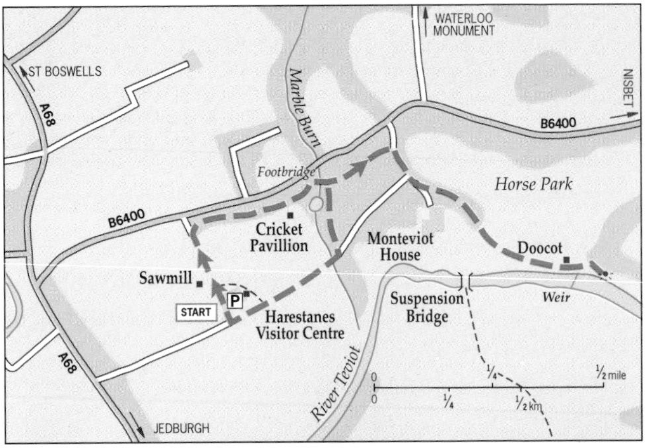

*The historic dovecote*

## The Waterloo Monument

The Waterloo Monument stands on Peniel Heugh, the site of an Iron Age fort. It is dedicated to the Duke of Wellington and the British Army and was erected in 1815 by the sixth Marquis of Lothian. The tower collapsed in the following year, and its replacement was eventually capped in timber in 1867. The wooden top is now rotting and, therefore, unsafe.

## The Doocot

Pigeons, or 'doos', used to be a valuable source of food in times of scarcity, and they were bred by landowners from the 16th century onwards in doocots (dovecotes). The doocot on this walk stands on a rise to the left of the path next to the river. The lower part dates from the 17th century. It is about 20 feet in diameter and is lined inside with stone nesting-boxes for hundreds of pigeons. Because it is in a dangerous condition, the doocot is not accessible to the public.

### What to look out for

The theme of the centre, based on the old home farm of a large country estate, is the use of wood. Needless to say, the woodland contains many species, both native and introduced. Next to the old mill lade on the River Teviot there is a magnificent purpose-built viewing platform, from where you can observe the area's many birds such as coal tits, buzzards and jackdaws.

The line of Dere Street, the old Roman Road from Newsteads to Corbridge, can be seen beyond the river.

# Hailes Castle and Traprain Law

**WALK 85**
LOTHIAN
NT592772

This walk takes you through the pleasantly rolling East Lothian countryside and touches on various aspects of the history of the area over the last 3000 years.

**Information**

The walk is about six miles long
Walking includes rough, narrow tracks which can be soft and muddy
Some road walking on quiet lanes – children and dogs should be under control
The climb to the summit of Traprain Law is steep but worth the effort
Cafés and pubs in East Linton

START
East Linton is 25 miles east of Edinburgh. Turn off the A1 into East Linton; just after passing under the railway bridge, turn left again into the village centre. There is ample parking in the village centre.

DIRECTIONS
From the village centre retrace your steps but instead of turning right under the railway bridge, turn left past the Red Lion Hotel, to cross the River Tyne on the 16th-century bridge which once carried the great mail road between Edinburgh and London. Turn right at Lauder Place to pass under the railway, and go up to the A1. The A1 can be very busy, so cross over with great care, and follow signs to Hailes Castle along the quiet, narrow road known as Brae Heads Loan. This road passes high above the River Tyne which flows through a deep valley below and gives excellent views west over the rolling countryside.
Just before reaching Hailes Castle, opposite the lay-by marked as parking for visitors to the castle, turn left up the lane. This is a well worn but rough track barred in places by gates which can be climbed or circumnavigated. The track winds its way between arable fields and rough ground eventually joining a minor road. Turn left onto this road; carry on past the first gate and stile on to the Law, to another gate and stile 200yds on, where there are some information boards – well worth reading before you start your ascent. The zig-zag path to the summit of Traprain Law is waymarked but leaves a lot to common sense. At the top take time to catch your breath and enjoy the views. Retrace your steps down the hill, and take the same track back to Hailes Castle. This walk in the opposite direction offers a whole new range of views to East Linton and beyond.

*Hailes Castle, once a medieval stronghold*

Pass Hailes Castle on the left, and head back along Brae Heads Loan for about 50 yards. Take the narrow path left, leading down towards the river, and cross via the wooden foot bridge.

Follow the rough path along the north bank of the river. The path is clearly defined: there is one stile and a series of wooden steps to overcome where the river passes through a steep, rocky gorge.

The path continues under the A1 and then passes along the edge of a garden before emerging into the village of East Linton, where you can return to the start point.

**What to look out for**

Although this area is heavily farmed there are still many hedges and small copses and patches of rough ground where a wide variety of wildlife can be found. The slopes of Traprain Law are particularly rich in plant life, and in spring the banks of the Tyne are carpeted in snowdrops, to be followed by wild daffodils.

**Hailes Castle**

This 13th–14th-century castle was built by the Earls of Dunbar, and then became a stronghold of the Gourlay family before passing to the Hepburns. James Hepburn, the Earl of Bothwell, brought Mary, Queen of Scots here in 1567. The castle was partially destroyed in 1650 by Cromwell's troops.

*The view from the castle*

**Traprain Law**

This great mound of volcanic rock rises to a height of over 700 feet. The summit was the site of a late Bronze Age settlement protected by turf ramparts. In about 700BC more substantial stone ramparts were built. Later it became the capitol of the Votadini tribe which ruled much of the Lothians and Borders around the time of the Roman occupation. The site came to prominence in the early part of this century when a horde of over 100 pieces of Roman silver was discovered.

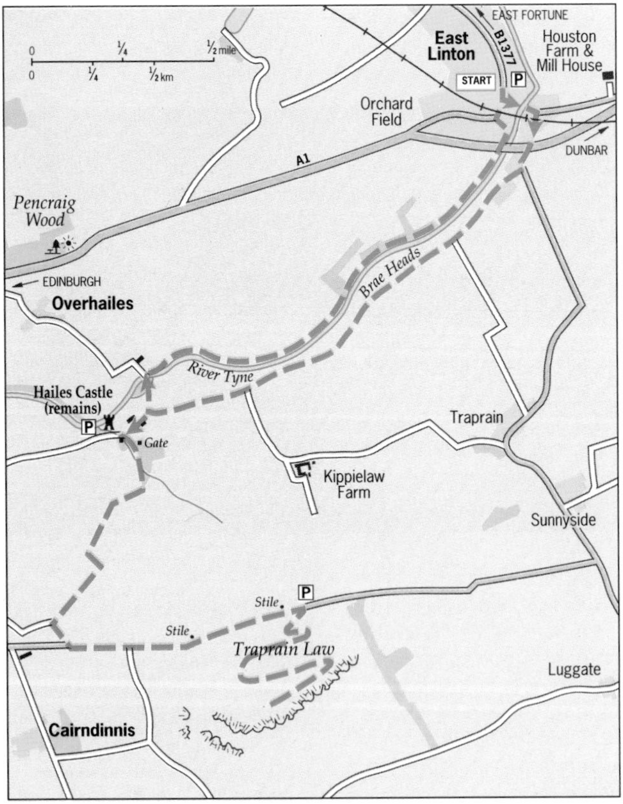

# The Pentland Hills

**WALK 86**
LOTHIAN
NT233631

An exhilarating hill walk only a few miles from Edinburgh, between two picturesque reservoirs in the Pentland Hills. The walk afford s spectacular views, as well as the chance to see a variety of plants and birds.

**START**
Park at the Flotterstone Visitor Information Centre. This is just off the A702, south of Edinburgh; turn right at the Flotterstone Inn and drive past the inn for about 100yds to reach the Visitor Centre and car park.

**DIRECTIONS**
From the Visitor Centre take the path through the woods,

**Information**

The walk is nine miles long and climbs about 450ft
Stout footwear is essential
Dogs should be kept on a lead
The Flotterstone Inn serves bar meals
Picnic area, barbecue facility and children's play area at Visitor Centre
Toilets at Visitor Centre

*Glencorse Reservoir*

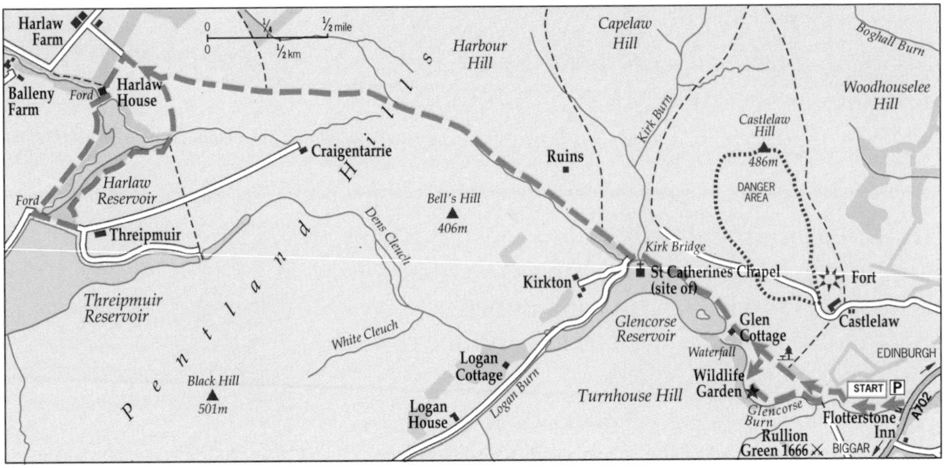


which runs parallel with and eventually joins the road. Carry on along the road, passing the firing range to your right and a wood and Glen Cottage to your left. About 1/2 mile after Glen Cottage the road curves left and crosses a stone bridge. Shortly after this bridge turn right through a gate (signposted 'Balerno, Currie and Colinton').

Follow this path up the hill. At the fork bear left (signposted to Currie and Balerno) and continue along this path, passing a ruined cottage to your right. When you reach the wall, cross using the stone stile and follow the path as it curves left and proceeds downhill to reach a gate. Cross the stile and go straight on (for 'Balerno'). Cross another stile and proceed along the edge o f a field. Follow the path as it curves left and shortly meets another path. Turn right onto this path.

Just before the metal gate turn left onto a tarmac road. Follow the road as it curves left, towards a house. Immediately past the house turn right. Cross the ford using the metal footbridge, and carry on along the path. Cross another ford and turn left , and follow the path through the wood, with the wall to your right. After about 200yds turn left and continue along the path around the edge of Thriepmuir Reservoir. When eventually you reach a wooden stile cross the wall. Turn left, cross another stile, and continue along the track, with a fence to your left. At a wooden post on your left turn right. Retrace your steps to Glen Cottage. Shortly beyond Glen Cottage, at the edge of the wood, turn right. Follow this path down through the wood and round a left curve. On your right you will see a Wildlife Garden and tree nursery. Carry on along the path until it rejoins the road and retrace your steps to the car park.

**Glencorse Reservoir**

The reservoir, built in 1822, contains the submerged remains of St Catherine's Chapel, a 13th-century chapel built by Sir William St Clair of Roslin.

The path through Maiden's Cleuch was an old drove road leading from Balerno and Currie to a sheep market at House o' Muir, just south of Flotterstone.

**What to look out for**

Birds that may be seen include red grouse, curlew, skylark and golden plover, and waterfowl such as goosander, tufted duck and geese.

Look out for the spectacular waterfall to your right just before the path curves left towards the Wildlife Garden.

# Strathclyde Country Park

**WALK 87**
STRATHCLYDE
NS733570

This is a satisfying walk along even paths, through scrubland which is brimming with wildlife. Along the way are views of a lovely loch and a little bit of Roman history.

**Information**

The walk is just over two miles long
Mostly even ground, with some hilly sections
No stiles
No pub; cafeteria close by (seasonal)
Good picnic places all along the walk

**START**

The country park, 1,650 acres which is split by the M74, is in the Clyde Valley between Hamilton and Motherwell, about ten miles south of Glasgow. Leave the M74 at junction 6 and follow signs on the A723. The walk starts from the Sandy Beach car park at the south-eastern edge of Strathclyde Loch.

*The Roman fort*

**DIRECTIONS**

From the car park cross the road, turn left and continue uphill along the pavement. At the first junction, after a row of houses on the right, turn left back downhill across the road. Continue along the path with Viewpoint car park on your right. Pass picnic tables and walk downhill through scrubland towards the loch. Keep right at the first junction, continue down and cross a footbridge. After the second footbridge, veer left into the open ground along the edge of the loch (several seats along here with good views).
Continue along the loch until the path swings right and takes you along the bank of the South Calder River. Visit the Roman Bath House here,

**What to look out for**

Strathclyde Park was the site of a Roman fort and the remains of their bath house is an attraction.
Watch for stonechats and linnets in the scrub; their song is especially noticeable in spring.

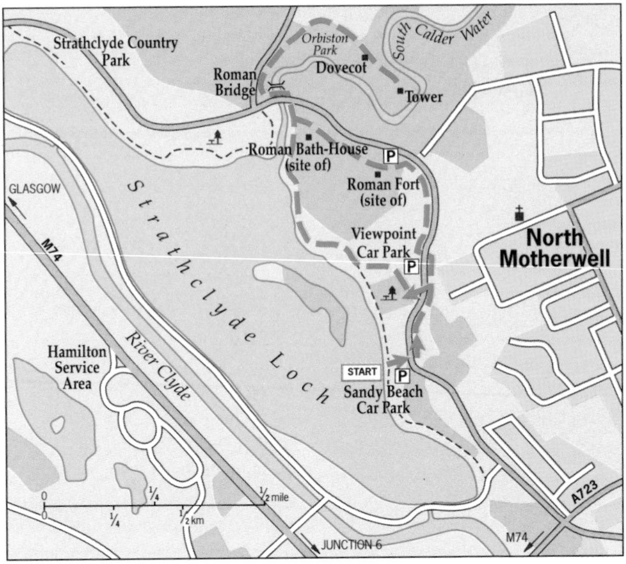


then cross Spine Road to see 'Roman Bridge' (actually of 18th-century construction). Return to the pavement and turn right towards the north of the park.

Take the path before Orbiston Spur to visit Orbiston Park. Walking past the swings with the golf course on your left, continue straight ahead at the junction and proceed downhill for about 80yds, taking a narrow path on the right into the woods to find the remains of Orbiston Tower. Retrace your steps to the swings and back downhill to Spine Road, turning left to rejoin the main route.

After a short distance cross over into scrubland again. Take the path between the Bath House and the road and follow it past the site of the Roman fort, past Viewpoint car park. The path now runs alongside the road. Follow the path across the road, turn right and continue back down to the starting point beside the loch.

**Roman Bath House and Fort**

The hill on the eastern side of Strathclyde Loch is the site of a Roman fort. Only faint traces remain, but in its day it would have housed a garrison of around 500 troops.

The bath house, discovered in 1973, would have been a kind of Turkish bath for the soldiers, to soothe away the stresses of life on the frontier.

**Orbiston Park**

The park is centred on the remains of Orbiston Tower or Castle. Historians are baffled about who occupied it, but evidence shows that they ate well. Mussel-beds were kept for the table, there is a dovecote nearby, where some 400 pigeons would have been bred for food, and there is a solidly-constructed ice house.

*A view across the loch*

**WALK 88**
STRATHCLYDE
NS428863

# The Banks of Loch Lomond

**Information**

The walk is about three and a half miles long
Quiet roads and paths
A few stiles
Dogs are not allowed in the nature reserve so are best left behind
Pub and café in Gartocharn
Toilets in Gartocharn

Loch Lomond is famed for its beautiful scenery and excellent wildlife. This walk crosses fields and goes along quiet lanes to reach a secluded corner of the loch.

**START**
The village of Gartocharn is on the A811, three miles north of Balloch and 20 miles north-west of Glasgow. At the public toilets turn left if coming from Balloch (right if coming from Drymen), then turn right past the police station. There is a small parking area by the church.

**DIRECTIONS**
Walk past the church and turn left down the track immediately past the community centre. Go through a gate and walk down the field, keeping the

*The view over the loch*

hedge on your right. Further down there are sections of boardwalk. Reach a small stream and turn right through a kissing-gate, keeping the stream on your left.

Turn left through another gate and cross the stream by a sleeper-bridge. Turn right, then left at the junction. In about 100yds there is a post box. Turn right here, signed 'Private Road'.

Go round two bends and at a junction continue straight ahead signed 'Nature Reserve' (good view of Duncryne, the hill above Gartocharn, on the right). At the next junction fork left and, keeping left, follow the track to the loch shore. Pass through a gate and go right with the track (this part can be muddy) and at the reserve take the left-hand gate.

Follow the footpath through

*Near Loch Lomond*

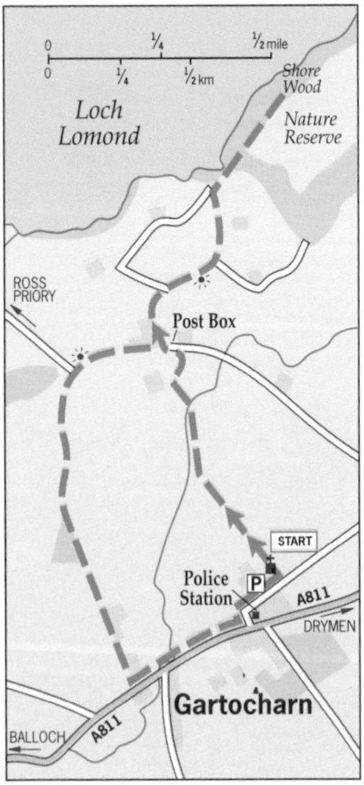


Shore Wood as far as the second stile. Retrace your steps from this point as far as the post box in the road. Turn right here and follow this road. The first two houses are Townhead of Aber and Aber Cottage ('aber' means estuary, and is found in Welsh as well as Scottish placenames). The road curves round past Ross Priory, an outstation of Strathclyde University, and gives a fine view back over the loch and its islands. Continue along the road for about ¼ mile. At the main road turn left, then left again at the public toilets to return to the start point.

**Loch Lomond**

This is the largest sheet of inland water in Britain and is over 23 miles long. The southern part is broad with a number of islands – from the walk you can see at least five. The wooded island called Inchcailloch ('the old woman's island') can be visited by boat from Balmaha on the east side of the loch. The islands are on the Highland Boundary Fault, which continues eastwards over Conic Hill, seen from the loch shore. The whole Loch Lomond area is now a Regional Park.

**Shore Wood**

The wood is part of the Loch Lomond National Nature Reserve, which also includes the islands, and is carefully managed to maintain its character and conserve the wildlife and the fine trees. The woodland has a rare atmosphere of great tranquillity, and in spring the floor of the wood is a rich carpet of bluebells.

**What to look out for**

The lake is a good area for birds – black-headed gulls and teal are found in summer, and look for parties of whooper swans and goldeneye in winter. Loch Lomond dock has its only British site here.

# The Fairy Hill

## WALK 89

CENTRAL
NN518003

**Information**

The walk is about one and a half miles long
Good paths and tracks to follow
No stiles
Dogs should be kept on leads until away from the houses
Inns, cafés, toilets and a tourist information centre may be found in Aberfoyle

This is a short walk to the top of a hill long associated with fairies, passing through pleasant woodland along the way. On the busiest summer weekend, when Aberfoyle is full of visitors, you may well find yourself alone up here.

**START**

From the A821/B829 junction in Aberfoyle, turn down Manse Road to cross the infant River Forth to a small parking area by the side of the road at Balleich.

**DIRECTIONS**

From the parking area follow the 'Fairy Trail' markers along a road which soon becomes a track leading to Doon Hill (good views of Aberfoyle, the forests and the former quarry above the village). Continue past a low wooden barrier and at a track junction go straight on.

In a further 70yds or so turn left on to the hill, following little toadstool signs. The path winds up the hill, passing lichen-covered boulders.

At a junction near the top, go right as indicated and climb up to the summit to find a cleared area. The tall pine tree is said to be the spirit of Robert Kirk.

Follow the toadstool markers off the hill and curve round with the path as it weaves through the woods, eventually depositing you on a side track. Turn left and in 50yds regain the outward route to retrace your steps to the parking area.

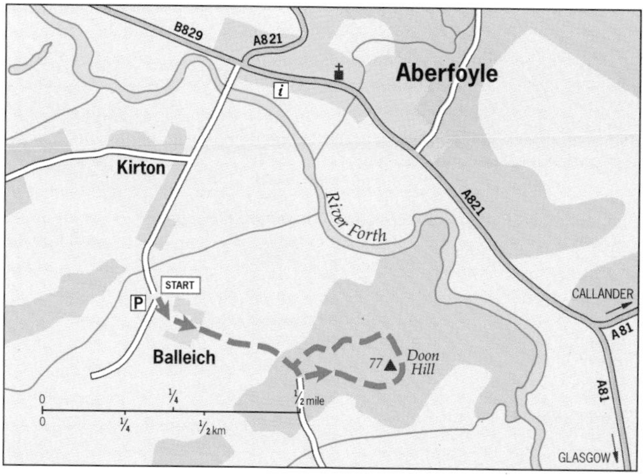


**The Man the Fairies Stole**

The Reverend Robert Kirk practised his ministry in these parts in the latter part of the 17th century. A Gaelic scholar, he was very interested in stories of the 'little folk' and it is said that he managed to gain communication with them, learning many of their secret ways and lore.

However, he could not resist broadcasting this information and his book, *The Secret Commonwealth of Elves, Fauns and Fairies* was published in

1691. The little people were, understandably, extremely annoyed at his betrayal of their trust, so while he was out walking on Doon Hill they spirited him away and he was never seen alive again. He did appear once at a relative's funeral, crying out that if a knife was thrown over his head, he would become flesh again, but his relatives and friends hesitated and the chance was lost forever.

*The wooded slopes of Doon Hill*

*A toadstool signpost*

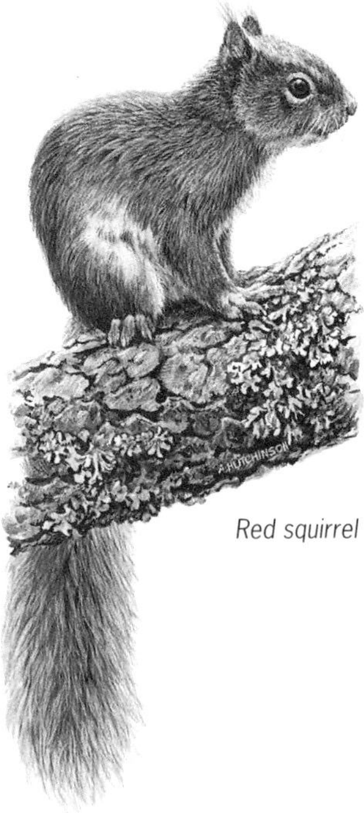

Red squirrel

**What to look out for**

Apart from the possibility of fairies, less fanciful residents of the woods to look out for include squirrels and roe deer, and woodland birds such as great tits, coal tits and nuthatches. Wood warblers are summer visitors.

# From Coalmine to Country Park

## WALK 90
FIFE
NT171961

### Information

The walk is about two and a half miles long
Mixed ground with good paths or tracks
No stiles
Dogs must be kept on leads
The visitor centre has displays and interesting leaflets
Café at visitor centre
Plenty of picnic tables, both by loch and in pit wheel area
Toilets at visitor centre

This walk in Fife is in a figure-of-eight, taking in the shores of an attractive man-made loch, an old cultivated area and the big wheel of the former pit.

**START**
Lochore Meadows Country Park is about four miles north of Cowdenbeath on the B920, accessed from either junction 3 or 4 of the M90 north of Edinburgh via the Forth Road Bridge. The entrance to the park is at Crosshill, between Lochgelly and Ballingry. The walk starts at the Visitor Centre.

**DIRECTIONS**
For the first loop, walk down towards the sailing club (The Lodge) and turn left on to a path to pass behind the building and its car park. The path swings left beside the outflow burn from the loch. Turn right over the bridge and at the far end turn right again. Go through a gate on to the Clune. Walk along the shore and continue round a small inlet. Scramble up on to the rocky knoll (with excellent views across the loch and its islands).
Drop down on the west side of the knoll and turn right on the lochside path to rejoin the outward route back to the Visitor Centre.
For the second loop, walk up the main path from the Visitor Centre northwards to the huge pit wheel of the former Mary Pit and the nearby colliery locomotive. Turn left, pass through a gate and turn left on to the rough road and walk along to the riding stables.
Just past the stables, turn left on a path fringing woodland back to the lochside. Turn left again and walk round the loch to the visitor centre.

**Lochore Meadows**
The country park has been reclaimed from former mining ground and now offers a range of recreational facilities including watersports, horse riding, golf and a 'trim trail'. Countryside events are also a regular feature.

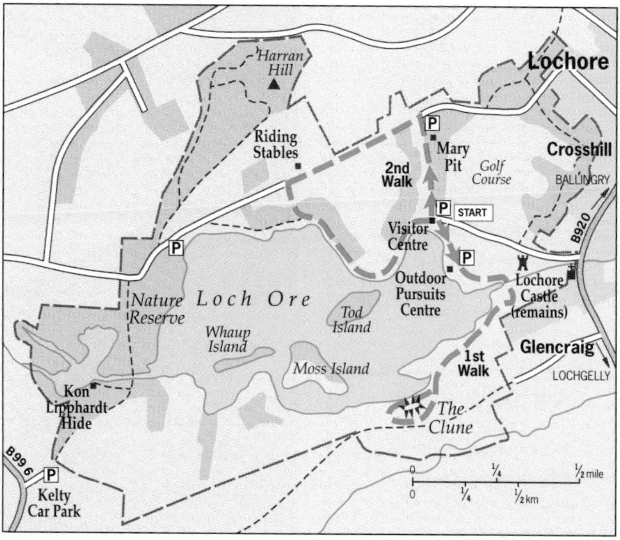

**Mary Pit**

At one time 350 men worked here, mining the coal deep under the ground; another 2,000 worked in pits near by. The mine-shaft was over 2,000 feet deep, beneath what is now the golf course. The colliery locomotive, called a 'pug', came from the former Michael Pit near Kirkcaldy.

*Around lovely Lochore*

At the heart of the park is Loch Ore, surrounded by woodland and open areas. The area south of the loch is on the 'Breaking the Ground' trail (leaflet from the visitor centre), which shows how the area was inhabited and cultivated centuries ago. The ring of stones on Clune Craig may be the remains of a hillfort.

**What to look out for**

The loch has water birds such as coots, mallards and tufted ducks, all year round, and these are quite commonly seen. However, in winter there are many more species to observe on the water here – goosander, scaup and long-tailed ducks are among the more unusual of these. The woodland is also home to many birds and small mammals. Watch out for flocks of siskins and redpolls during the winter months.

# A Ramble on the Lomond Hills

**WALK 91**
FIFE
NO253075

A moderately energetic walk to the summit of East Lomond Hill, site of a prehistoric fort, starting from the delightful village of Falkland.

**START**
The car park in Falkland, situated near the centre of the village, is signposted from the A912.

**DIRECTIONS**
Leave the car park at the entrance, passing the public toilets to your right. Turn left at the T-junction, then almost immediately right, up Horse Market. At the end of the street turn left. Go straight on at the crossroads, signposted `Footpath to Lomond Hills' and proceed up the road and onto the gravel track. At the fork bear right, and after about 50yds turn left, up the wooden steps.
Follow the path up through the wood, going straight on at the crossroads (between two stone markers) and eventually through a wooden horse barrier. Continue climbing towards the edge of the wood. From the end of the wood follow the path south-west (diagonally right) towards the summit. Aim for the gate in the fence and on reaching it cross the stile. Continue straight on up the steep hill until you reach the summit.

*A pepperpot tower of Falkland Palace can be seen behind the church in this view of the village*

**Information**

The walk is about five and a half miles long
Steep in parts; stout footwear is essential
Dogs must be kept on leads at all times
Wide selection of pubs and tearooms in Falkland
Toilets at car park
Picnic sites at the Craigmead and East Lomond Relay Station car parks
Large groups should contact the Ranger Service in advance (0592 741212)

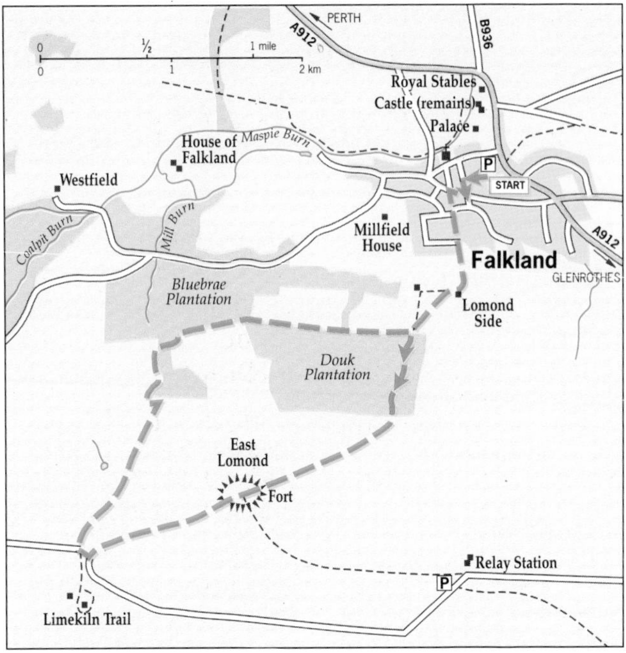


From here continue south-west and regain the path, leaving the summit roughly in line with the right-hand end of the distant reservoir. Follow the path as it winds down the hill (quite steep in parts; may be slippery) until you come to a gate. (Take the Limekiln Trail opposite for a 20-minute detour, returning to the gate.)
Don't go through the gate, but bear right down a grassy track. Turn left at the fork and continue to a ruined wall. Follow the wall until it ends at a corner with another wall. From here descend diagonally left, bearing for a radio mast on the next ridge of hills until you meet a clear path again. Turn right along this, passing a spring on your left, and through old quarry heaps. Soon the path passes between two stone markers. Follow the path diagonally right towards an unfenced spit of trees which projects from the main plantation below. When you reach the trees turn left and walk around the edge.
Shortly before the main plantation (and just before a large mass of boulders in your path) turn right into the trees. Once through the trees, cross the stile to your left, and turn right.
Follow the path down, passing a ruin to your right. When you reach the rough road, turn right and proceed to the junction with your outward route. Turn left and retrace your steps back to the car park.

**East Lomond Hill**
This is the site of a prehistoric fort, dating from between the late 1st millennium BC and the early 1st millennium AD. The summit is crowned by a large Bronze Age cairn, and there are remnants of the ramparts lower down. Once part of the hunting forests of Falkland Palace, a 'Ranger' was appointed in 1605 to protect deer and discourage the public. Now the area is part of Fife Regional Park, and a modern day Ranger Service operates.

**What to look out for**

Roe deer and red and grey squirrels are found in the woods. The moor is home to red grouse (the only site for them in Fife), and curlews, skylarks, meadow pipits, wheatear and whinchats may also be seen on the hill.

# The Hermitage and Ossian's Cave

This short walk visits Ossian's Cave and The Hermitage, both built in the 19th century for one of the Dukes of Atholl and now owned by the National Trust for Scotland. The Hermitage is above the splendid Falls of Braan.

**WALK 92**
TAYSIDE
NO013422

**START**
The National Trust for Scotland car park is off the A9, one mile north of Dunkeld (signposted).

**DIRECTIONS**
Rather than heading directly for The Hermitage from the car park, take the forest track that heads uphill beside the main road, signposted 'Craigvinean'. (Across the A9 is the prominent cliff of Craig y Barns, used by climbers.) At the top of the rise the track swings left by a field. (The Perth to Inverness railway runs under your feet in a tunnel here.)
Continue through fine woodland for about ½ mile.

*The Falls of Braan*

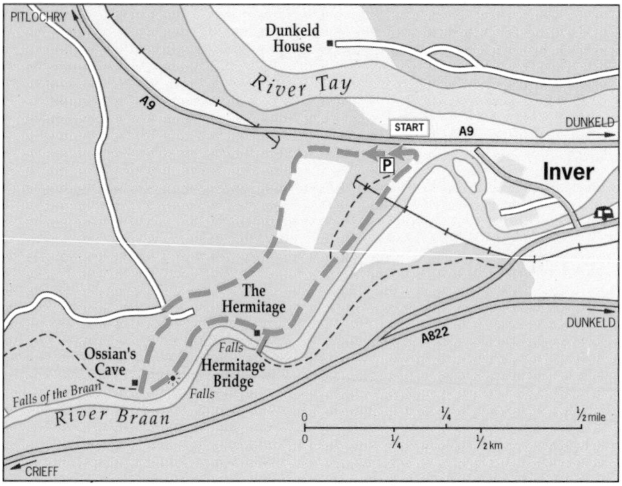


## Information

The walk is about two miles long
Mainly good paths, but some rough stretches
Dogs should be kept on leads
Nearest café in Dunkeld, but ice-cream, drinks and snacks van sometimes parked
Hermitage leaflet available at an 'honesty box' in the car park
Nearest toilets in Dunkeld

At a junction of tracks a sign points left to The Hermitage. Follow this path and in 30yds take the right fork onto a slightly rougher path.
You soon reach Ossian's Cave, in an area of huge boulders with the River Braan rushing past below. Turn left along the riverside path and in a few yards reach a viewpoint on the right above the river. Continue through a Norway spruce plantation to reach the main falls and the Hermitage.
(From here a longer signposted route leads through woods to Inver and back to the car park.)
Our walk returns over the bridge and along by the river on the main path, back to the car park.

Wren

**Ossian's Cave**
This is a folly built in the 18th century and named after the legendary Celtic bard. It is well made, with a corbelled roof, and it is quite safe to go inside.

**The Hermitage**
Another folly, set high above the waterfall, the Hermitage is also called Ossian's Hall. It was built in 1758 by the third Duke of Atholl before he succeeded to the title – apparently as a delightful surprise for his uncle, the second Duke.
In those early days, visitors would have entered to see a painting of Ossian on the far wall. When a hidden pulley was operated, the painting slid into a recess, giving entry to a smaller room. Here, the walls and ceiling were covered with mirrors and coloured glass, and the reflections of the waterfalls below were truly amazing. The bridge dates from the same period.

## What to look out for

The woods contain many fine trees including old Douglas and silver firs. If you are lucky you may see Britain's smallest bird, the goldcrest, and other woodland birds include long-tailed tits, wrens and willow warblers.
Wild fruits include blackberries and bilberries in season.

# Neptune's Staircase

**WALK 93**
HIGHLAND
NN112769

This is an easy and interesting walk with a mixture of attractions – boats on a canal, the site of an ancient castle and marvellous views to the highest mountain in Britain.

**START**
Banavie is about four miles north of Fort William via the A82 and the A830. In Banavie turn right onto the B8004 and soon reach the large car park at the foot of a series of canal locks known as Neptune's Staircase.

**DIRECTIONS**
Leave the car park passing to the right of the Moorings Hotel on to the canal towpath. A series of eight locks ('Neptune's Staircase') lifts vessels over 70ft at the head of Loch Linnhe.
Cross over at one of the lock gates to the far side of the canal and turn left to follow the easy towpath for almost two miles.
Where you see a row of

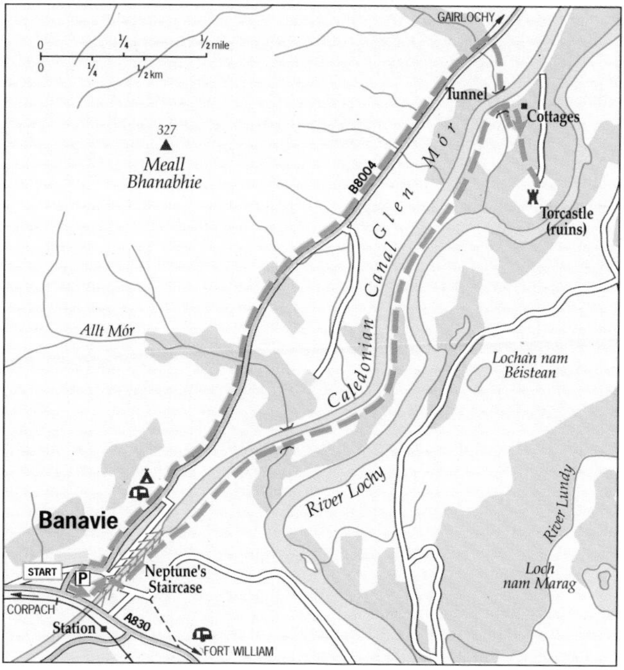


### What to look out for

The canal is a busy waterway and many enjoyable hours can be spent watching the boats negotiating the locks.
There are superb views of Ben Nevis, Aonach Mor and Carn Mor Dearg and the distant Grey Corries mountains, some of the highest mountains in the country.
Look out for a variety of ducks, such as mallards and tufted ducks, on the canal itself, and you will often see buzzards and ravens flying over the woods around Torcastle.

### Information

The walk is four and a half miles long
Easy walking along a canal towpath
Some road walking on return, but on a very quiet road
Hotel near the car park at Banavie
Picnic on grassy areas alongside the canal and at Torcastle by the River Lochy

*The view on a brilliant day of Ben Nevis, from Banavie*

cottages down a steep bank to the right of the towpath, turn right down a narrow path and then left onto a track which leads to the ruins of Torcastle. From the castle, return to the canal and go through the tunnel below it. Where the track joins the B8004, turn left to return to Banavie and the start of the walk. All along this road there are superb views of Ben Nevis, Britain's highest mountain, and the surrounding peaks.)

**Banavie**

In 1948 the parish priest of Glenfinnan, the Rev Father P J O'Regan published a small book in which he claimed that Banavie was the birthplace of St Patrick. He was quoting a 10th-century writer who said that 'St Patrick belonged to the village of Bannavie, not far from the western sea'.

**Torcastle**

The ruins of the 19th-century Torcastle stand on the site of a very ancient fort, Tor Castle. In 1630, an anonymous author wrote, 'There was ane ancient castle builded whaire this Torcastle is which was called Beragonium and this Torcastle was builded last by ane which is called Ewen MacAllane the Chief of Clan Cameron'. It has also been suggested that this is the site of Torc Castle, the capital of the Dalriadic Scots. In 1947 Torcastle opened as a hotel, but it was destroyed by a fire in 1950 and never rebuilt.

**The Caledonian Canal**

Thomas Telford's Caledonian Canal, running from Corpach, just north of Fort William, to Inverness, was completed in 1847. Its purpose was to provide a navigable waterway between the Firth of Lorne on the west coast and the Moray Firth on the east, saving shipping the long journey all around the north coast of Scotland. It is still used by some commercial boats and fishing boats, but is largely used nowadays by pleasure craft. The waterway also takes in Loch Linnhe, Loch Lochy, Loch Oich and Loch Ness. The series of locks on the canal at Banavie was christened 'Neptune's Staircase' by Telford, and the name has stuck.

# The Bow-Fiddle Rock

A short walk on the lovely Morayshire coast linking two attractive towns, passing a famous offshore landmark and crossing a superb stretch of sandy beach.

**WALK 94**
GRAMPIAN
NJ513671

### Information

The walk is about four miles long
Good paths, with a section along beach
Some road walking
Dogs should be kept on leads on the road sections
Cafés and pubs in Cullen and Portknockie
The Cullen Bay Hotel serves morning coffee, lunch and afternoon tea; families welcome
Picnic tables below the viaduct near the start and at Cullen Bay
Toilets at the start and at Cullen Bay

**START**
Cullen is on the A98, 20 miles east of Elgin. Park in the square.

**DIRECTIONS**
From the square, walk downhill towards the sea, passing under the railway viaduct (fine view over Cullen Bay) and continue left with the main road above Seatown. Turn right at the Royal Oak Hotel, overlooked by the viaduct. Pass a row of houses and turn left down a slip road, back towards the viaduct. Cross the footbridge over the Burn of Cullen, pass under the viaduct and turn right onto the main road.

Continue along the road to the Cullen Bay Hotel. Leave the road here to join the old railway track, now a footpath, and walk towards Portknockie, with the golf course and beach below to the right.

Continue into Portknockie. The path rises to Bridge Street. Walk down it and continue down either New Street or Victoria Street, passing the Victoria Hotel. At the end, turn left along Patrol Road for a short way to see Portknockie's picturesque harbour.

Return along Patrol Road. At the end fork left. Pass a small boatyard and turn left onto a track towards the sea. In a further 50yds turn right to find a path running alongside a fence on the cliff top. (There is soon a superb close-up of the Bow-Fiddle Rock.) Follow the cliff-top path (fine views) until Cullen Bay comes into view. Where a path joins from the right, go left down the steps to reach the shore.

The path reaches the broad, firm sands of Cullen Bay. Once across the sands, go right up steps to a small

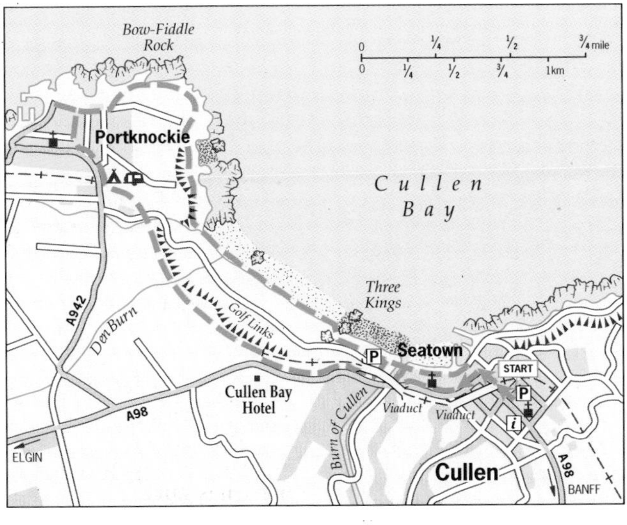

promenade. Cross the Burn of Cullen by the footbridge, just below the railway viaduct, and enter Seatown. Either walk along the front or explore the maze of lanes between the houses. At the harbour turn right and left to reach a path climbing up to the main road and return to the square.

**The Cullen Viaducts**
The railway viaducts are here because the Countess of Seafield refused to allow the line to cross the policies of Seafield House, a little way inland.

**The Bow-Fiddle Rock**
This large rock stack has been eroded by the sea, forming the natural archway from which it gets its name, though from the Cullen side it looks rather more like a whale's tail. A large number of sea birds can usually be seen on the rock.

**Cullen Seatown**
The houses of the former Invercullen are mostly 18th- and 19th-century, and are tightly grouped in a maze of narrow lanes. The famous smoked fish soup, Cullen Skink, originated here.

**What to look out for**

There is plenty of birdlife offshore here, including cormorants and eiders. Look for birds on the beach such as oystercatchers and a variety of gull species. Turnstones and purple sandpipers appear in the winter months.

*The distinctive Bow-Fiddle Rock*

# The Giant's Causeway

**WALK 95**
ANTRIM
C945439

A walk which includes both the spectacular Giant's Causeway, one of Europe's finest geological sites, and the magnificent cliffs of the Antrim coast.

**Information**

The walk is about five miles long
Route steep in parts and may be muddy, so strong footwear recommended
No road walking
Café and toilets at Visitor Centre
There are several possible picnic spots along the route

**START**
Park at the Causeway car park, which is just off the B146, about 7 miles east of Portrush.

**DIRECTIONS**
Enter the Visitor Centre and pass through to the open ground overlooking the sea. Take the cliff path on the right (signposted). In wet weather this path may be muddy, and special care is needed along exposed parts when strong winds are blowing.
After about ¼ mile, a path and steps to the left (the

*The curious hexagonal columns of the Giant's Causeway form a natural pavement*

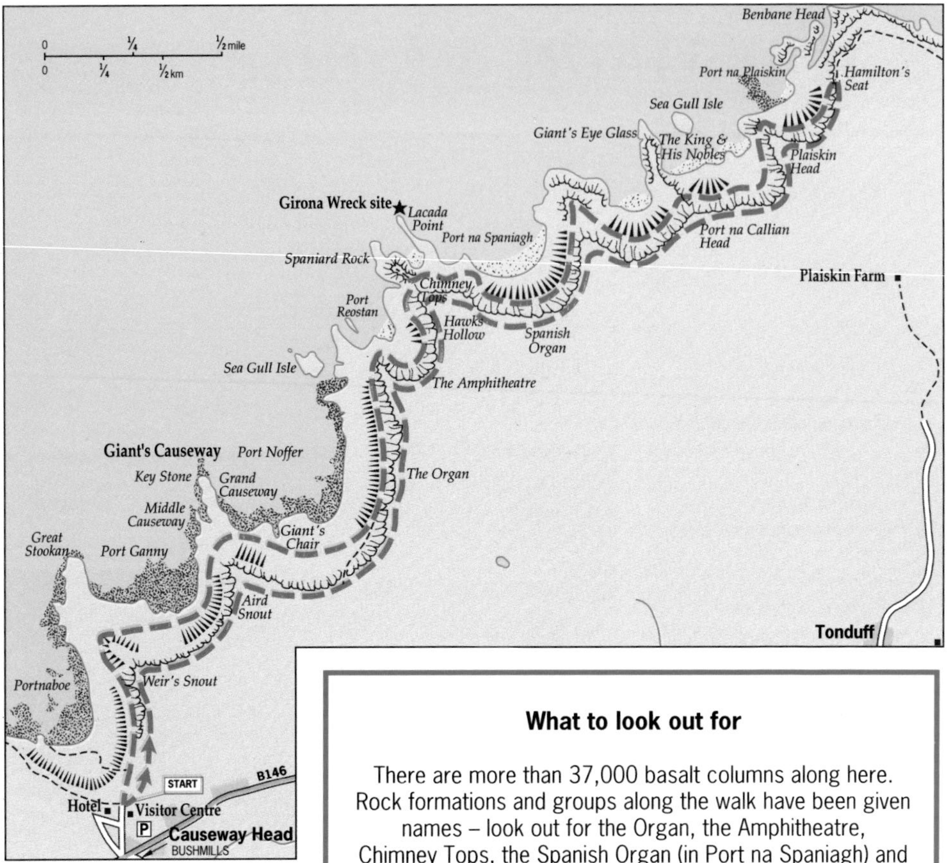


**What to look out for**

There are more than 37,000 basalt columns along here. Rock formations and groups along the walk have been given names – look out for the Organ, the Amphitheatre, Chimney Tops, the Spanish Organ (in Port na Spaniagh) and the King and His Nobles.

Shepherd's path) leads down to the shore; go past this turning, and continue along the cliff path to Weir's Snout and Aird Snout, where there are excellent views of the cliffs, and of the Causeway below.

Continue for about 1 mile, past the bay of Port na Spaniagh, to Hamilton's Seat (signposted). Here take the path on the left which descends to the shore. Follow this path to the Grand Causeway, and then take the wide, clear path which leads back along the cliffs to the Visitor Centre.

**The Giant's Causeway**

Geologists would have you believe that the extraordinary hexagonal columnar formations of basalt along this stretch of coastline were created millions of years ago by volcanic action.

Locals, however, will tell you that the Causeway was built by the great giant, Finn MacCool, who wanted to cross quickly to the island of Staffa, off the west coast of Scotland, in order to fight a rival giant.

**Port na Spaniagh**

The largest ship of the Spanish Armada was wrecked on the rocks of Lacada Point here in October 1588, with the loss of as many as 1,300 lives. It happened that the *Girona* was carrying treasures from two other vessels as well as its own; over the years, thousands of objects have been recovered from the wreck site, and may be seen displayed at the Ulster Museum, in Belfast.

# Exploring Gortin Glen Forest

**WALK 96**
ULSTER
H485821

This is an enjoyable walk along paths through a conifer forest and beside a mountain stream, close by the famous Ulster History Park.

**What to look out for**

The woodland is full of wildlife – look for signs of hedgehogs, red squirrels, badgers and sika deer. Birds include redwing, tree-creeper, goldfinch, kestrel, and both long-eared and barn owls.

**START**
Gortin Glen forest lies about 6 miles from Omagh. Park at the Gortin Glen Forest car park, which is just off the B48, and near the Visitor Centre.

**DIRECTIONS**
From the car park, turn down over the small bridge and follow the Ladies View Trail and Pollan Trail.
Follow the path through the forest, along the pretty Pollan Burn.
At the waterfall turn off to the right, following the Ulster Way sign, and go down the steps to the bridge. Cross the bridge and continue on up the next set of steps, crossing and recrossing the Pollan Burn several times by rustic bridges.
Continue to follow the Ulster Way signs until the tarmac of the Scenic Drive is reached. Turn left here, following the blue arrow and Ulster Way up through the forest. On reaching the forest drive turn right, then soon turn left up through the trees to the Ladies' Viewpoint. There is a marvellous panoramic view from here over the forest; the hills beyond are called Mary Gray and Bessie Bell – hence the name of the viewpoint.
From here take the path signposted 'Ladies View Trail', which runs down through

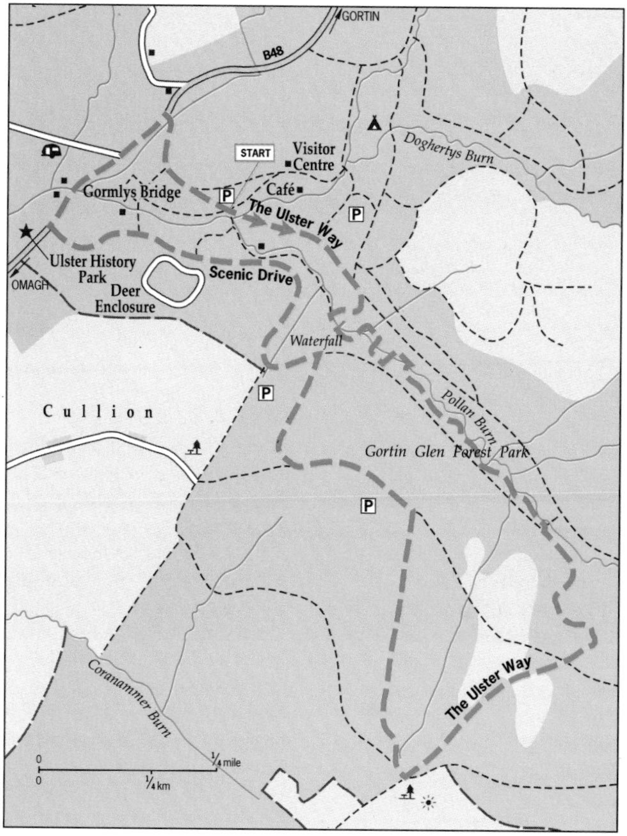

### Information

The walk is four and a half miles long
Fairly easy walking on forest paths
One short stretch of road walking
No stiles
Café and toilets at Gortin Glen Visitor Centre
Several likely picnic spots, including Ladies' Viewpoint

*A view of the forest and park*

the woods to a forest road. Turn left at the road and follow it down to join the Scenic Drive once more. Turn right and keep to this road, passing the deer enclosure on your left. Where the Scenic Road comes out at the main B48, either turn left and cross over to visit the Ulster History Park, or turn right and in about ¼ mile turn right again to return to the forest Visitor Centre car park.

**Gortin Glen Forest Park**
The forest park covers at total area of some 3,500 acres, of which about half has been planted. It is criss-crossed by a network of paths and scenic drives, and more information is to be found at the Visitor Centre.

**The Ulster History Park**
This fascinating site, open all year, contains full-size replicas and reconstructions of some of Ireland's most ancient buildings. These include a round tower, a crannog (an ancient artificial island built in a lake for protection, with thatched huts lying within a wooden palisade), a Norman motte and bailey castle, a neolithic house and a dolmen. Other features of interest include an original ogham stone, with its curious writing, which was found locally.

# A Walk Across the Howth Peninsula

The Howth Peninsula lies on an attractive peninsula across the bay from Dublin, but the sea cliffs and rocky hillsides traversed on this walk could be a thousand miles away.

**WALK 97**
DUBLIN
0288392

**START**
Howth (Binn Éadair) lies about nine miles east of Dublin, on the northern edge of the peninsula. Park in the village, and start the walk at the east pier of the harbour.

**DIRECTIONS**
Walk up East Balscadden Road, with views of the two islands of Ireland's Eye and, further out, Lambay. Lambay is a bird sanctuary, and was the first landing place of the Norse invaders of Ireland.

Pass a house once lived in by W B Yeats, and at the end of the road take the cliff path which forms its continuation.
Within sight of the Bailey Lighthouse (on a nose of land to the south, reaching out into Dublin Bay), the cliff path joins a track. Continue straight ahead, cutting across the headland.
Cross the tarmac road, and on the far side follow the path just to the left of a house called 'Gale Point'; in a few yards turn right, still on a path. Turn left at the T-junction where a plaque at ground level indicates a right of way.
Take the right path at the first fork, to stay above the cliffs. There is another fork

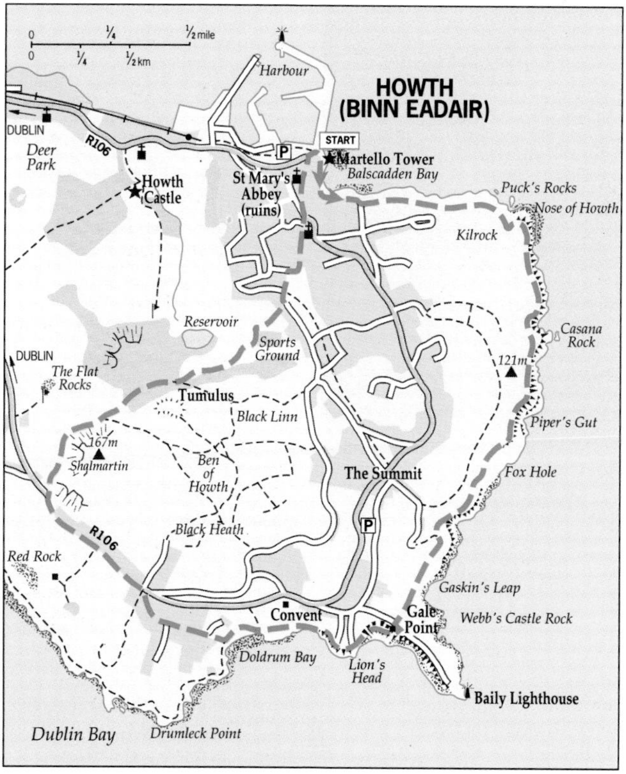


**Information**

The walk is five and a half miles long
Some walking along quiet roads
Possible picnic spots along the path, or on the Ben of Howth

*Looking along the rugged shore of the Howth Peninsula*

further on at the edge of a garden, to the left of which is a continuation of the coastal path, but ignore this and turn right onto the tarmac at Ceanchor Road (bollards marking the end of the road will be just about visible from the path).

At the end of Ceanchor Road turn left onto Thormanby Road, and a few yards beyond the last house on the right, turn right uphill at a path to face a summit of Howth Head.

Do not take the main path which heads resolutely uphill. Instead, take the minor left turn and walk up through gorse and ferns (which can grow tall in summer) to round the hill, with views across to Bull Island.

At a ruined house at the edge of the golf course, follow the line of white stones across the course, and so enter a narrow valley beyond, with a rocky spur of Howth Head on the right and a small wood on the left.

The path tends to break into a maze of tracks towards the end of the wood, so keep on lower ground, to the right of a second golf course, and watch out for goal posts just beyond.

Keep the playing field close on your right to descend on a short, narrow path to Balkill Road. Turn left here and walk down through Howth to return to the start point.

**What to look out for**

Seabirds nesting on the cliffs include herring and black-backed gulls, kittiwakes and cormorants. Many geese and waders are attracted to the saltmarshes of Bull Island.

**Howth**

This attractive village is today one of Ireland's busiest fishing ports. The prominent lighthouse was built in 1814; the castle, however, is much older in origin. While the castle itself is not open to the public, the castle gardens certainly are, and appear particularly splendid when the rhododendrons are flowering.

# Glendalough – the Medieval Heart of Ireland

This lovely walk reveals the magnificent beauty of Glendalough, as well as the monastic settlements which have made this once remote valley a famous centre of medieval Ireland.

**WALK 98**
CO WICKLOW
GRID REF

**Information**

The walk is about five miles long
Paths are mostly forest tracks
No stiles
Facilities at the Visitor Centre, towards the end of the walk

**START**
The road to Glendalough is off the R756, between Laragh and Holywood. The walk starts from the upper car park, about ¼ mile beyond the round tower.

**DIRECTIONS**
From the car park take the path skirting the park to the nearby Upper Lake, with a spectacular waterfall at the far end. Follow the path, with the lake on your right, passing a footbridge before reaching two bridges which span the turbulent stream. Take the right-hand bridge – the footbridge – and continue on the path to reach the 11th-century Reefert Church.
From here, continue on the path, signed Poulanass Waterfall, and turn right on to a forest track. Followthis track into the narrow valley through which the Poulanass Waterfall tumbles in a series of spectacular

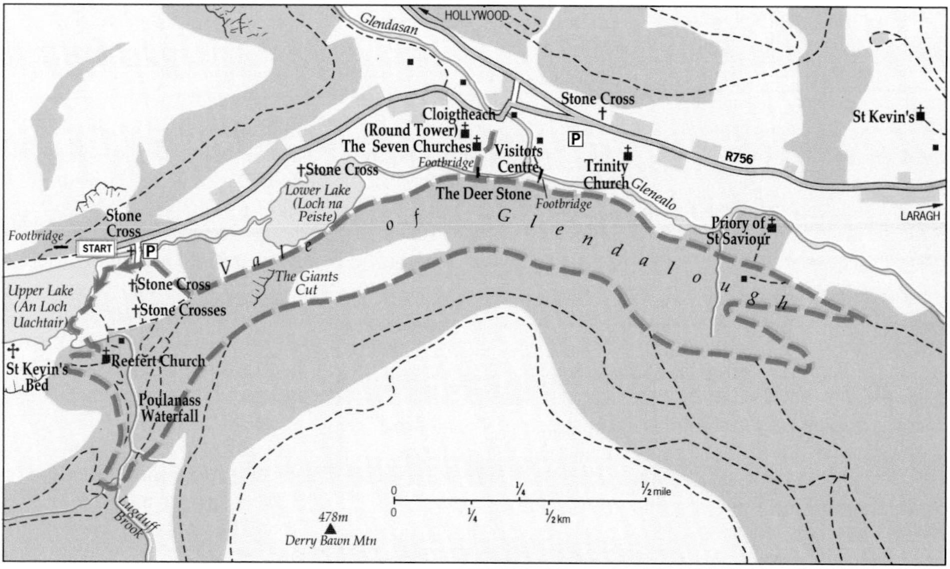

*Looking along the beautiful valley of Glendalough*

cascades in a deeply-cut bed.

Ignoring the path back to the car park, take the first turn left, thereby crossing two bridges. Between the bridges, a pillar on the right displays samples of local rock.

Take the right fork immediately after the second bridge and stay on the main track. After about ¾ mile, take the track on the left which zig-zags down to the valley floor. Turn left here on to a path, and continue to the second bridge.

Turn right here to visit the monastic settlement.

Return to the path and continue along it to pass the Lower Lake on your right; take the right turning, signposted to the car park, to return to your starting point.

### What to look out for

The ancient woodland of this valley is one of the very few remnants of the ancient forests which once covered most of Ireland, and it is a conservation area. Look out for mixed woodland of oak, beech and holly.

**Glendalough (Gleann dá Loch)**

The 'Valley of the Two Lakes' is a famous beauty spot. Once there was only one lake, but silt washed down from the hills and carried by the Poulanass Waterfall formed a delta in the valley, gradually splitting the lake into two.

**Ancient Settlements**

The main concentration of the medieval monastic ruins lies close to the Visitor Centre. Each ruin is fully described at its site, and they include several churches, a gateway and an impressive round tower which stands about 100ft high. Further remains and early crosses may be seen on the walk.

# Exploring Waterford Harbour

On tracks and country roads between the attractive villages of Passage East and Cheekpoint, this walk takes you along high ground above the estuary which was formed by the meeting of three of Ireland's great rivers; the return is through a wood and pleasant agricultural land.

**WALK 99**
CO WATERFORD
S703103

**Information**

The walk is about eight miles long
Steep steps at Passage East
Some road walking – dogs should be kept under strict control
Tracks may be overgrown or muddy in places

START
The walk starts from Passage East, about 5 miles east of Waterford, at the end of the R683. Park in the square close to the ferry crossing.

DIRECTIONS
Walk along the main road (R683) from Passage East, taking the first track right after 1 mile. Follow this track through a mixed wood to the crest of a hill, descend beyond it into a small valley and continue upwards on the same track to a T-junction close to a school. Turn right here and walk towards Cheekpoint, turning left (rather than taking the cul-de-sac straight ahead) near the village to reach the estuary bank.
Walk through the village, with the estuary on your right, and at the far end follow the road uphill. Take the first turn right, a narrow turning after a 90-degree bend to the left.
At the first fork, either go right and take the path which forms its continuation through a field and into a wood, or if thick summer vegetation has made this field impassable, take the left fork on a track leading to a T-

*The ferry at Passage East*

junction. Turn right, then left, to rejoin the main road close to the village of Faithlegg. (A short detour down the first right turn leads you to a fine viewpoint.) If you decide to risk the field route, ignore the fork left just inside the wood and continue along the main path high above the River Suir. Continue on this path, through a gap in a stone wall, and shortly beyond this turn left to go steeply uphill on a forest path. At its end, on tarmac, turn right to reach a viewing point. Take the track running left which starts just below the front of the viewing point. It ends on tarmac; turn right here to reach the main road close to Faithlegg. Pass the church on your left (the graveyard is worth another detour), and beyond it turn left towards Passage East. Walk along this road for 1¼ miles and turn left at the T-junction.

Continue for ½ mile and take the first track on the right. Ignoring the right turn, continue to a T-junction, turn left here and take the steps which lead steeply down into Passage East, to return to the start.

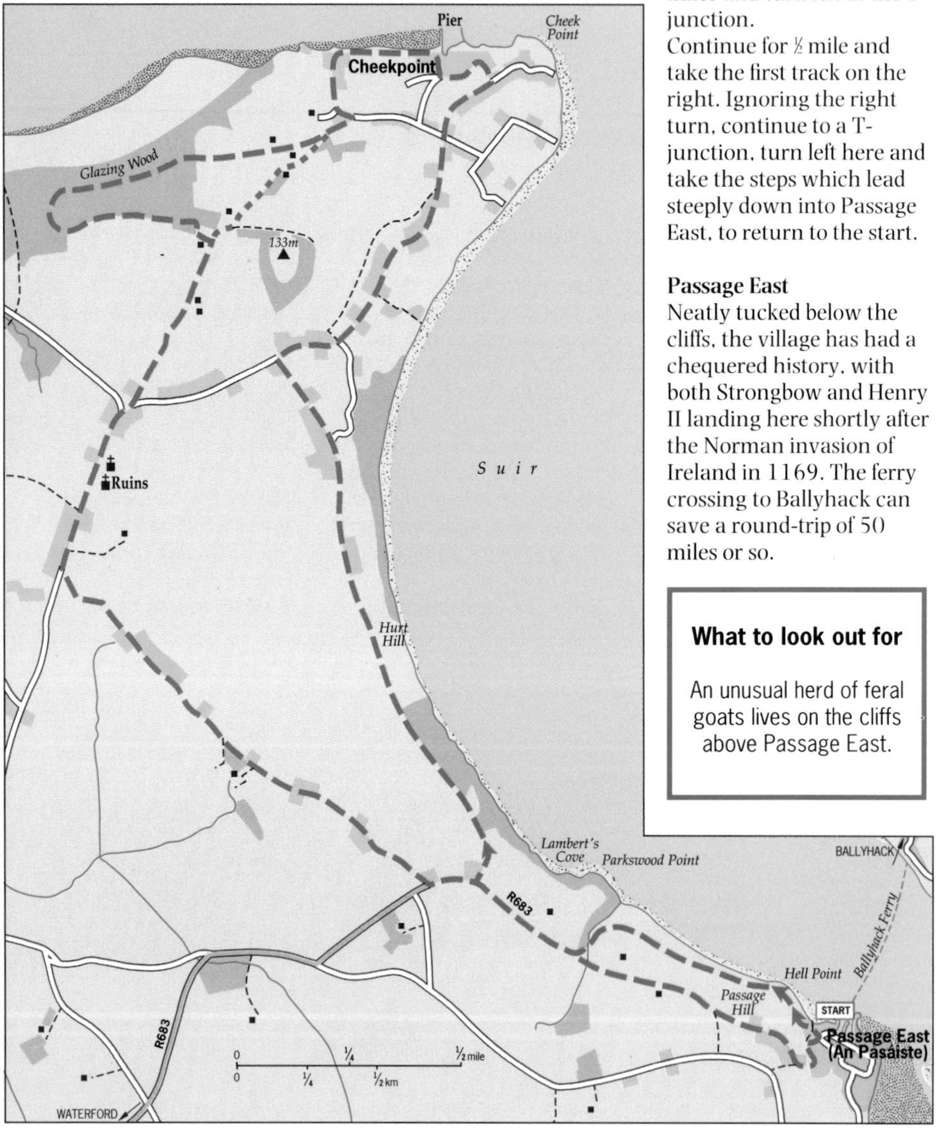


**Passage East**

Neatly tucked below the cliffs, the village has had a chequered history, with both Strongbow and Henry II landing here shortly after the Norman invasion of Ireland in 1169. The ferry crossing to Ballyhack can save a round-trip of 50 miles or so.

**What to look out for**

An unusual herd of feral goats lives on the cliffs above Passage East.

# *Dooks on Dingle Bay*

**WALK 100**
CO KERRY
GRID REF

This gentle walk around the townland of Dooks (Dooaghs) introduces a variety of habitats – moor and bogland, sand dune and seashore, with an opportunity for swimming or golf.

**Information**

The walk is four and a half miles long
Easy walking on level ground.
Some walking on quiet roads, and along a sand and shingle beach
Check tide times for the last stretch of the walk
Pubs at Cromane and Glenbeigh

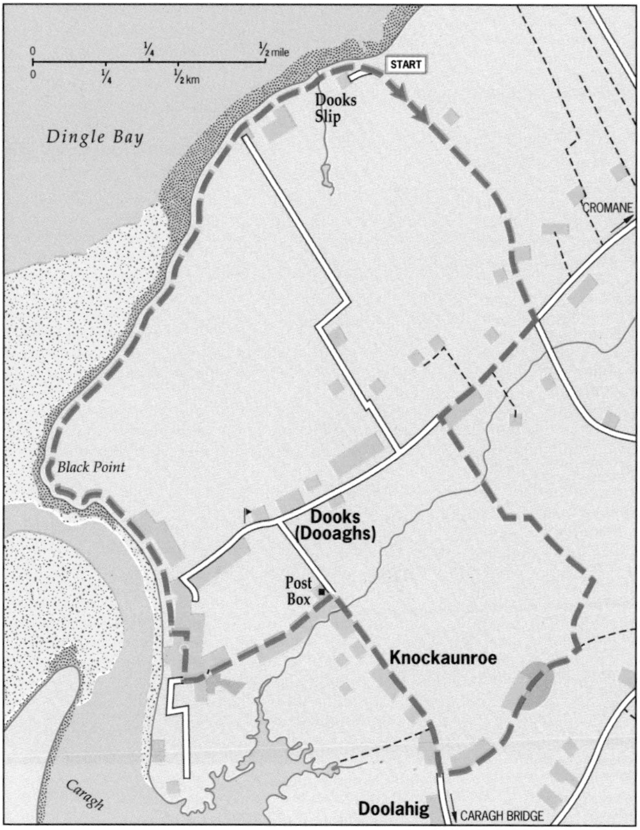


**START**
The walk starts at Dooks Slip (unsigned), about 5 miles from Killorglin, off the N70, on the southern side of Dingle Bay. Park with care near the slipway, and check tide times for your return along the beach before setting off.

**DIRECTIONS**
Retrace your route to the slipway along Burkett's Road for about ¼ mile. Turn right at the crossroads, and 300 yards later watch for the narrow entrance on the left to a grassy road, bordered mainly with gorse. Follow this, bearing slightly left at the entrance to bogland. Approaching the 'mountain', circle right with the green road, with fine views to the north and west. As the green road meets a semi-surfaced lane, a copse of trees gives temporary shelter on a hot day.
Continue to the T-junction. Turn right and after about ½ mile turn left beside a pillar with a post-box. Pass Buncar House on your left, and go right and then left to the mouth of the Caragh River and the beach. Go right along the beach and around Black Point, skirting Dooks Golf Club.
Continue along the beach. If the tide is high, it may be necessary to leave the sand

and walk on the boulder and pebble beach for short stretches, or to walk along the edge of the sand dunes. Return in this way to the start point at the slipway.

**Dooks Slip**

The mooring point for little open boats of the fishermen who ply the Caragh River, Dooks also boasts a popular family beach for swimming and windsurfing. North of here, in 1902 the *Manchester Merchant* sank on its maiden voyage from São Paulo to Liverpool when its cargo of cotton spontaneously ignited.

*Looking north along the bay to Black Point*

**What to look out for**

Dooks Golf Club, apart from its claims to be the oldest in Ireland, has also been specially adapted to create a safe haven for the increasingly rare natterjack toad.

The green road across the bogland, teaming with wildlife, leads to an area of intensive turf-cutting.

This region is warmed by the Gulf Stream – look out for subtropical plants, including lush fuschia hedges.

# Index
## (numbers refer to walk numbers)

# T



# U



# V



# W



# Y



The Automobile Association wishes to thank the following photographers and libraries for their assistance in the preparation of this book.

J Baxter 85b
Images Colour Library Ltd Cover

All remaining pictures are held in the Association's own library, with contributions from:
P Baker 9; V & S Bates 10, 17, 18, 19, 27, 28, 31, 32, 55a, 56; M Birkitt 41, 49; I Burgum 52, 53, 54, 55b, 58; J Carnie 91, D Corrance 85a, D Croucher 57, 61, 62, 63, 65, 66; S Day 92, 93; A Edwards 50, E Ellington 94, D Forss 11, 20, 21, 22, 23, 25, 26, 33, 34, 35, 36, 37, 39, 40, 42, 43, 73b, 74, 75; P Goodrum 1, 2, 4, 5; A Hopkins 79, 81; J Jennings 96; T Kelly 97; S King 78; A Lawson 6b; S & O Mathews 38b; C Mellor 44, 45, 46, 47; J Morrison 68, 69, 71, 72, 76; R Moss 3; G Munday 95; K Paterson Spine, 82, 83, 84, 86, 87, 88, 89, 90; N Ray 6a, 7, 8, 12, 13; P Sharpe 77; M Short 14, 15, 16, 29, 30, 98; A Stonehouse 100

Section Titles: D Forss The West Country; D Forss South and South-east England; P Baker Central England and East Anglia; D Croucher Wales and the Marches; S Gregory Northern England: A Baker Scotland; L Blake Ireland

Illustrations by Andrew Hutchinson
Introduction Illustration on page 10 by Richard Draper and Ann Winterbotham